GOD'S GIFT FOR YOU

Caleb Stahl

GOD'S GIFT FOR YOU

ARE YOU DECEIVED?

CALEB STAHL

God's Gift For You by Caleb Stahl
Copyright © 2022 by Caleb Stahl
All Rights Reserved.
ISBN: 978-1-59755-665-1

Published by: ADVANTAGE BOOKS™ www.advbookstore.com

This book and parts thereof may not be reproduced in any form, stored in a retrieval system or transmitted in any form by any means (electronic, mechanical, photocopy, recording or otherwise) without prior written permission of the author, except as provided by United States of America copyright law. form without permission in writing from the copyright owner.

Scripture quotations are taken from The Holy Bible, King James Version, which is public domain.

Library of Congress Catalog Number: 2022936199

Names:	Stahl, Caleb, Author
Title:	God's Gift For You: Are you deceived? / Caleb Stahl
Publisher	Advantage Books, 2022
Identifiers:	ISBN (print): 9781597556651
	(mobi, epub): 9781597556798
Subjects:	Christian Life: Inspirational

First Printing August 2022
22 23 24 25 26 27   10 9 8 7 6 5 4 3 2 1

Table of Contents

Preface 7
Chapter 1: I Corinthians 12 11
Chapter 2: I Corinthians 13 27
Chapter 3: I Corinthians 14 49
Chapter 4: The Gift Of Prophecy 75
Chapter 5: The Gift Of Healing 89
Chapter 6: Passages That Prove The Gifts Are For Today 111
Chapter 7: Some Misused Passages & Objections To The Charismatic Movement 137
Chapter 8: The Baptism Of The Spirit 189
Chapter 9: The Gift Of Tongues 233
Notes 257

Caleb Stahl

Preface

The first thing I wanted to note was my intent in writing this book. Before, I disclose that, I should probably explain what my intent isn't. I do not want to try to condemn anyone, especially other believers seeing that there is no condemnation to them which are in Christ Jesus *Romans 8:1 - There is therefore now no condemnation to them which are in Christ Jesus, who walk not after the flesh, but after the Spirit.* The meaning of those who walk not after the flesh in that verse is referring to the chapter right before it. It means those who are trying to keep the law in the flesh to earn salvation. I'm not writing to people who are trying to keep the law in their flesh. I am writing to born again believers. Christ has already taken the punishment for sin, and God has already poured out his wrath and condemnation upon Christ when he was on the cross. In so doing, he condemned sin in the flesh. *Romans 8:3 - For what the law could not do, in that it was weak through the flesh, God sending his own Son in the likeness of sinful flesh, and for sin, condemned sin in the flesh.* Christ has become sin for us, and imputed to us his own righteousness to the point that we have actually become the righteousness of God in him. *II Corinthians 5:21 -For he hath made him to be sin for us, who knew no sin; that we might be made the righteousness of God in him.* If that is true, then who am I to condemn another Christian? I am writing this book because I believe that the truth has been distorted on this matter concerning spiritual gifts. I want to give Charismatic Christians a tool to use to help them understand the Scriptures, and so they have something to stand on so they understand why they believe in the spiritual gifts. I also want to give Christians that don't believe in the spiritual gifts something to consider.

I will be writing a rebuttal to B.F. Cate's book, *The Nine Gifts of the Spirit are Not in the Church Today.* I'm using that book because it was given to me by my godly pastor who didn't believe that the signs and gifts were for today. I want to mention that he is godly man, and he had good intentions by giving me that book. I am not trying to tear B.F. Cate down in any way. Neither am I trying to soil his reputation. In fact, I personally think that he has written one of the best defenses of the cessationist position that I have ever seen. I also simply believe that the truth has been distorted on this matter and I'm trying to write about it to help correct it.

With that being said the Bible says in *I Timothy 4:1 - Now the Spirit speaketh expressly, that in the latter times some shall depart from the faith, giving heed to seducing spirits, and doctrines of devils.* I am not saying that every Christian that doesn't believe in all the spiritual gifts are of the devil. In fact I am saying just the opposite. It is seducing spirits that are deceiving people by telling these lies. I am saying that I do believe that he has deceived many people concerning this topic. There are doctrines of devils. That is just a fact. I believe that the belief that the spiritual gifts are not in the church today is one of them. *James 3:15-16 - This wisdom descendeth not from above, but is earthly, sensual, devilish. 16 For where envying and strife is, there is confusion and every evil work.* These verses tell us that there is wisdom out there that is devilish. It is from the devil, and not from God. It is the source of envy, strife, confusion, and every evil work. In this discussion of the spiritual gifts, there has been much contention. It is full of emotion, anger, and confusion. It sounds to me like the devil has his hand in this matter. How does he handle the Scriptures? We get a glimpse of it in *Matthew 4:5-6 - Then the devil taketh him up into the holy city, and setteth him on a pinnacle of the temple, 6 and saith unto him, If thou be the Son of God, cast thyself down: for it is written, He shall give his angels charge concerning thee: and in their hands they shall bear thee up, lest at any time thou dash thy foot against a stone.* First of all we can see here that he quoted from the Scriptures. The devil knows the Scriptures very well, and he knows how to distort them. He quoted from *Psalm 91:11-12 - For he shall give his angels charge over thee, to keep thee in all thy ways. 12 They shall bear thee up in their hands, lest thou dash thy foot against a stone.* The context of this verse is found in *Psalm 91:1 - He that dwelleth in the secret place of the most High shall abide under the shadow of the Almighty.* This is a man that is in the Lord's will following his path. When the devil quotes this passage in Matthew 4 and again in Luke 4, he purposely leaves out four words. *Psalm 91:11-12 - For he shall give his angels charge over thee, to keep thee <u>in all thy ways</u>. 12 They shall bear thee up in their hands, lest thou dash thy foot against a stone.* These four words make all the difference. These four words say that God would command his angels to protect the man that walks in the ways of the Lord, not in any way that he chooses. That is how the devil was trying to tempt

Jesus. He was twisting the Scriptures by purposefully leaving words out for his own purpose. He does the same thing today, and many of those doctrines of devils have been made the same way. Many times this is how false doctrines arise. Let's look to the Scriptures and handle them correctly and sincerely and ask God to guide us to the right answer. I encourage you, as the reader to sincerely pray and ask God to guide you into truth as you read this book!

I also encourage you as the reader to ask yourself, "Am I believing the Bible, or am I believing what I'm believing about the Bible?" A good way to test whether or not this is true in your life is if you could use the Scriptures and prove what you believe. If we are just believing what we believe about the Bible without any Scriptural proof, then how do we know what we are believing is true?

Let me give you an analogy. If I wanted to drive to California from Pennsylvania, but I drove South on Route 81, I would never make it to my destination. However, I can write off or reinterpret the road signs telling me that I'm heading in the wrong direction, and can even convince myself that I made it to my destination when I arrive in Florida because I see palm trees and a beach. It may even feel like I'm in the right place, even though I've ignored the signs the whole trip. My point is no matter how much we desire to arrive at truth, if we start off with the wrong presupposition about truth, it won't matter what the truth really is, we will just believe our presupposition of it. Because we have such a strong presupposition, we can even write off, and reinterpret the Scriptures believing that we are on the right track the whole way. If you don't believe me, look at how much time a cessationist tries to prove that the Scriptures which deal with the Spiritual gifts don't apply to us today, instead of trying to interpret them like any other passage of Scripture. That is not meant to be condemning, it is meant to make you think as the reader. For example read the verse below through a cessationist lens of Scripture without reading what I've written about it, and see what your interpretation will be.

Romans *1:11 - For I long to see you, that I may impart unto you some spiritual gift, to the end ye may be established.* The spiritual gifts are given to us by God to establish us. They are given to us by our Heavenly Father as a gift. This is the same Heavenly Father that loved us so much that he sent his holy, precious, and beloved Son Jesus to come into the world to die a horrible death on our behalf. They are nothing to be afraid of. Would our Heavenly Father give us something bad? Doesn't He want the best for us? He wants to establish us. Why not pray about this topic as you read this book that God would bring you to the right conviction concerning these gifts?

Chapter 1

I Corinthians 12

I Corinthians is the book that primarily deals with the spiritual gifts. There are other books and sections of books that deal with the spiritual gifts such as *Romans 12:4-8*. I would recommend that you look at that passage. One thing is certain when I look at the spiritual gifts. Every believer has at least one spiritual gift. Because every believer has at least one spiritual gift, they have a purpose in the body of Christ. Therefore, they should be using it. *I Corinthians 12* is the chapter that outlines the spiritual gifts and their use in the church. I would be willing to guess that many people don't understand the spiritual gifts and haven't read much about them or even looked at *I Corinthians 12* and *I Corinthians 14* because they have been taught that they don't apply to them anyway. Whether the body of Christ as a whole has read these two chapters or not is irrelevant. What is important is what they teach, and how they apply to believers. With that in mind, we will take a look at both of these chapters in depth, verse by verse, to put everything in context so that we get a fuller grasp and understanding of what they are about.

I Corinthians 12:1 - Now concerning spiritual gifts, brethren, I would not have you ignorant. Paul opens up this chapter by writing that he did not want them to be ignorant of the spiritual gifts. It is interesting that there is so much confusion and so much ignorance concerning these same gifts today. Yet, if we fulfill Paul's wish concerning these gifts, we must look at what the Scriptures really teach.

I Corinthians 12:2-3 - Ye know that ye were Gentiles, carried away unto these dumb idols, even as ye were led. 3 Wherefore I give you to understand, that no man speaking by the Spirit of God calleth Jesus accursed: and that no man can say that Jesus is the Lord, but by the Holy Ghost. Paul speaks directly to the Gentiles that were involved in paganism. They saw many spiritual things when they were involved in paganism because they were interacting with devils. *I Corinthians 10:19-21 - What say I then? that the idol is any thing, or that which is offered in sacrifice to idols is any thing? 20 But I say, that the things which the Gentiles sacrifice, they sacrifice to devils, and not to God: and I would not that ye should have fellowship with devils. 21 Ye cannot drink the cup of the Lord, and the cup of devils: ye cannot be partakers of the Lord's table, and of the table of devils.* Apparently some people involved in the pagan religions spoke in a form of gibberish which is similar to speaking in the unknown language while using the gift of tongues. Paul is comforting these believers by telling them that anyone speaking by the Spirit of the Lord, whether it be speaking with the gift of tongues or speaking any other language, will not be engaging in pagan spirituality. Reinhard Bonnke writes in his book *Taking Action,*

> An objection has been raised that tongues have been heard among those who are not Christians. Mormons can produce their own cases of tongues. No doubt. In fact, as mentioned earlier, the oracles at the temples of pagan gods sometimes gave forth their pronouncements in gibberish through the vestal lips of virgins, which priests purported to interpret. The devil, like the magicians of Egypt can counterfeit the miracles of God and supernaturally impart utterances. [1]

He writes earlier in his book,

> Some have suggested that because speaking in tongues is heard among non-Christians, such as Spiritualists, and Buddhists, all who speak with tongues are of the devil. It does not follow that if a Spiritualist speaks with tongues, then everybody who speaks with tongues is a Spiritualist. We may as well say that because burglars use a steal jimmy, everybody who uses a steal jimmy is a burglar. The fact that there is a counterfeit should not lead us to reject the genuine. [2]

Let me clarify some things that Bonnke wrote. When he is saying that speaking in tongues is heard among non-Christians like Spiritualists, and Buddhists, he is referring to those supernatural utterances which are given to them by demons. But the point remains, just because other people receive supernatural utterances from demons, that does not mean that we can't receive supernatural unknown utterances from the Spirit of the living God, and just because we do receive those supernatural utterances from the

Spirit of the living God, that doesn't mean that the utterance itself is demonic because others have received supernatural utterances of demons.

Others have claimed that people who are speaking in tongues could be speaking curse words in another language. I will not deny the fact that there have been reported cases of such things happening. I'm sure that there have also been cases in which people have received supernatural utterance from the devil in a Charismatic church service. In those cases, the answer is simply those who have spoken curse words in another language were probably speaking out of the flesh to gain approval of their peers, and sad to say that does happen. But the truth is that they just weren't speaking under the influence of the Spirit, nor would someone who received a supernatural utterance from a demonic source in charismatic service. A question then arises. What would demons be doing in a church service? The answer is simple. Probably the same thing that they were trying to do in the synagogues while Jesus was on earth. They are probably trying to cause disruption. The fact that a demon is trying to cause disruption in a Charismatic church service is actually a sign that that particular church is on the right track because they are facing opposition from the enemy. That particular church was causing disruption in the enemy's camp so the enemy fought back. If they were such a disruption, then they wouldn't be facing the same opposition.

I Corinthians 12:4-6 - Now there are diversities of gifts, but the same Spirit. 5 And there are differences of administrations, but the same Lord. 6 And there are diversities of operations, but it is the same God which worketh all in all. The basic idea of these verses is that there are a diversity of gifts, but the same God. Paul may be speaking of the trinity, but he doesn't necessarily have to be. In verse 4, he says that there is the same Spirit among the brethren. In verse 5, he speaks of the same Lord which could be a reference to Jesus. And in verse 6, he speaks of the same God which could be a reference to the Father. It doesn't have to be a reference to the trinity, but either way he does say that God is the one working. This tells me two things. First of all, it is God that does the work. It always is God that does the work. It is God that does the work in ministry, but especially when it relates to the sign gifts and to miracles. Second, when the sign gifts are exercised and miracles are performed, it is God that is doing it. Which means He approves of them. If God approves of them, then we probably should too.

I Corinthians 12:7-11 - But the manifestation of the Spirit is given to every man to profit withal. 8 For to one is given by the Spirit the word of wisdom; to another the word of knowledge by the same Spirit; 9 to another faith by the same Spirit; to another the gifts of healing by the same Spirit; 10 to another the working of miracles; to another prophecy; to another discerning of spirits; to another divers kinds of tongues; to another the interpretation of tongues: 11 but all these worketh that one and the selfsame Spirit, dividing to every man severally as he will. Spiritual gifts are given for our benefit and profit. They are not given to harm us. Paul repeats this same concept in *Romans 1:11 - For I long to see you, that I may impart unto you some spiritual gift, to the end ye may be established.* The spiritual gifts are given for our betterment, not to harm us. Paul said that they help establish and edify believers, not tear them down. I am convinced that the church is supposed to be functioning in all the gifts of the Spirit today. With that being said, I will be getting the definitions for the gifts of the Spirit from Jon Courson. He is the pastor of Applegate Christian Fellowship, and he has been a pastor since 1977 when he founded Applegate Christian Fellowship. He has authored several books, and is a well-known speaker. Jon Courson writes in his application commentary, "The word of wisdom doesn't come from one's ability to figure out a situation. It is supernaturally given to answer a question or solve a problem."[3] In one sense a word of wisdom is given by God to help us figure out life's difficult circumstances. Courson writes,

> Because he laid all of His power when He came to earth (Philippians 2:7-8), Jesus was a Man just like you and me – but without sin. So when He moved in the arena of the miraculous and operated in the realm of the supernatural, it was not because he was Jesus. Rather, it was because he was walking with the Father and was empowered by the Spirit – just as we can be.[4]

Whether or not someone wants to argue with this statement of Jon Courson, they cannot argue with Scripture. Even if Jesus performed miracles because He was God, it doesn't matter. He said in *John 14:12 - Verily, verily, I say unto you, He that believeth on me, the works that I do shall he do also; and greater works than these shall he do; because I go unto my Father.* Jesus said verily (or truly) twice. Probably because the statement that he was just about to make would be unbelievable unless He said it. He said that we will do the same works that he did and even greater works if we would just believe. In context, Jesus was speaking of the miracles. *John 14:10-11 - Believest thou not that I am in the Father, and the Father in me? the words that I speak unto you I speak not of myself: but the Father that dwelleth in me, he doeth the works. 11 Believe me that I am in the Father, and the Father in me: or else believe me for the very works' sake.* Jesus said that "the Father that dwelleth in me, he doeth the works." The Greek word for "works" is the same Greek word translated as "works" in *John 5:39 - But I have greater witness than that of John: for the works which the Father hath given me to finish, the same works that I do, bear witness of me, that the Father hath sent me.* What works was Jesus talking about? He was talking about miracles. The miracles bore witness "that the Father had sent him". What else was Jesus talking about in this passage when he says "the Father that dwelleth in me, he doeth the works"? If that is the context of this passage, then it indicates that Jesus truly was referring to the miracles when he said "He that believeth on me, the works that I do shall he do also; and greater works than these shall he do". Some people might object by asking what greater work can be done than raising the dead or calming a storm. I don't know, but I believe it. I can tell you that Paul did greater works than Jesus in this sense, a woman with an issue of blood touched the edge of his garment and was healed, but in the book of Acts they simply took Paul's handkerchiefs or aprons to those who were possessed by demons or sick, and they were healed whether he was present or not. There have also been other saints in the Old Testament who have done exploits by faith. *Hebrews 11:32-35 -And what shall I more say? for the time would fail me to tell of Gedeon, and of Barak, and of Samson, and of Jephthae; of David also, and Samuel, and of the prophets: 33 who through faith subdued kingdoms, wrought righteousness, obtained promises, stopped the mouths of lions, 34 quenched the violence of fire, escaped the edge of the sword, out of weakness were made strong, waxed valiant in fight, turned to flight the armies of the aliens. 35 Women received their dead raised to life again: and others were tortured, not accepting deliverance; that they might obtain a better resurrection:* What does it even mean to quench the violence of fire? I'm pretty sure that this is referring to Shadrach Meshach, and Abed-nego, but it doesn't specifically say so. All of these feats are amazing feats. It should be encouraging to see what faith can actually do! *Joshua 10:12-13 -Then spake Joshua to the Lord in the day when the Lord delivered up the Amorites before the children of Israel, and he said in the sight of Israel, Sun, stand thou still upon Gibeon; and thou, Moon, in the valley of Ajalon. 13 And the sun stood still, and the moon stayed, until the people had avenged themselves upon their enemies. Is not this written in the book of Jasher? So the sun stood still in the midst of heaven, and hasted not to go down about a whole day.* Joshua stopped the sun by faith which affected the entire solar system. What you define as "greater works" is a matter of semantics, but I choose to believe the plain reading of the text. I don't know what is possible, but I do know what Jesus said to a man whose son was possessed with a devil that came to Jesus when he was coming down from the mount of transfiguration. He was asking Jesus for His help personally since his disciples couldn't cast the devil out. Jesus replied to him in *Mark 9:23 - Jesus said unto him, If thou canst believe, all things are possible to him that believeth.* I don't know what greater works can be done than that which was done by Jesus, but I do know what the Scriptures say, and I believe it. The Bible says, "all things are possible to him that believeth".

Courson continues on by saying, "…Jesus knew what could not have been known apart from revelation. He spoke a word of knowledge."[5] He was speaking about when Jesus was with the woman at the well and he supernaturally knew that she had been married to five husbands. That was a word of knowledge. Concerning the gift of faith Courson writes, "There are those, however, who move in the supernatural arena of faith, where, because of an exercise of faith, things happen that wouldn't happen otherwise…"[6] He continues writing, "The operation of faith is the ability to step out in response to the leading of the Spirit and do something you would have never done otherwise."[7] This is given in certain circumstance and situations. This gift should not be confused with the faith required to walk with God. It is our job to exercise faith in our walk with God. *II Corinthians 5:7 – (for we walk by faith, not by sight:)* The gift of healing is self-explanatory. It doesn't need much explanation. Just look at Jesus. Many people were healed by him in different ways. The working of miracles is as it sounds, it is working diverse miracles that aren't prophetic, or healing in nature.

Courson defines the gift of prophesy by writing, "The operation of prophecy is not to foretell the future, but to "forth-tell" God's heart. Prophecy consists of words of edification, exhortation, or comfort spoken at the very time they are most needed."[8] I would like to add that prophecies are something that could not be known by natural means. *I*

Corinthians 14:24-25 - But if all prophesy, and there come in one that believeth not, or one unlearned, he is convinced of all, he is judged of all: 25 and thus are the secrets of his heart made manifest; and so falling down on his face he will worship God, and report that God is in you of a truth. The gift of prophecy is evident in the passage. What is the result? "The secrets of his heart are made manifest." The purpose of prophecy is to reveal the secrets of a person's heart. It's not to embarrass them, but rather to comfort them. More precisely Paul writes in *I Corinthians 14:3 - But he that prophesieth speaketh unto men to edification, and exhortation, and comfort.* Prophecy reveals the secrets of a person's heart in order to speak words of edification, exhortation, and comfort to them. I remember one of the first times that I was attending a charismatic service. The man that gave the message spoke about loving the Lord with all our heart, soul, and mind. It was a great message. After words he prophesied speaking words of edification, exhortation, and comfort to individual people that the Lord wanted to care for. I remember this one lady there was struggling with some major issues. I don't remember what those issues were, but it was significant. I don't think that the specifics were even given to protect her. If I remember correctly, the man spoke to her about specific areas of her life in general terms. Either way, I do know one thing. I do know that the Lord was ministering to her deeply. I can vividly remember her on knees just weeping. The Lord was specifically, very personally, and carefully revealing the secrets of her heart to speak words edification, exhortation, and comfort to her. I had never seen anything like that in my entire life. Most people are carrying something when they walk into a church service, but I had never seen someone on their knees weeping as the Lord himself was ministering to her in such a moving way. That is the Lord that I know. He ministers to people's souls in a way that no one else can. I've also personally given prophetic words that have brought tears to someone's eyes. It is a powerful gift that ministers deeply to a person's soul.

Prophecy also may be foretelling the future, but it doesn't have to be. In such cases prophecy still shows God's heart. Such was the case when Agabus prophesied that Saul was going to be arrested in Jerusalem. It was an event in the future, but the prophecy showed God's heart concerning his servant Paul. We'll look at that passage in depth later on as well. The discerning of spirits is pretty self-explanatory. It is simply discerning spirits. It could be discerning the spirit of a man, the Holy Spirit, or even the devil and his demons. This can be manifested many times through the words that are said. Courson explains the usefulness of this gift to pastors when he writes, "Especially as we're involved in pastoring – caring about people, sharing with people, and helping people – we need to discern if what they are saying is coming from the Lord, the influence of demons, or simply the result of their own human wisdom."[9] The gift of tongues is simply the ability to be able to speak in a language that is not known by the speaker. The interpretation of tongues is the ability to interpret a language that the interpreter does not know. It is abused many times. Unfortunately many have used the gift of tongues incorrectly according to the outline given about their use in *I Corinthians 14:27-28*. We will talk about this passage in depth later on. Believers are not the ones that make any of this happen. The Spirit is the one that causes all of the manifestations of these gifts.

I Corinthians 12:12-13 - For as the body is one, and hath many members, and all the members of that one body, being many, are one body: so also is Christ. 13 For by one Spirit are we all baptized into one body, whether we be Jews or Gentiles, whether we be bond or free; and have been all made to drink into one Spirit. The church is commonly referred to as the body of Christ. It is called the body of Christ for a reason. A body is unified. It is one. It has many different parts but it is still one body. It is the same way in the body of Christ. We are the members of the body of Christ and serve different functions based on what part we are and what gift we've been given. The Spirit is the one that baptizes us into the body of Christ. It doesn't matter whether we're Jews or Gentiles, we are all one in Christ. This is important to note. Many have said this passage refers to the baptism of the Spirit by quoting *Matthew 3:11 - I indeed baptize you with water unto repentance: but he that cometh after me is mightier than I, whose shoes I am not worthy to bear: he shall baptize you with the Holy Ghost, and with fire.* The Greek words translated as "with the Holy Ghost" are ἐν πνεύματι ἁγίῳ. It is particularly said that the word πνεύματι is an instrumental of agency which would mean that Jesus would be using the Holy Spirit to baptize us. This verse is then used as a cross reference with *I Corinthians 12:13* to prove that baptism of the Spirit refers to the baptism which takes place at the moment of salvation when a believer is baptized into the body of Christ. The problem with that logic is that Jesus told the disciples that they would be baptized with the Spirit in *Acts 1:5 - For John truly baptized with water; but ye shall be baptized with the Holy Ghost not many days hence.* This was after they had already received the Spirit in *John 20:21-22 - Then said Jesus to them again, Peace be unto you: as my Father hath sent me, even so send I you. 22 And when he had said this, he breathed on them, and saith unto them, Receive ye the Holy Ghost.* This fact also refutes the argument that the baptism of the Spirit, and the baptism by the Spirit into the body of Christ occurs at the same time. They can occur at the same time as seen in *Acts 10*, but that is not to say that they are the same baptism. When that does happen, they are two different distinct baptisms occuring at the same time. That same Greek word πνεύματι found in *Matthew 3:11* could be locative of sphere. In which case, Jesus would be baptizing us into the Spirit. I believe this is a better translation of this word because of the fact that the disciples were baptized into the body of Christ, and received the baptism of the Spirit on two different occasions. This means that *I Corinthians 12:13* does not refer to the baptism of the Spirit.

The baptism of the Spirit is when Christ baptizes us into the Spirit. In this baptism the Spirit is baptizing us into Christ. The roles are reversed in these two baptisms. They are two different baptisms.

I Corinthians 12:14-16 - For the body is not one member, but many. 15 If the foot shall say, Because I am not the hand, I am not of the body; is it therefore not of the body? 16 And if the ear shall say, Because I am not the eye, I am not of the body; is it therefore not of the body? A body is made up of many different parts. This is the same way with the body of Christ. We are all different members of the body of Christ, and therefore serve different functions. A foot can't say that because it isn't the hand, it isn't part of the body. The foot serves a function just like the hand does. It is very important. If the foot doesn't function the way that it is supposed to, the body won't be able to adequately function. The hand has a function, and it certainly is important as well. But it is not more important than the foot. They both serve a function and therefore are equally important in allowing the body to function the way that it should. The same is true with the eye and the ear. They both serve a function and are therefore equally important. The body of Christ is very similar. Every person has at least one spiritual gift, and therefore they serve a function and are important. No member of the body of Christ is more important than the others because all the members contribute to help the body of Christ function properly.

I Corinthians 12:17-22 - If the whole body were an eye, where were the hearing? If the whole were hearing, where were the smelling? 18 But now hath God set the members every one of them in the body, as it hath pleased him. 19 And if they were all one member, where were the body? 20 But now are they many members, yet but one body. 21 And the eye cannot say unto the hand, I have no need of thee: nor again the head to the feet, I have no need of you. 22 Nay, much more those members of the body, which seem to be more feeble, are necessary: If the whole body were an eye. It wouldn't be able to hear. If the whole body were an ear, then it wouldn't be able to smell. Something would be missing. God has placed every single person into the body of Christ. He places people into a local body and gives them all a particular gift. If they do not function in the gift that God gives them, then there will be something missing. This means that every member is dependent upon each other to function properly. God probably does this to establish relationships with each other. It also means that every member should be serving. Every single person has been given a spiritual gift by God, and therefore should be using it. This also means that one member shouldn't be the sole focus and focal point of the church. It is really easy to let the pastor become the focal point of the ministry. That should not happen. Too often I believe this may happen because the pastor is taking on took many responsibilities. It may be that he doesn't want to share the load with his congregation. It could also be that the congregation doesn't want to share the load with the pastor. Both of this situations are detrimental to the function of the church. God did not design the church to function this way. The pastor needs to share the responsibilities with the church members, and the church members need to accept the responsibilities if the church is going to function properly. Even the members that don't seem to have a function, or that it doesn't seem like they contribute much, do contribute. They do contribute and should be honored for their contribution instead of being treated like they are not needed. An eye can't say to a hand that it is not needed. Neither can the head say to the feet that they are not needed. The same is true with the body of Christ. All serve a function and therefore all are needed. The reason why this is focused on so much is because the tendency is to highlight one member of the body and not the other. It is so easy to focus on the pastor and deacons and put them on a pedestal. The same can be done with those with the gift of prophecy and the gift of healing. But it should not be done. Even the person that serves behind the scene should be recognized for their service. They deserve just as much credit for faithfully serving where they are at. This leads me to conclude that we do not go to church to be served, but we go to church to serve. When the pastor is done preaching and the service is over, the members of the congregation have a great opportunity to serve each other by loving each other and praying for one another. This should greatly help the unity of the church when every member functions the way that God designed them to. God has designed every member to be needed! Everyone is needed in the body of Christ and should be treated like it! I think it is pretty obvious here that spiritual gifts are needed and should be exercised. If someone was paralyzed from the waist down, it would be a handicap. If someone had an ear infection, then treatment would be needed. If someone had liver failure, then it could be fatal. If we as the body of Christ don't believe in all the spiritual gifts it can paralyze the church. If the members of the church don't function in the gifts that they have been given then it can be fatal. Many have denied the gift of healing and the gift of prophecy in the church today. In those same churches there are people walking around wondering if God is still with them, or if He is even listening to their prayers when He wants to speak to them directly to their hearts through a prophecy. Instead of spending all the time at prayer meeting praying for revival and the salvation of many people's souls, a major prayer request that comes up is the need of healing. This is because there are so many people both believers and unbelievers who need healing. God wants to directly heal that person through his church, so that He can personally touch believers in need of healing and give other believers an opportunity to share the gospel with unbelievers. I'm not saying we shouldn't pray for healing, but I am saying that if we believed in the gift of healing, then we would be able to spend more time praying for the salvation of souls, and for revival. This is not meant to be condemning, but it meant to be challenging. I am trying to challenge the way we think to line up with what Paul is telling us in this passage.

I Corinthians 12:23-24 - and those members of the body, which we think to be less honourable, upon these we bestow more abundant honour; and our uncomely parts have more abundant comeliness. 24 For our comely parts have no need: but God hath tempered the body together, having given more abundant honour to that part which lacked: Paul states that there is a possibility that we may think one member to be less honorable than another because of the gift that they have been given. Paul simply says that we bestow more abundant honor on those members of the body. God doesn't want us to honor some in the church such as the leadership and not honor other members of the body of Christ. All the members of the body should be honored for what they could contribute to the body of Christ. In fact that is one reason why we should honor every single member of the body of Christ. They have been given a spiritual gift, and because of it they should be treated as such. When their gift is used additional honor should be given to that member for their faithfulness. Paul says that we should honor the uncomely parts with more comeliness. This really has to do with our perspective. Comeliness is charm, elegance, or external beauty. We are to honor those that don't seem to have the same charm, elegance, or external beauty because Christ can still be seen through them. Those that don't seem to be anything special, are supposed to be viewed as special by the other members of the body. The reason why we should honor each other in the body of Christ is because we all have been given a spiritual gift. The gift itself is not the reason we are to honor each other. We are to honor each other because through these gifts we can see Christ in different ways. We are all members of the body of "Christ". We see Christ in different ways, because Christ shows Himself differently in different members of the body of "Christ". For this reason we are to honor each other. We are to honor the members of the body of Christ that do appear to have charm, elegance, or external beauty, but not above any of the other members. Remember we are not to honor them for the charm, elegance, or external beauty given to them by Christ. We are to honor them because Christ is seen through the charm, elegance, or external beauty given to them. In fact, it is not about their charm, elegance, or external beauty. It is about Christ. In focusing on Christ, we see Christ's charm, elegance, and beauty seen in them. This is the real charm, elegance, and beauty. They are to be honored just as every other member because all members picture Christ. One is his hand, one is his foot, one is his eye, but all are members of His body. Paul says that God has united us together by giving honor to those that lack honor for this reason. Again, this promotes unity. It is simply caring for those that seem to be lacking in the body of Christ by seeing them as members that picture Christ. This is God's heart for His church.

1 Corinthians 12:25-27 - that there should be no schism in the body; but that the members should have the same care one for another. 26 And whether one member suffer, all the members suffer with it; or one member be honoured, all the members rejoice with it. 27 Now ye are the body of

Christ, and members in particular. These verses tell us why Paul writes this. So that there wouldn't be a schism in the church, but rather there should be unity in the church, or the body of Christ. He wants His church to care for one another, and to love each other. We are to love each other equally. How does this work? Paul writes that if one member suffers, then all the members of the church suffer with that member. On the other hand, if one member is honored, then all the members are to rejoice with him. Christ is seen through these actions. This is greatly needed in the body of Christ. Why are we supposed to do this? Because we are all part of the body of Christ. We are one unit, as a body, and as a family. But we are also individual members in that body that contribute to the body, and to the family. If that is not done it is not because God doesn't want us to. If it is not done, then it is a result because of sin. Too many times there is backbiting and cutting down in the body of Christ, and this should not be the case. For a long time I saw this in the body of Christ. I didn't like what I saw. As a result I didn't want to be a part of the body. After studying this passage of Scripture, and experiencing His true design, I see that this is not God's design for the church. It is sin. God's design for the church is glorious. We should view the church as such, and we should have faith to believe the Scriptures description of the church in this passage, and to act accordingly.

I Corinthians 12:28-30 - And God hath set some in the church, first apostles, secondarily prophets, thirdly teachers, after that miracles, then gifts of healings, helps, governments, diversities of tongues. 29 Are all apostles? are all prophets? are all teachers? are all workers of miracles? 30 have all the gifts of healing? do all speak with tongues? do all interpret? How are we supposed to contribute to the body of Christ, if we believe that our God-given gifts are not in the church today? Many have said that there are no prophets and apostles in the church today. Some say that there are none that have the gift of healing today, and that God does not use his servants to do miracles today. Those beliefs are in direct contradiction to this passage. To believe so, requires us to to deny the plain meaning of these verses. A cessationist is then forced to deny what the Bible clearly teaches and reinterpret it to mean the exact opposite of the plain meaning of it. A very similar passage is found in *Ephesians 4:11-12 - And he gave some, apostles; and some, prophets; and some, evangelists; and some, pastors and teachers; 12 for the perfecting of the saints, for the work of the ministry, for the edifying of the body of Christ:* He gave them to the church.

To say that that he didn't is to deny the authority of the Scriptures. This proves how much some teaching has influenced us when we have a hard time believing the clear statements of the Scriptures. That statement is not meant to condemn, but it is meant to confront beliefs that contradict the Scriptures. The office of a prophet and an apostle are given to edify the body of Christ so that He can be seen through them. How else can Christ directly speak today to His children unless He speaks through someone's mouth such as a prophet?

Paul then asks some questions in the next two verses. They are rhetorical questions with obvious answers. No, not everyone is an apostle or a prophet, not everyone is a teacher. Not everyone is a worker of miracles. Not all have the gift of healing. Not everyone is to be speaking in tongues or to interpret tongues. But some do have those gifts. God has set them in the church to edify the church, and to help establish the church. If everyone was supposed to prophesy to teach then there would be no one left in the church to listen. That would violate all the principles that he just wrote relating to the body of Christ. If everyone had the same gift, then the church would not function the way that it was meant to function. Not everyone functions in the same gift, but all are to be functioning in at least one gift.

Many times there are abuses and errors in doctrine and practice the body of Christ, and some react to those errors by teaching and practicing the exact opposite. This almost never leads to the right conclusion. We must not base our practice or doctrine on personal beliefs and opinions which many times end in error, as do the reactions to those errors. One error concerns the gift of tongues. Many people misuse and abuse it, and teach false doctrine about it to the point that it is believed that one must speak in tongues in order to be saved. That teaching flat out denies *Ephesians 2:8-9 - For by grace are ye saved through faith; and that not of yourselves: it is the gift of God: 9 not of works, lest any man should boast.* Salvation is not by our work, nor has it ever been or will be by our works, and this includes speaking in tongues. It is an error that should be confronted. This verse also seems to indicate that not all in the body of Christ speak in tongues in the setting of the church though they be assuredly saved. The answer is that not everyone needs to speak in tongues to be saved. It is an error in doctrine and belief, and that teaching should be shunned. On the other side many have seen the abuse and the false doctrine concerning the gift of tongues, and have completely rejected the gift altogether which has also ended in error. The gift of tongues is just that, it is a gift to be used in the right context and way, and to reject it for the abuses and errors concerning it is like saying that Christians don't need grace because some have abused it as a license to sin. Grace is not meant to be a license to sin, yet it has legitimate uses for the Christian. In the same way, the gift of tongues has been abused, but it also has legitimate purposes for the Christian.

1 Corinthians 12:31 - But covet earnestly the best gifts: and yet shew I unto you a more excellent way. Many people who oppose the modern charismatic movement have used this verse as a reason for their opposition. They say that love is the more excellent way, therefore love should be focused on instead of the gifts. Love is the more excellent way. It should be our focus. But if we deny the gifts, then we are not allowing Christ to be seen through the gifts He gives to the church. Remember they are Christ's gifts to give, or to hold back. John the Baptist said in *John 3:27 - John answered and said, A man can receive nothing, except it be given him from heaven.* These gifts are given from heaven by Christ to the children of God so He can be seen through them. If love is the more excellent way, then that means the spiritual gifts are excellent because they are Christ's gifts. Paul wrote in *Philippians 1:9-10 - And this I pray, that your love may abound yet more and more in knowledge and in all judgment; 10 that ye may approve things that are excellent; that ye may be sincere and without offence till the day of Christ.* Paul prayed that their love would abound, but that it would abound according to knowledge and judgement that comes from God. But the way that it would abound was by approving those things that were excellent in each other which were Christ's. These excellent things included His love, His grace, and His mercy. When they saw those things of Christ that were excellent they were to approve of them in order that they would be sincere and without offence until the day of Christ. That includes but is not limited to the God-given spiritual gifts as we have seen from *1 Corinthians 12:31*. According to this verse these gifts were excellent. And as we have seen they were given by Christ to the children of God so that Christ could be seen through them. The Philippian believers would actually be loving on their brothers and sisters in Christ by approving their gifts. In doing so, they actually are partaking of the more excellent way of love. They were to approve of these things until the day of Christ. The day of Christ hasn't happened yet, and so we are to approve of those same gifts. He is not writing that love is more excellent to the point that they pursue love at the exclusion of the spiritual gifts. In fact this passage teaches that they should pursue both with a higher emphasis on love. The Greek word for covet is in the imperative mood in the Greek which is used primarily to express commands. It can be used to entreat others to do something, but whether it is a command or an entreaty, we know that God wills for us to covet the best gifts. We should therefore covet the best gifts with the greater priority given to love. The greatest priority for the Christian is to love. *Matthew 22:37-40 - Jesus said unto him, Thou shalt love the Lord thy God with all thy heart, and with all thy soul, and with all thy mind. 38 This is the first and great commandment. 39 And the second is like unto it, Thou shalt love thy neighbour as thyself. 40 On these two commandments hang all the law and the prophets.* If you get nothing else from this book, understand this. The two greatest priorities for a Christian is to love the Lord with all of our heart, soul, and mind, and to love our neighbor as ourselves. When you take a step back, that's what this chapter is about. It is about the God-given spiritual gifts that are to be used to contribute to the church. We come to church not to be served, but rather to serve. This chapter paves the way for the next chapter in which Paul talks about love. Every single believer has been given a spiritual gift, and they are expected to use it. But every believer is to use their gift in love!

Chapter 2

I Corinthians 13

I Corinthians 13 is commonly referred to as the love chapter. Why? Because it speaks to us about charity or love, ἀγάπη love. It tells us of the importance of love in the first three verses. In the next four it tells us of a description of love. But many have used *I Corinthians 13:8-10* as the reason for why they don't believe in the spiritual gifts. I believe that interpretation is faulty. Let's look at the whole chapter.

I Corinthians 13:1-13 - Though I speak with the tongues of men and of angels, and have not charity, I am become as sounding brass, or a tinkling cymbal. 2 And though I have the gift of prophecy, and understand all mysteries, and all knowledge; and though I have all faith, so that I could remove mountains, and have not charity, I am nothing. 3 And though I bestow all my goods to feed the poor, and though I give my body to be burned, and have not charity, it profiteth me nothing. 4 Charity suffereth long, and is kind; charity envieth not; charity vaunteth not itself, is not puffed up, 5 doth not behave itself unseemly, seeketh not her own, is not easily provoked, thinketh no evil; 6 rejoiceth not in iniquity, but rejoiceth in the truth; 7 beareth all things, believeth all things, hopeth all things, endureth all things. 8 Charity never faileth: but whether there be prophecies, they shall fail; whether there be tongues, they shall cease; whether there be knowledge, it shall vanish away. 9 For we know in part, and we prophesy in part. 10 But when that which is perfect is come, then that which is in part shall be done away. 11 When I was a child, I spake as a child, I understood as a child, I thought as a child: but when I became a man, I put away childish things. 12 For now we see through a glass, darkly; but then face to face: now I know in part; but then shall I know even as also I am known. 13 And now abideth faith, hope, charity, these three; but the greatest of these is charity.

In the first three verses Paul speaks of the importance of love. *I Corinthians 13:1-3 - Though I speak with the tongues of men and of angels, and have not charity, I am become as sounding brass, or a tinkling cymbal. 2 And though I have the gift of prophecy, and understand all mysteries, and all knowledge; and though I have all faith, so that I could remove mountains, and have not charity, I am nothing. 3 And though I bestow all my goods to feed the poor, and though I give my body to be burned, and have not charity, it profiteth me nothing.* He writes that if he could speak in tongues (the languages of men and of angels), but he doesn't have charity, then he is just making noise. He said that he could have the best spiritual gift which is the gift of prophecy. He could know all mysteries and knowledge. He could even have faith to move mountains. But all this would be meaningless if he did have charity. He'd still be nothing if he didn't have love. If he gave up everything he had to feed the poor, and he died a martyr's death by being burned, but he didn't have charity, even then all these things wouldn't profit him. Paul is showing us the importance of charity. It is more important than the gifts of tongues, the gift of prophecy, understanding of all mysteries and knowledge, faith that can move mountains, giving to the poor, and even dying a martyr's death. He says that in God's economy love is the most important quality that we can have. It reigns supreme. This is something that I do want to point out. Love is so important. Love is the most important thing we can ever do. The Bible tells us in *Matthew 22:37-40 - Jesus said unto him, Thou shalt love the Lord thy God with all thy heart, and with all thy soul, and with all thy mind. 38 This is the first and great commandment. 39 And the second is like unto it, Thou shalt love thy neighbor as thyself. 40 On these two commandments hang all the law and the prophets.* Jesus said that the two greatest things that we can ever do is to love Him with all our heart, soul, and mind, and then to love our neighbor as ourselves. In the body of Christ returning to our first love is greatly needed today. Our Christian lives, and our entire lives really should be about Him. He should be our God, and our love, and our true hearts desire. The greatest thing we can ever do is to love him! We also need to put a high priority on loving each other. It is for this reason that I am writing this. I do not want to tear anyone else down. I am just zealous for the Word of God. I love Him and His Word, and want things to be set straight.

After explaining the importance of love, Paul then gives a description of love. *I Corinthians 13:4-8a - Charity suffereth long, and is kind; charity envieth not; charity vaunteth not itself, is not puffed up, 5 doth not behave itself unseemly, seeketh not her own, is not easily provoked, thinketh no evil; 6 rejoiceth not in iniquity, but rejoiceth in the truth; 7 beareth all things, believeth all things, hopeth all things, endureth all things. 8 Charity never faileth...* Paul said that charity or love suffereth long. The Greek word for this is μακροθυμέω makrothyméō, mak-roth-oo-meh'-o; to be long-spirited, i.e. (objectively) forbearing or (subjectively) patient:—bear (suffer) long, be longsuffering, have (long) patience, be patient, patiently endure. It simply means to be patient. Unfortunately, there is only one way to gain patience, and that is through tribulation (Romans 5:3-4). Yet, patience is still worth the cost. It is the Father's loving hands that molds us in those times. He says that charity is kind. The Greek word for kind is χρηστεύομαι chrēsteúomai, khraste-yoo'-om-ahee; to show oneself useful, i.e. act benevolently:—be kind. By definition loves shows itself useful. This means that this kindness gets to work! *Titus 2:7 - In all things shewing thyself a pattern of good works: in doctrine shewing uncorruptness, gravity, sincerity.* Paul wrote to Titus that he would shew himself a pattern of good works, to be constantly doing them. This is what charity is supposed to do. Love looks like something, and that something practically manifests itself in good works. The Greek word for envy is †ζηλόω zēlóō, dzay-lo'-o; to have warmth of feeling for or against:—affect, covet (earnestly), (have) desire, (move with) envy, be jealous over, (be) zealous(-ly affect). It has a burning desire for something that is prohibited. It literally means to covet. This is something that charity or love does not do because it makes itself busy giving to others, that it doesn't have time to covet something for itself. The Greek word for vaunteth itself is περπερεύομαι perpereúomai, per-per-yoo'-om-ahee;—vaunt itself. Charity does boast. It doesn't brag because it is too busy approving those things which are excellent in others. *Philippians 1:10 - that ye may approve things that are excellent; that ye may be sincere and without offence till the day of Christ.* The Greek word for puffed up is φυσιόω physióō, foo-see-o'-o; in the primary sense of blowing; to inflate, i.e. (figuratively) make proud (haughty):—puff up. It is not puffed up because it doesn't boast or vaunt itself. It doesn't have a big head. Again this emphasizes the fact that charity is not proud. The Greek word for behave itself unseemly is ἀσχημονέω aschēmonéō, as-kay-mon-eh'-o; to be (i.e. act) unbecoming:—behave self uncomely (unseemly). This can be hard to understand, but simply, put charity is polite. The phrase seeketh not her own is made up of a couple Greek words. But they are self-explanatory and it doesn't need to be shown. It means exactly what it sounds like. Love doesn't seek its own desires. It seeks the desires of another. It is not self-centered. This is probably one of the most important qualities of love, because it is the foundation for all the others. It is not trying to accomplish its own desires and goals, but the desires and goals of the one that it is loving. If we are to love God with all our heart, all our soul, and all our mind, and to love our neighbor as ourselves then we need to seek to do the will of God for our lives and to help accomplish the goals of others, and find the will of God for their lives. The Greek word for is "easily provoked" is παροξύνω paroxýnō, par-ox-oo'-no; to sharpen alongside, i.e. (figuratively) to exasperate:—easily provoke, stir. This means that it can be. It does not get angered easily, but it can. How? Look at Jesus. He is perfect love. What was he provoked by? The scribes and Pharisees. He was provoked by their hypocrisy. This tells me that true love is provoked by empty, corrupted religion. True religion is not corrupt. *James 1:27 - Pure religion and undefiled before God and the Father is this, To visit the fatherless and widows in their affliction, and to keep himself unspotted from the world.* True religion doesn't try to find out why people are fatherless and widows, but it actually tries to help them. Some might think that it might be ridiculous to condemn and judge the fatherless and widows, and those that are destitute. But sad to say, many times Christians do judge the poor, and find a reason for why they are poor in order to excuse themselves from reaching out to them, helping them, and showing them grace. This should not be the case. John writes against this in *I John 3:16-18 - Hereby perceive we the love of God, because he laid down his life for us: and we ought to lay down our lives for the brethren. 17 But whoso hath this world's good, and seeth his brother have need, and shutteth up his bowels of compassion from him, how dwelleth the love of God in him? 18 My little children, let us not love in word, neither in tongue; but in deed and in truth.* John writes about how Jesus laid down his life for us. Since he has sacrificed so much, we are supposed to be sacrificing for the brethren as well. If we have this world's good, or the resources to help someone and we see that person has a need, (especially if it be a fellow child of God) We should be seeking to provide for them. If we don't try to provide, if we look the other way, if we turn away from them and don't have compassion to them, then we just don't have the love of God in us. This is a tall order. This is very convicting. How many Christians actually make a conscious effort to reach out to feed the poor? We have Birthday parties and share presents, we have coffee every day, we strive to have the newest cars all the while some of our fellow children of God are out on the streets, without food to eat or a place to stay. I have talked to a single mother who had seven children that was working and struggling to provide for herself and her children. I don't know what happened. It may be easy for us to jump to conclusions, but ultimately we don't know. It may have been that she sinned, and that's why she had seven children. It could've been that she got married, but her husband left her, or was killed. Either way, it is not our responsibility to find reasons for why she is in that situation in order to use "wisdom" to decide whether or not we should help her. John clearly says if we shut up our bowels of compassion then we do not have the love of God in us. As I was talking to her, she said she had gone to seven different churches for help to provide for her children. All seven of them turned her away. That should not be. Paul said in *Romans 12:9 - Let love be without dissimulation...* Dissimulation is hypocrisy. We are not to have hypocrisy when we love. Here's the problem. Most of us believe that we should be caring for the poor, but how many Christians go out of their way to do it? *James 4:17 - Therefore to him that knoweth to do good, and doeth it not, to him it is sin.* If we do not attempt to provide for our poor brothers and sisters in Christ, then it is sin, and we do not have the love of God in us.

The Greek word for "thinketh" is λογίζομαι logízomai, to take an inventory, i.e. estimate (literally or figuratively):—conclude, (ac-)count (of), + despise, esteem, impute, lay, number, reason, reckon, suppose, think (on). This is an accounting term. It counts something. What is it counting in this context? It accounts for evil. The Greek word for evil is κακός kakós, kak-os'; apparently a primary word; worthless (intrinsically, such; i.e. (subjectively) depraved, or (objectively) injurious:—bad, evil, harm, ill, noisome, wicked. Paul is saying that love doesn't account for the wrong done against it. It doesn't keep lists of the wrong done. It is not Christian to hold offenses done against the one who committed it. Instead the Bible says in *Proverbs 17:9 - He that covereth a transgression seeketh love; but he that repeateth a matter separateth very friends.* The word "but" in that verse means that there's a contrast. A contrast between covering a transgression, and repeating a matter, between seeking love and separating friends. In this context, when Solomon says "repeateth a matter", he's probably referring to a transgression. The person that always is bringing up the faults and failures of others is causing separation. When the Bible says, "covereth a transgression", it means to conceal it. We are to conceal the transgressions of others. We're not concealing the transgression so we don't have to deal with it. We're not concealing it, because we're brushing it under the rug. We're not concealing it so that you can continue in sin so that grace can abound. We are not concealing it so that we can sin as much as we want after we're saved. This is talking about our relationships with each other, specifically with our relationships with our friends. This is something that we can incorporate in our relationships with our friends to strengthen them. We are concealing someone else's transgression so that something else can be seen. There is something good that we can find about them if we choose to look. It doesn't take much to see something wrong, but we should be focusing on what's right or good about them. If nothing else, the image of God has been stamped on that person's life. They have the potential to be conformed to the very image of Christ. They have been created by God, and they are fearfully and wonderfully made. When we see people like that we can say that is a person worth loving, no matter who it is. We're not seeing what's wrong with people. We're seeing what's right with that individual, and we're doing our best to draw out their strengths. We are trying to help them with what they're missing. It might seem spiritual to always be finding what's wrong with someone, but it's not. It's spiritual to see what's right with an individual and to see their potential and try to draw it out. The Greek word for rejoice is χαίρω chaírō, khah'-ee-ro; to be "cheer"ful, i.e. calmly happy or well-off; impersonally, especially as salutation (on meeting or parting), be well:—farewell, be glad, God speed, greeting, hail, joy(- fully), rejoice. Whereas the Greek word for "iniquity" is ἀδικία adikía, ad-ee-kee'-ah; (legal) injustice (properly, the quality, by implication, the act); morally, wrongfulness (of character, life or act):—iniquity, unjust, unrighteousness, wrong. The Greek word for iniquity is in the Dative case in the Greek. It seems as though it is a Dative of Respect. All that means is that love does not rejoice in respect to iniquity or si Love does not rejoice in sin. Whether that sin be done against it, against someone else, or against God. Neither does it rejoice when bad circumstances are happening in other people's lives as a result of sin, even if that person causes irritation in their lives. This is exactly why it doesn't rejoice in sin. Sin hurts people, and love does not desire that for anyone. The Greek word for "truth" is ἀλήθεια alḗtheia, al-ay'-thi-a; truth:—true, × truly, truth, verity. This word is also in the Dative case in the Greek. It is also a Dative of Respect meaning that Love rejoices or takes joy in the truth. Between these two statements, it tells me that ἀγάπη love is holy. In fact, one cannot love without being sanctified. Why? How are we supposed to love someone if we are sinning against them? Jesus is always are perfect model. He loved others even when they were opposed to him. Praise God for the Lord Jesus Christ, the holy Son of God, and our loving Savior! The Greek word for "beareth" is στέγω stégō, steg'-o; to roof over, i.e. (figuratively) to cover with silence (endure patiently):—(for-)bear, suffer. It goes back to the fact that it is longsuffering, it is patient. It is the outworking of the fact that it is longsuffering. It bears all things. It bears with people in the midst of their faults, and failures. The Greek word for "believeth" is πιστεύω pisteúō, pist-yoo'-o; to have faith (in, upon, or with respect to, a person or thing), i.e. credit; by implication, to entrust (especially one's spiritual wellbeing to Christ):—believe(-r), commit (to trust), put in trust with. It simply means to trust the other individual. Charity or love believes the best about an individual no matter what happens. The Greek word for "hopeth" is ἐλπίζω elpízō, el-pid'-zo; to expect or confide:—(have, thing) hope(-d) (for), trust. It means that charity hopes the best for the individuals of the lives around them. The Greek word for "endureth" is ὑπομένω hypoménō, hoop-om-en'-o; to stay under (behind), i.e. remain; figuratively, to undergo, i.e. bear (trials), have fortitude, persevere:—abide, endure, (take) patient(-ly), suffer, tarry behind. This means exactly what it says. It is enduring. Jesus is a great example of this quality of charity. *John 13:1 - Now before the feast of the passover, when Jesus knew that his hour was come that he should depart out of this world unto the Father, having loved his own which were in the world, he loved them unto the end.* At the last supper when Jesus had broken bread, he said that this was his body that was to be broken. When he took the cup, He said that it was his blood that was to be spilled for them. He knew that he was going to the cross and he still loved them until the end. That is amazing. Think about it. He's using an illustration to show them what is going to happen to him. The Bible tells us in the night that he broke bread he was betrayed. He broke the bread and passed the cup knowing that Judas was going to betray him, and yet he still loved them to the end. That is amazing! The last quality that Paul gave about love is that it never fails. The Greek word "faileth" is ἐκπίπτω ekpíptō, ek-pip'-to; to drop away; specially, be driven out of one's course; figuratively, to lose, become inefficient:—be cast, fail, fall (away, off), take none effect. If it doesn't take none effect, then it means that it always has an effect. It means that it really does never fail. If we understood this then it would change the way that we witness. The best way to witness to someone is to love them. Why? Because love never fails. People might not remember a debate about

Christianity vs. Atheism. But they will remember when you visit them in the hospital. They will remember when you baked them a pie as a sign of your care for them as your neighbor. They will remember acts of love. Why? Because love never fails. It also means that it won't pass away. This is amazing. This means that we will always love. How? We will always love each other and the Lord in heaven. This is the context of *I Corithians 13:8-10 - Charity never faileth: but whether there be prophecies, they shall fail; whether there be tongues, they shall cease; whether there be knowledge, it shall vanish away. 9 For we know in part, and we prophesy in part. 10 But when that which is perfect is come, then that which is in part shall be done away.* This is the passage that people use to prove that the spiritual gifts are not in the church today. The context of this passage has nothing to do with spiritual gifts. The context is love. B.F. Cate writes in his book, *The Nine Gifts of the Spirit are not in the Church Today*,

> Now let us read beginning with the 8th verse. Paul said, "Charity [love] NEVER FAILETH." This implies that the gifts WOULD FAIL; so he continues by saying, "but whether there be prophecies, they SHALL FAIL; whether there be tongues, they SHALL CEASE; whether there be knowledge it shall VANISH AWAY. For we know IN PART, and we prophesy IN PART" (Verses 8-9). The reason they knew only in part was because what is now written in the New Testament was not then fully revealed. "But" says Paul, "when that which is PERFECT [completion of the New Testament] is come, then that which is IN PART [prophecy, etc.] SHALL BE DONE AWAY" (verse 10). Then he illustrates this by saying, "when I was a child, I spake as a child, I understood as a child, I thought as a child: but when I became a man, I PUT AWAY childish things" (verse 11). In the early days of this dispensation, when this epistle was written, they were as children; but the time was fast approaching should "PUT AWAY childish things" (nine gifts), and walk by faith in the "more excellent way" of "love" and in the light of God's complete revelation. Paul illustrates again, saying, "For NOW [when this epistle was written] we see through a glass, darkly [know in part]; but THEN [when God's revelation to man was completed] then face to face; now I know in part; but then shall I know even as also I am know" (verse 12). To "know even as also I am

known" means, that God's revelation is complete, we do not "know in part" any more, but we know God's mind (for this dispensation) even as He knows our mind. To be sure that we understand this, Paul tells us exactly what was to abide after the spectacular, or the sign gifts, ceased. "And now ABIDETH faith, hope, love, these THREE; but the greatest of these is love" (Verse 13). To be doubly sure that we understand him, Paul adds up to THREE, not NINE, as listed in the 12th chapter. Thus he shows that the NINE gifts went out of the church as the New Testament came in. Some think that the gift of faith was a spectacular gift that only some Christians had. Read again I Corinthians 12:8-11. We may have great faith, in our day, according to the way we apply ourselves to the teachings of the New Testament, not by a special gift of faith.[10]

I quoted word for word the entirety of B.F Cate's interpretation of *I Corinthians 13:8-13* found in his book. I do not want to take any of his words out of context. Before I interpret this passage of Scripture, I want to point out the flaws of this interpretation. The whole argument is based on the belief that prophecy was what God used to give the Scriptures. In fact later on B.F Cate states,

All the Word of God is prophecy. Those parts usually spoke of as prophecy those parts usually spoken as prophecy are predictive prophecy. The same thing is true of the prophets. People usually think of a prophet as one who foretold the future. But, as we shall see later, a prophet was one who received the Word of God by divine revelation.[11]

It is evident that some believe that prophecy is what God used to reveal his word to man. I looked up the words "predictive prophecy" in a Bible search engine, and I found zero results. I looked up the word "predictive" in the same Bible search engine. I still found zero results. That is a theological term created to fit the presuppositions that someone had before they come to the Bible. Like I said in the preface, many people don't actually believe the Bible, they believe what they believe about the Bible. Let's stick with what the Bible says about prophecy.

I Corinthians 14:3 - But he that prophesieth speaketh unto men to edification, and exhortation, and comfort. Paul said that the purpose of prophecy is edification, exhortation, and comfort. There you go, let's establish that right now. The purpose of the gift of prophecy in the New Testament is edification, exhortation, and comfort. Now let's take a look at B.F. Cate's interpretation. Cate says,

> Now let us read beginning with the 8th verse. Paul said, "Charity [love] NEVER FAILETH." This implies that the gifts WOULD FAIL; so he continues by saying, "but whether there be prophecies, they SHALL FAIL; whether there be tongues, they SHALL CEASE; whether there be knowledge it shall VANISH AWAY. For we know IN PART, and we prophesy IN PART" (Verses 8-9).[12]

I do not disagree with this. It is not disputed that prophecy would fail or pass away. I'm not arguing that tongues won't cease or that knowledge won't vanish away. The question is not whether all these things will pass away, but when will they pass away.

> The reason they knew only in part was because what is now written in the New Testament was not then fully revealed. "But" says Paul, "when that which is PERFECT [completion of the New Testament] is come, then that which is IN PART [prophecy, etc.] SHALL BE DONE AWAY" (verse 10).[13]

The problem that I have with this interpretation is that it also says that "we know in part". When that which is perfect is come then that which is in part shall be done away. What's in part? Prophecy and knowledge are in part. If prophecy was done away with at the completion of the Word of God, then so was what we know. If prophecy was what God was using to reveal his Word, then in context what they knew was the Scriptures, which would be done away when they were revealed. What did they know at this time? They knew the Old Testament. Someone could very easily use this passage to prove that we don't need the Old Testament anymore. I mean after all, we have the New Testament right?

I guess you could say that the phrase "we know in part" refers to the partial knowledge of the Word, not the actual Word, which would be done away when the Word of God was completed. But to be consistent with our interpretation, then that means that partial prophesy, not the actual gift was done away when the word of God is completed. If that interpretation is taken to be true, then partial prophecy would refer to its use in revealing the Word of God. In which case, it would still have a use to reveal the secrets of men's hearts to speak edification, exhortation, and comfort to them. No matter what interpretation is taken, the Word of God itself tells us in *I Thessalonians 5:19-20 - Quench not the Spirit. 20 Despise not prophesyings.* The same Paul tells the Thessalonian believers not to quench the Spirit. How do we quench the Spirit? When we despise prophesying. Many times it is said that the word "prophesyings" really means preaching. We are not to despise preaching. That's just not what it says. The Greek word for "prophesyings" is προφητεία prophēteía, prof-ay-ti'-ah; ("prophecy"); prediction (scriptural or other):—prophecy, prophesying. It means prophesyings when it says prophesyings. This is the same word used in *I Corinthians 13:8 - ... but whether there be prophecies, they shall fail.* Does that mean that Paul was saying that they weren't supposed to despise prophesyings at least until it was done away? If this word in *I Thessalonians 5:20* means preaching, then why wouldn't it mean preaching in *I Corinthians 13:8*? I mean after all, if we have that which is perfect, the complete Word of God, then why do we still need preaching? We can read it ourselves. There's obviously some issues. Why don't we just take the Word of God for what it says when it says that we aren't supposed to despise prophesyings. By the way, the Greek word for "despise" in *I Thessalonians 5:20* is in the imperative mood meaning that it is a command. He is commanding them not to despise prophesyings. We need to respect the commands of God, therefore we should accept the gift of prophecy. B.F. Cate writes,

> Then he illustrates this by saying, "when I was a child, I spake as a child, I understood as a child, I thought as a child: but when I became a man, I PUT AWAY childish things" (verse 11). In the early days of this dispensation, when this epistle was written, they were as children; but the time was fast approaching should "PUT AWAY childish things" (nine gifts), and walk by faith in the "more excellent way" of "love" and in the light of God's complete revelation.[14]

Cate here describes the spiritual gifts as childish. Paul wrote something else. *Romans 1:11 - For I long to see you, that I may impart unto you some spiritual gift, to the end ye may be established.* He longed or desired to see the Christians in Roman so that he could impart a spiritual gift to them for the purpose that they would be established. The writer of Hebrews agrees with Paul in *Hebrews 6:1-2 - Therefore leaving the principles of the doctrine of Christ, let us go on unto perfection; not laying again the foundation of repentance from dead works, and of faith toward God, 2 of the doctrine of baptisms, and of laying on of hands, and of resurrection of the dead, and of eternal judgment.* He writes that "laying on of hands" is a fundamental principle of Christ.

The verse that Cate is referring to when he speaks of the "more excellent way" is *I Corinthians 13:31 - But covet earnestly the best gifts: and yet shew I unto you a more excellent way.* This is the last verse in I *Corinthians 12*. He tells the Corinthians in this that he will show them a more excellent way speaking of love in *I Corinthians 13*. I agree with that because that is what Paul said. But if love is the more excellent way that means that spiritual gifts are excellent themselves. Do you know what we are to do with things that are excellent? *Philippians 1:9-10 - And this I pray, that your love may abound yet more and more in knowledge and in all judgment; 10 that ye may approve things that are excellent; that ye may be sincere and without offence till the day of Christ.* Paul writes that the Philippians would have discernment and that their love would abound. But he also prays that they were to approve those things that are excellent until the day of Christ. If he is speaking directly to the Philippian believers then he is also directly speaking to us because we are both part of the church. We are to approve those things that excellent in each other including our God-given spiritual gifts until the day of Christ.

Cate writes again,

> Paul illustrates again, saying, "For NOW [when this epistle was written] we see through a glass, darkly [know in part]; but THEN [when God's revelation to man was completed] face to face; now I know in part; but then shall I know even as also I am know" (verse 12). To "know even as also I am known" means, that God's revelation is complete, we do not "know in part" any more, but we know God's mind (for this dispensation) even as He knows our mind.[15]

I have one question about this interpretation. What does it mean by "face to face"? Cate does not answer this question, and it is a very important phrase in determining the meaning of this passage. With that being said, I fully disagree with that statement that we know God's mind as he knows our mind. Even if he simply meant that we know his mind for this dispensation now that the Word of God has been completed. First of all, God did not reveal all his knowledge to us in the Scriptures. He said so in *Proverbs 25:2 - It is the glory of God to conceal a thing: but the honour of kings is to search out a matter.* This verse teaches that God has concealed some things, so that we would search them out. Many kings have been wise by promoting science and the discovery of knowledge. Other verses that prove that no one fully understands the mind of God is found in *Romans 11:33-34 - O the depth of the riches both of the wisdom and knowledge of God! how unsearchable are his judgments, and his ways past finding out! 34 For who hath known the mind of the Lord? or who hath been his counsellor?* Paul is asking a rhetorical question. When considering the depth of the wisdom and knowledge of God, His unsearchable judgements, and his ways past that are past finding out, the obvious answer to his question is no one. No one fully understands and knows the mind of the Lord. In fact in this same epistle Paul writes in *I Corinthians 2:16 - For who hath known the mind of the Lord, that he may instruct him? But we have the mind of Christ.* Paul clearly is pointing to the fact that no one can know the mind of the Lord, and no one, no matter how smart they think they are, can instruct him. Then he says that we have the mind of Christ. This means that the method that the Holy Spirit uses to speak to us is through thoughts. In context, Paul is writing about the Holy Spirit. *I Corinthians 2:9-10 - But as it is written, Eye hath not seen, nor ear heard, neither have entered into the heart of man, the things which God hath prepared for them that love him. 10 But God hath revealed them unto us by his Spirit: for the Spirit searcheth all things, yea, the deep things of God.* He is writing about the Spirit's ministry of revealing the deep things of God to us. The Holy Spirit knows all the deep things of God, but it is like a filing cabinet which he searches to reveal the right thing at the right moment to his people. *I Corinthians 2:13 - Which things also we speak, not in the words which man's wisdom teacheth, but which the Holy Ghost teacheth; comparing spiritual things with spiritual.* The Holy Spirit teaches us. This is an important topic that is repeated in several places in the Word of God, and it is probably my favorite ministry of the Holy Spirit. I love when the Holy Spirit teaches us new things through the Word of God! Praise God for his glory, and the work and ministry of the Holy Ghost! It is obvious then that no one truly knows the whole mind of God. But, it is also obvious from this passage that when Paul wrote, "we have the mind of Christ" He is specifically referring to the Holy Spirit indwelling us, not the Word of God. To say that to be "known even as also I am known" means to know the mind of God for this dispensation because we have the completed Word of God is just not Scriptural because no one can know the mind of God, and the mind of God according to the Scriptures is not the Word of God, but the Spirit of God.

The biggest reason that I disagree with Cate's interpretation is found in *I Corinthians 1:4-8 - I thank my God always on your behalf, for the grace of God which is given you by Jesus Christ; 5 that in every thing ye are enriched by him, in all utterance, and in all knowledge; 6 even as the testimony of Christ was confirmed in you: 7 so that ye come behind in no gift; waiting for the coming of our Lord Jesus Christ: 8 who shall also confirm you unto the end, that ye may be blameless in the day of our Lord Jesus Christ.* Paul thanked God for the grace that God had given to them. Why? Because His grace is thankworthy! His grace allowed them to be enriched in everything including their words and their knowledge. It was through their words, knowledge, and life which was being enriched by him that their testimony was confirmed in them. The Greek word for "come behind" is ὑστερέω hysteréō, hoos-ter-eh'-o; to be later, i.e. (by implication) to be inferior; generally, to fall short (be deficient):—come behind (short), be destitute, fail, lack, suffer need, (be in) want, be the worse. It is a resultative infinitive in the Greek text, and it is functioning as a verb. This means that the result of receiving his grace to be enriched in all things, including in knowledge, and in speech to the point that their testimony was confirmed in them was that they would be destitute of no gift, lack no gift, suffer need of no gift, or to be in want of no gift. How long? The Greek word for "waiting for" ἀπεκδεχομένους. It is most likely a temporal contemporaneous time participle. As a participle, this word contains a verbal aspect. The verbal action of a temporal contemporaneous time participle happens at the same time as the main verb of the sentence, phrase, or clause. They, as do we, wait for the coming of the Lord. This verbal action is happening at the same time as the main verb in this phrase. What is the main verb? The word ὑστερεῖσθαι is the word that is function as the main verb in this phrase. They were waiting at the same time that they were coming behind in no gift. As long as they were waiting they would also be coming behind, or lacking no gift. How long were they waiting? They were waiting their entire lives as do believers wait today for the coming of our Lord Jesus Christ. As believers we will stop waiting for the coming of our Lord Jesus Christ when he literally comes in the rapture. This means that according to this verse. As believers we will not lack any of the spiritual gifts until he comes back. At that time is when tongues will cease, and prophecies will fail, but not until then.

My goal is not to tear down B.F. Cate in any way. I'm sure that he was a godly man that served God and loved Him very much. I just disagree with his conclusions on the spiritual gifts and am trying to help guide people to the truth concerning them. I want us as Christians to believe the Bible for what it plainly says. I'm going to give my interpretation of *I Corinthians 13:8-10*. We have already seen the context of verses 8-13. The context is love. He speaks of the importance of love in the first three verses and the qualities of it in the next four. Let's look at it again. *I Corinthians 13:8-13 - Charity never faileth: but whether there be prophecies, they shall fail; whether there be tongues, they shall cease; whether there be knowledge, it shall vanish away. 9 For we know in part, and we prophesy in part. 10 But when that which is perfect is come, then that which is in part shall be done away. 11 When I was a child, I spake as a child, I understood as a child, I thought as a child: but when I became a man, I put away childish things. 12 For now we see through a glass, darkly; but then face to face: now I know in part; but then shall I know even as also I am known. 13 And now abideth faith, hope, charity, these three; but the greatest of these is charity.* I do not question if prophecies shall fail, if tongues shall cease, if knowledge shall vanish away, but I do question when. Paul says "we know in part, and we prophesy in part". What does that mean? To know in part means to know Him in part. Then what's it mean to prophesy in part? Well if we prophesy in part, it means that we don't prophesy in full. It means that we don't prophesy the whole of human history. We only prophesy what God gives us which is part of the future, but not the whole of it. If he gave us all of human history, then we wouldn't need to walk by faith. What is that which is perfect? I believe that it is Jesus. Why do I say that? Because Jesus is perfect love. I've heard it said that if it was Jesus it would say that if that which is perfect was Jesus, then it would say, "when that which is perfect is come again". That's just semantics. What would be the difference in saying, "Jesus is coming" and, "Jesus is coming again"? In fact the Greek word for "is come" is in the aorist tense. The aorist tense describes undefined action. This means that this could very well be Jesus because we have no idea when he is to come back. Paul has been speaking about love this entire chapter. When he says that which is perfect, he's referring to perfect love which is Jesus. When Jesus comes back, then his method of exhorting, edifying, and comforting us through the gift of prophecy will be done away, as will our method of knowing him through the word will be done away.because we will be in his very presence *I Corinthians 13:11 - When I was a child, I spake as a child, I understood as a child, I thought as a child: but when I became a man, I put away childish things.* The Greek word for "child" is νήπιος népios, nay'-pee-os; from an obsolete particle νή- nḗ-; not speaking, i.e. an infant (minor); figuratively, a simple-minded person, an immature Christian:—babe, child (+ -ish). It is the same Greek word translated as "children" in *Ephesians 4:14 - that we henceforth be no more children, tossed to and fro, and carried about with every wind of doctrine, by the sleight of men, and cunning craftiness, whereby they lie in wait to deceive;* Since this is the same Greek word, it means that they are both describing the same thing. Children are tossed to and fro by every wind of doctrine, and are carried about by the doctrines of men.

The Bible also tells us in *I John 2:14 - I have written unto you, fathers, because ye have known him that is from the beginning. I have written unto you, young men, because ye are strong, and the word of God abideth in you, and ye have overcome the wicked one.* The word "know" is the word is ἐγνώκατε which comes from γινώσκω. This word is the same word used in *I Corinthians 13:9*. John writes that mature Christians know God. The Apostle Paul was a child for a season of his life. He spoke as one that was one that was tossed to and fro by the doctrines of men. He was a Pharisee. Jesus spoke about the Pharisees in *Matthew 15:9 - But in vain they do worship me, teaching for doctrines the commandments of men.* They worshipped him in vain because they taught the doctrines and commandments of men instead of the commandments and doctrines of God. Before he was saved, Paul knew the Old Testament, he knew the Jewish traditions, he knew all the religious rules and commandments, but he didn't know Christ. He eventually realized it and he said in *Philippians 3:8-10 - Yea doubtless, and I count all things but loss for the excellency of the knowledge of Christ Jesus my Lord: for whom I have suffered the loss of all things, and do count them but dung, that I may win Christ, 9 and be found in him, not having mine own righteousness, which is of the law, but that which is through the faith of Christ, the righteousness which is of God by faith: 10 that I may know him, and the power of his resurrection, and the fellowship of his sufferings, being made conformable unto his death.* This is in the immediate context of him speaking about his qualifications as a Pharisee. Though Paul was a child for a season of his life when he was carried about, tossed to and fro by the doctrines of men, he gave up everything to know Christ when he met him. He said, "I count all things but loss". He gave up everything for the "excellency of the knowledge of Christ Jesus my Lord." That is not the only thing he said in this passage. He said that he wanted to be "found in him, not having my own righteousness" but rather he desired the "righteousness which is of God by faith". We will never ever be able to have a relationship with God based on our ownmerit. We have to realize that God has imputed his own righteousness to us. That fact is the basis of our relationship with Him. It is the foundation. It has nothing to do with us, at all. When someone gets a real good picture of what Christ did for them, and they realize that it has nothing to do with them, it takes away all pride. Paul knew this. He gave up everything, and wanted to be found in the righteousness of Christ that he would know Christ! This word "know" is also the same word used for know in *I Corinthians 13:9. I Corinthians 13:11 - When I was a child, I spake as a child, I understood as a child, I thought as a child: but when I became a man, I put away childish things.* Paul is an example of someone that was a child, but that put away childish things for Christ. He spoke as one who was carried about by the doctrines of men, he understood as one who was carried about by the doctrines of men, and he thought as one who was carried about by the doctrines of men. But, He put away his speech, understanding, and thoughts as a child. But, he gave up everything including his life as a Pharisee to know Christ. At the point he was mature, and he became a man. *I Corinthians 13:12 - For now we see through a glass, darkly; but then face to face: now I know in part; but then shall I know even as also I am known.* As we have already seen when Paul says that he knew in part, he is saying that he knew Christ in part. What does that mean? Paul said we see through a glass darkly. The Greek word for glass is ἔσοπτρον ésoptron, es'-op-tron; a mirror (for looking into):—glass. It is a mirror. Paul says that we are looking into a mirror darkly. The only other time that this word "glass" is used in the Bible is in *James 1:22-24 - But be ye doers of the word, and not hearers only, deceiving your own selves. 23 For if any be a hearer of the word, and not a doer, he is like unto a man beholding his natural face in a glass: 24 for he beholdeth himself, and goeth his way, and straightway forgetteth what manner of man he was.* This word is translated as "glass" here in verse 23. James writes that if a man hears the word but doesn't do it he is like a man that looks in the mirror and sees something wrong with his appearance and doesn't do anything about it. He is keeping with the analogy that the Word of God is like a mirror. This tells me that Paul is doing the same thing by comparing the Word of God with a mirror in *I Corinthians 13:12*. Nobody that I know looks at a mirror to look at a mirror. People don't use mirrors like that in our day, neither did people use mirrors like that in Paul's day. They look at a mirror to see what it pictures. Paul is saying that we look into the Word of God and get a darkly or obscure picture. What picture do we see? We see Jesus in the mirror. *II Corinthians 3:18 - But we all, with open face beholding as in a glass the glory of the Lord, are changed into the same image from glory to glory, even as by the Spirit of the Lord.* Paul writes about "beholding as in a glass". These five English words are all one Greek word, and that Greek word has the same root of the word translated as "glass" in *I Corinthians 13:12*. What do we see when we look or behold in the "glass"? We see the glory of God and the image of God. In this verse it clearly says that we are beholding the glory of God, but it also says that we are changed into the "same image". If there is a duplicate, then there has to be an original. Whose image are we to be conformed to? We are to be conformed to the image of Christ. We are seeing the image of God and the glory of God which are both wrapped up in Christ. *Hebrews 1:1-3 - God, who at sundry times and in divers manners spake in time past unto the fathers by the prophets, 2 hath in these last days spoken unto us by his Son, whom he hath appointed heir of all things, by whom also he made the worlds; 3 who being the brightness of his glory, and the express image of his person, and upholding all things by the word of his power, when he had by himself purged our sins, sat down on the right hand of the Majesty on high;* God spoke in many different ways at different times to the Jewish people by his servants the prophets. But in this time period he has spoken to us by his Son. Jesus is the brightness of His glory and the express image of His person. Jesus is the glory of God and the image of God wrapped up in one. When we look into the glass we are seeing Jesus. The reason why James says that we see ourselves in the mirror is because Christ is who we are supposed to look like, and we need to continually partner with the Holy Spirit to make those changes to become more Christ-like. *I Corinthians 13:12 - For now we see through a glass, darkly; but then face to face: now I know in part; but then shall I know even as also I am known.* Paul is saying that when he was a child he was carried about to and fro by the doctrines of men, but when he became mature, when became a man, he got into the

Word himself to know Christ. He actually wanted to know him instead of just being taught by the doctrines of men. That's the difference between a child and a mature Christian. A child simply believes everything they are taught and is content with that, but a mature Christian gets into the Word for themselves to know Him. We know Him in part by what we can see in the Word of God, but then we will know him face to face. When is that? When that which is perfect is come, when perfect love is come, when Jesus is come back. *I John 3:2 - Beloved, now are we the sons of God, and it doth not yet appear what we shall be: but we know that, when he shall appear, we shall be like him; for we shall see him as he is.* God has shown us so much love by adopting us as his own children. Right now we are the sons of God. But when Jesus comes back we will be perfectly like him. Because we will see him as he really is! When Jesus comes back we will not need to prophesy, we won't need to know him through the Word because we will see him face to face, and He will speak words of edification, exhortation, and comfort to us personally as he will do to the saints that come out of tribulation. *Revelation 7:17 - For the Lamb which is in the midst of the throne shall feed them, and shall lead them unto living fountains of waters: and God shall wipe away all tears from their eyes.* When Jesus comes back we will know him as he knows us. How does he know us? *Psalm 139:1-2 - O Lord, thou hast searched me, and known me. 2 Thou knowest my downsitting and mine uprising, thou understandest my thought afar off.* The Lord searches us and knows us. He knows when we sit down and when we stand back up. He has his eyes on his children. But we will know him that intimately. We will be in the very presence of God himself when Jesus comes back. We will see him sit down on his glorious and majestic throne, and will see Him face to face! *I Corinthians 13:13 - And now abideth faith, hope, charity, these three; but the greatest of these is charity.* Then we will see him face to face, but for now we have something to help us through life. We have faith, hope and love. We have faith in what the Word says about Him right now. We have hope that one day we'll see Him face to face, and we love him now, and love our neighbors as ourselves. *Mark 12:28 - And one of the scribes came, and having heard them reasoning together, and perceiving that he had answered them well, asked him, Which is the first commandment of all? 29 And Jesus answered him, The first of all the commandments is, Hear, O Israel; The Lord our God is one Lord: 30 and thou shalt love the Lord thy God with all thy heart, and with all thy soul, and with all thy mind, and with all thy strength: this is the first commandment. 31 And the second is like, namely this, Thou shalt love thy neighbour as thyself. There is none other commandment greater than these.* Jesus said the greatest commandment in all the Bible is to love God with all our heart, soul, mind, and strength. He said the second greatest is to love our neighbors as ourselves. The Greek words for "love" come from the word ἀγαπάω which is the verb form or a cognate of the Greek word ἀγάπη. The greatest of all the commandments is to love the Lord our God and all our soul and all our mind. So then why is love the greatest out of faith, and hope? I couldn't agree more with B.F. Cate on this point. Because faith and hope will both pass away once Jesus comes back. We won't need faith when Jesus comes back because we will see him face to face. We won't need hope when he comes back because our hope will become reality, but we will always love. It will never pass away. We will always love our brothers and sisters in Christ, and our Lord that bought us for all of eternity. The same Lord that we are eagerly waiting for and love with all our heart, soul, mind, and strength today, is the one that we will love for all of eternity. A thousand years from now, we will still be able to tell him, "I love you." Love is the greatest because love is eternal.

I think you can see that the context is not talking about the Word of God but about loving and knowing Christ. Paul is not saying that when the New Testament is complete, then spiritual gifts will pass away off the scene. He's saying that once Christ comes back we won't need them anymore when we see Him face to face! I am not ready to take three verses out of context to prove that the chapter right before this and the chapter right after this doesn't apply to us. Really it is taken out of context to prove that an entire topic of the Bible doesn't apply to us. This is the only time that I am aware that Scripture is used to prove that other parts of the Scripture don't apply to believers. I am not ready to do that. This is also one of the main reasons why I don't believe in cessationist doctrine because it uses the love chapter as a main source of their doctrine which causes division in the body of Christ.

If someone takes the interpretation that ascribes, "that which is perfect" to the Word of God, then they will miss a great blessing of hope that one day we'll see Him face to face and love Him and our brothers and sisters in Christ for all of eternity. I am not writing this to condemn B.F. Cate or anyone else that holds to his interpretation of this passage. The very fact that he or anyone that holds to his interpretation of this passage points to the fact that they are in the Word of God and probably have godly convictions! As you read this book please seek God, and ask Him to show you the truth about Himself and about this topic. Ask Him to convict you of it personally no matter what interpretation you come to!

Caleb Stahl

Chapter 3

I Corinthians 14

In this chapter, Paul writes to the Corinthians about the use of the gift of prophecy, and the gift of tongues. Many people that oppose the charismatic movement point to this chapter as part as the whole of book of Corinthians. The argument goes like this. The book of Corinthians was written to carnal believers that needed to correct many things in their church. Since Paul corrects their use of the gifts in this chapter, therefore he is discouraging them from using the gifts. Though he does give them regulations on how to use them, he does not discourage them from using the gifts. To use this as an argument is not very good logic. If we took that same logic and applied it to Paul's teaching on the Lord's Supper in *I Corinthians 11*, then Paul would also be discouraging them from partaking of it. If we use that as an argument that we shouldn't use the gifts, then we should be consistent and agree that we shouldn't partake of the Lord's Supper. No one would agree to that. No matter what your view of the Lord's Supper is, most born again believers would agree that the Lord's Supper is necessary. If we wouldn't do that with the Lord's Supper, then why would we agree to that reasoning when it comes to the Spiritual gifts? To be sure, the Corinthian believers did misuse the spiritual gifts, and I am not advocating for the misuse of the gifts, but I am advocating for the use of them according to how the Scriptures teach. Paul is very self-explanatory, and straightforward in his teaching about the use of these gifts. Hopefully this chapter will clear up a lot of misconceptions about both of these gifts.

I Corinthians 14:1 - Follow after charity, and desire spiritual gifts, but rather that ye may prophesy. After his talk about love, Paul said that they were to follow after it. The Greek word for "follow after" is an inflection of the word διώκω diṓkō, dee-o'-ko; to pursue; by implication, to persecute:—ensue, follow (after), given to, (suffer) persecute(-ion), press forward. This word is in the imperative mood in the Greek meaning that it is a command. This is how important love is. Paul commands the Corinthian believers to purse after charity as if they were hunting it down. Paul and God both place a high priority on love. To love God and to love are neighbors as ourselves really are the greatest things that we can ever do. It can be challenging, but needless to say, we still need to do it. He doesn't just say, follow after charity. He also says desire spiritual gifts and especially the gift of prophecy. Many people don't desire the spiritual gifts because they are afraid of them. There is nothing to be afraid of. They are called spiritual gifts for a reason. They are gifts from God given to us to benefit the church. The Greek word for desire is also in the imperative mood which is primarily used for giving commands, though it can be used to make entreaties. Paul could be giving a command, or be entreating the Corinthians, and by application, us as well, to desire the spiritual gifts. Either way we know that it is godly to desire spiritual gifts. He'll explain why prophesying should be desired. He is about to compare the gift of prophecy with the gift of tongues.

I Corinthians 14:2 - For he that speaketh in an unknown tongue speaketh not unto men, but unto God: for no man understandeth him; howbeit in the spirit he speaketh mysteries. Paul says that the gift of tongues can be spoken in an unknown language. The Greek word for tongue is γλῶσσα glōssa, gloce-sah'; of uncertain affinity; the tongue; by implication, a language (specially, one naturally unacquired):—tongue. This word can imply a language. In this context, I believe this word could be translated as "language" in this case. We are talking about an unknown tongue. Some take this verse to be a reproof of the believers at Corinth because they were using the gifts to edify themselves instead of edifying the church. The words that are in italics in the King James Version (KJV) are not in the originally manuscripts, but were supplied by the translators for clarification. Some have pointed to the fact that the word "unknown" is in italics in the KJV. Therefore the word is not in the original manuscripts. They may say because of this that Paul not referring to an "unknown" tongue, but a tongue or language that was known. I will admit that the word "unknown" is in italics in the King James Version. (I have put all the Scripture that I have quoted in italics to signify that I am quoting from the Scripture). The truth is that the King James translators probably had a reason for why they supplied the word "unknown". I would ask the same people who believe that Paul wasn't speaking about an unknown tongue a question. If Paul was not referring to an unknown language, but to a language that can be understood, then why isn't it spoken to men? If Paul is referring to the gift of tongues in this context as a gift that allows the person using it to speak a language that they don't know to share the gospel with other people, then why isn't it spoken to men? Why is this tongue or language spoken to God then? For sake of argument, let's just say that Paul was speaking about using the gift of tongues to speak in a language that is not known by the speaker in order to share the gospel. Why then does Paul say that we are supposed to be speaking to God? The gospel originated with Him. Jesus Christ is the author and finisher of our faith. This would imply that God gave this gift to his church so that they could speak the gospel that He originated back to Him in a language that they could not understand. This doesn't make sense at all. I do believe that the gift of tongues was given to the church by God so the person using this gift could speak in a language that they didn't understand in order to preach the gospel. The difference is between speaking in the tongues of men and of angels. Speaking in the tongues of men was and still should be used to preach the gospel. Speaking in the tongues of angels was and still should be used to edify ourselves and the church. It would make sense that Paul truly is speaking about an unknown language because it is not spoken to men, but to God. No one can understand him because it is not meant for them. It is meant to be spoken to God. He is actually speaking in the Spirit mysteries. These mysteries are hidden things and secrets. This is why there is a need for an interpreter in order that the church can benefit from someone speaking this language.

Some make a distinction between speaking in tongues, and their prayer language. I don't see that difference Scripturally. He that speaks in an unknown tongue is speaking to God. What is prayer? Speaking to God. I understand that God may move during a service when everyone is speaking in tongues, but that is because he is working in spite of our behavior, not because of it. He sees our hearts, and moves because we have a desire for him. Why not pray out loud prayers that could be understood, if you are trying to stir yourself up? I promise you that unbelievers, and those who don't believe in the gifts will be more receptive to what is said in the service. The reason why we continue to do it is because it is a tradition passed down through generations, and not necessarily because we are trying to adhere to the Word of God. If you disagree, I challenge you to find where Paul gives permission for everyone to speak in tongues all at once without any interpreters. I don't care about who says what, or what traditions we may have, I care about what the Word of God says!

I Corinthians 14:3 - But he that prophesieth speaketh unto men to edification, and exhortation, and comfort. Paul clearly writes what the purpose of prophecy is. It is edification, exhortation, and comfort. Edification, exhortation, and comfort are all in the accusative case in the Greek. Specifically they are accusatives of purpose. The purpose of prophesying is edification, exhortation and comfort. The purpose of prophecy was not and is not the giving of Scripture to his people. I don't know of a verse that says that. If the purpose of prophecy was the giving of Scripture, then what book did Agabus the prophet write? What about Silas? He was a prophet. If the gift of prophecy was used for the purpose of giving the Scriptures to God's people then the prophets that the Bible calls by name should have written books, but they didn't. Therefore, the gift of prophecy was not used in the giving of Scripture, but rather it was used to exhort, to edify, and to comfort. Remember what the Bible says in *I Corinthians 14:24-25 - But if all prophesy, and there come in one that believeth not, or one unlearned, he is convinced of all, he is judged of all: 25 and thus are the secrets of his heart made manifest; and so falling down on his face he will worship God, and report that God is in you of a truth.* Paul wrote that when the gift of prophecy is in use, the "secrets" of a person's heart are made manifest. They are made manifest in order to speak to them edification, exhortation, and comfort. The Lord didn't use the gift of prophecy to reveal his word, He uses it to speak to his people in a very personal, careful, and encouraging way.

I Corinthians 14:4 - He that speaketh in an unknown tongue edifieth himself; but he that prophesieth edifieth the church. The person that speaks in tongues or in this unknown language edifies himself. Why is that? Because it takes faith to do it. By faith they are speaking mysteries in the spirit. By faith they are giving praise to God. This is why the person speaking in this unknown language edifies himself. Speaking in tongues is not something mystical, or an ecstatic spiritual experience. It simply is an exercise of faith that edifies the person doing it. This unknown tongue is a language. How does someone speak any other language? They do it by exercising their own will power, and so it is when they are speaking in tongues. The person that prophesies edifies the church because he is speaking words that they can understand in order to exhort, edify, and comfort them. This seems to indicate that speaking in tongues really should be used in a devotional sense instead of being used in the church. I speak in tongues all the time, but it is almost always when I'm outside of church, and I'm speaking to the Lord. Prophecy is to be done in the church to edify, to exhort, and to comfort.

I Corinthians 14:5-6 - I would that ye all spake with tongues, but rather that ye prophesied: for greater is he that prophesieth than he that speaketh with tongues, except he interpret, that the church may receive edifying. 6 Now, brethren, if I come unto you speaking with tongues, what shall I profit you, except I shall speak to you either by revelation, or by knowledge, or by prophesying, or by doctrine? Paul flat out told the Corinthian believers that he wanted them to speak in tongues. Why? He wanted them to speak in tongues because they would be acting in faith edifying themselves in doing it. Again, speaking in tongues seems to be more of something done in a devotional sense to edify ourselves. Paul is going to make the same point over and over again in this passage of Scripture. The point he is going to make is the importance of being understood in the church service setting. If someone is speaking in tongues without an interpreter, then no one is going to be edified. He is emphasizing the need for edification. The point of speaking in this unknown tongue in a church service is to edify the church through an interpreter. If there is no interpreter, then it shouldn't be done. Paul is going to make the point over and over again that being understood is necessary for the edification of the church. Tongues should be used in a devotional sense to edify themselves by exercising faith believing that they are speaking mysteries in the Spirit and praise to God. It can also be done in the church setting, but it is not going to edify anyone else in the church unless there is an interpreter. If there is an interpreter then the church can receive edification. If it is done in the proper way, speaking in tongues can be beneficial to all the church. Therefore it should be done in the Bible way. If there is no interpreter, then prophesy should be given the priority because it is a gift specifically given by God for edification, exhortation, and comfort. Paul writes that if he would come to them speaking in tongues without an interpreter, he wouldn't profit them. The fact that there needs to be an interpreter when someone is speaking in tongues points to the fact that it is a viable language. If there is an interpretation, then there will be edification. If there's no interpretation, then there will be no edification. Again this points to the fact that prophecy should be given the priority instead of speaking in tongues. The only way that they are going to receive some type of profit is if he was speaking to them in a language that they could understand. This is self-explanatory. Tongues should not be used in the church unless there is an interpreter so that the church can be edified by the one speaking in tongues. He says that the only way that he is going to profit them is if he speaks to them in a way and in a language that they understand. He gives four useful ways to communicate. The Greek word for "revelation" is ἀποκάλυψις apokálypsis, ap-ok-al'-oop-sis; disclosure:—appearing, coming, lighten, manifestation, be revealed, revelation. This is the illumination of the Holy Spirit. A good example of this is found in *Ephesians 3:3-6 - how that by revelation he made known unto me the mystery; 4 (as I wrote afore in few words. whereby, when ye read, ye may understand my knowledge in the mystery of Christ) 5 which in other ages was not made known unto the sons of men, as it is now revealed unto his holy apostles and prophets by the Spirit; 6 that the Gentiles should be fellowheirs, and of the same body, and partakers of his promise in Christ by the gospel:* God made known a mystery or a hidden truth to Paul by revelation. Paul had written to the Ephesian believers so that they could understand his knowledge in the truth that God had revealed to Paul. A mystery is something that has always been true, but wasn't previously revealed by God. As Paul said this mystery was not made known to the sons of men but was revealed to the apostles and prophets. Specifically the mystery was that the Gentiles would be fellowheirs, of the same body (the body of Christ), and partakers of his promise in Christ by the gospel. In other words the mystery was that the Gentiles could be saved and have equal rights as do the Jews. I will admit that Paul wrote that this revelation was revealed to prophets, but it was also revealed to apostles. But he also specifically tells us that this truth was given to him by revelation, not by prophecy. The Greek word for "revelation" in *Ephesians 3:3* is the same Greek word used for "revelation" in *I Corinthians 14:6*. Paul differentiates between "revelation" and "prophecy" in this verse proving that prophecy is not what God used to give the truth to his church. Revelation was what God used to give truth to his church. The Greek word for "knowledge" is γνῶσις gnōsis, gno'-sis; knowing (the act), i.e. (by implication) knowledge:—knowledge, science. It is simply knowledge. Knowledge is something very important. Whether it is Bible knowledge or any other type of knowledge it certainly is profitable. It is very useful and very important. We can use knowledge to make our lives better, and better serve the Lord. Greek word for "prophesying" is προφητεία prophēteía, prof-ay-ti'-ah; ("prophecy");

prediction (scriptural or other):—prophecy, prophesying. This is pretty self-explanatory. We already talked about prophesy in chapter 1, and we talk about it more in depth in the next chapter. It is important to know that prophecy could be understood by the Corinthian believers and therefore was edifying to them. The Greek word for "doctrine" is διδαχή didaché, did-akh-ay'; instruction (the act or the matter):—doctrine, hath been taught. We know what doctrine is, it simply means teaching. We do not find our doctrine from revelation, we find our doctrine from the Word (*II Timothy 3:16*), but many times God can give us illumination or revelation to help us understand doctrine. All of these four are spoken in a language that can be understood. All of them are edifying to the church. Therefore, they should be spoken in the church. On the other hand, speaking an unknown language and without an interpreter cannot be understood. Therefore it should not be spoken in church without an interpreter. Paul emphasizes this point by making some analogies.

I Corinthians 14:7-8 - And even things without life giving sound, whether pipe or harp, except they give a distinction in the sounds, how shall it be known what is piped or harped? 8 For if the trumpet give an uncertain sound, who shall prepare himself to the battle? and none of them is without signification. Paul now makes an analogy about inanimate objects. He speaks about musical instruments giving a distinction. I don't know that much about music, but I do know that if all the instruments in an orchestra are playing the exact same notes, then there will be no harmony. Every instrument will simply be playing the same notes instead of the part that it was designed to play. To the untrained ear, it will be impossible to make a distinction between them. No one will be able to pick out the harp from a wind instrument. If a trumpet that is used in war to direct an army is instead used to play a note that the army is unfamiliar with, then the whole army will be confused. The harp, a wind instrument and the trumpet all have a specific purpose, but they can be abused if they are not used for that purpose. In the same way in a church setting the gift of tongues has the purpose of edification if there is an interpreter. If it is not used to edify the church through an interpreter, then it will be abused. Being understood is essential for the edification of the church.

I Corinthians 14:9-10 - So likewise ye, except ye utter by the tongue words easy to be understood, how shall it be known what is spoken? for ye shall speak into the air. 10 There are, it may be, so many kinds of voices in the world, and none of them is without signification. 11 Therefore if I know not the meaning of the voice, I shall be unto him that speaketh a barbarian, and he that speaketh shall be a barbarian unto me. 12 Even so ye, forasmuch as ye are zealous of spiritual gifts, seek that ye may excel to the edifying of the church. Paul is making his point again. Being understood is necessary for edification. He tells the Corinthian believers that unless they spoke in a language that can be understood by everyone that is hearing them speak, then no one is going to understand what they were saying. If they spoke in tongues without an interpreter then they will be abusing the gift of tongues by using it in the church for a purpose that it was not intended. Others will not be able to understand what is being said and they will speak words into the air. There are many different voices and many different languages in the world. Every one of them is different. Every one of them is distinct. The trained ear can recognize any particular language. He says if he doesn't know the meaning of the voice or language of the person speaking to him, then the one speaking would be like a barbarian to him. Paul would be like a barbarian to the one speaking. It is almost as if they were different nationalities. In the very least they wouldn't be able to understand what is being said by each other. Have you ever tried to talk to someone that speaks a different language? I have. I went on a missions trip down to Honduras, and the nationals spoke Spanish. There's nothing wrong with that. The problem was not with the people or the language, the problem was that I didn't understand Spanish and they didn't understand English. I know exactly what Paul is saying here. The gift of tongues benefits no one if there is no interpreter because everyone else will not be able to understand what is being spoken. Paul is emphasizing the point that being understood is necessary for edification. Paul told the Corinthian believers that they were zealous of spiritual gifts. Notice that he doesn't rebuke them for being zealous. He just redirects their zeal. The focus of their zeal should be directed towards edification. Speaking in tongues is something that should be done in the church in the right context, in the right way, and for the right purpose. It should be done to edify the church. If that is going to happen then there needs to be an interpreter. Ultimately, the purpose of using the spiritual gifts in a church setting is for edification of believers. The spiritual gifts are not given for an experience, but for edification. Many times this is not why they are used. Many people use the spiritual gifts as a way to have a new experience instead of edifying the church. This should not be the case. The just shall live by faith, not emotions, experiences or anything else.

I Corinthians 14:13 - Wherefore let him that speaketh in an unknown tongue pray that he may interpret. It only makes sense if the purpose of the spiritual gifts is to edify the body of Christ. If someone wants to speak in tongues when there is no interpreter present in the service, then he should pray to interpret what he's saying. Again this verse emphasizes the point that being understood is necessary for edification.

I Corinthians 14:14 - For if I pray in an unknown tongue, my spirit prayeth but my understanding is unfruitful. This is an interesting verse. Apparently, it is possible not to just speak in tongues, but also to pray in tongues. If we pray in tongues then our spirit is praying, but we won't understand what we are praying. What would possibly be the purpose of that? Let's look back at what Paul said in *I Corinthians 14:2 - For he that speaketh in an unknown tongue speaketh not unto men, but unto God: for no man understandeth him; howbeit in the spirit he speaketh mysteries.* Paul said here that he that speaks in and unknown tongue is speaking "in the spirit". If speaking in tongues is speaking in the spirit, then wouldn't praying in tongues be praying in the spirit? Paul also wrote in *Romans 8:26 - Likewise the Spirit also helpeth our infirmities: for we know not what we should pray for as we ought: but the Spirit itself maketh intercession for us with groanings which cannot be uttered.* The Greek word for infirmities is ἀσθένεια asthéneia, as-then'-i-ah; feebleness (of mind or body); by implication, malady; morally, frailty:—disease, infirmity, sickness, weakness. The Spirit helps our feebleness and our weakness especially in times when we do not know what to pray for. The Spirit itself prays for us making intercession for us with groanings. The Spirit groans for us, when we are in such a position that we don't even know what to pray for. Have you ever been there? Were you ever in a place that you didn't know what to pray for? I have and it was challenging. I used to go to a rehabilitation program for young men in the juvenile justice system. I remember that there was one young man that had messed up in his life. He had children with three different young ladies. I had no idea how to pray for him. In those times when we have no idea what to pray for as we ought, we can pray in the spirit. The Spirit will help us and direct our prayers. In those times that we don't know what to pray, we can trust the Spirit to help us pray when we don't even know what to pray for. We can pray in the spirit or pray in tongues at that point in time when we need it the most.

I Corinthians 14:15 - What is it then? I will pray with the spirit, and I will pray with the understanding also: I will sing with the spirit, and I will sing with the understanding also. Apparently it is possible to sing in tongues as well. It is a language. We can pray, sing, and talk to each other in English. Why would it be any different in tongues or an unknown language? This also indicates that Paul did both. He would pray, speak, and sing in tongues. But he would also pray, sing, and talk to others with his understanding, probably in Greek or Hebrew. If Paul did both, then we probably should as well.

I Corinthians 14:16-17 - Else when thou shalt bless with the spirit, how shall he that occupieth the room of the unlearned say Amen at thy giving of thanks, seeing he understandeth not what thou sayest? 17 For thou verily givest thanks well, but the other is not edified. Paul keeps going back to the same concept driving the point home. Paul refers to speaking in tongues as blessing with the spirit. In this context, it seems as though speaking in tongues is referred to as giving thanks. He tells them that no one will be able to say Amen when you give thanks in an unknown tongue because they won't understand what is being said. It is interesting that he refers to those that don't understand what is being said in tongues as spoken as the unlearned. This will come up in the next couple verses, and we will deal with those verses in a later chapter. They would be giving thanks, but no one would be edified. There must be an interpreter when someone speaks, prays, or sings in tongues.

I Corinthians 14:18-19 - I thank my God, I speak with tongues more than ye all: 19 yet in the church I had rather speak five words with my understanding, that by my voice I might teach others also, than ten thousand words in an unknown tongue. Paul said that he spoke in tongues more than all of them, even though they were zealous of spiritual gifts. Paul is an example to us. If he spoke in tongues, then we probably should as well. It seems as though he didn't speak in tongues during a church setting. He also said that he would rather speak five words with his understanding than ten thousand in an unknown tongue. He is emphasizing the importance of being understood when we speak. Five words that are understood are more valuable than ten thousand words spoken in tongues that are not understood. Paul keeps emphasizing the fact that we need to be able to understand each other when we speak to each other in the church.

I Corinthians 14:20 - Brethren, be not children in understanding: howbeit in malice be ye children, but in understanding be men. This is not what Paul was talking about in *I Corinthians 13:11*. The reason that we know this is because the word for "children" in *I Corinthians 14:20* is a different word than the word that was used for "child" in *I Corinthians 13:11*. The word for "man" in this verse is also different from the word that was used for "man" in *I Corinthians 13:11*. He wanted them to be mature in understanding but not in malice or any sin for that matter.

I Corinthians 14:21-25 - In the law it is written, With men of other tongues and other lips will I speak unto this people; and yet for all that will they not hear me, saith the Lord. 22 Wherefore tongues are for a sign, not to them that believe, but to them that believe not: but prophesying serveth not for them that believe not, but for them which believe. 23 If therefore the whole church be come together into one place, and all speak with tongues, and there come in those that are unlearned, or unbelievers, will they not say that ye are mad? 24 But if all prophesy, and there come in one that believeth not, or one unlearned, he is convinced of all, he is judged of all: 25 and thus are the secrets of his heart made manifest; and so falling down on his face he will worship God, and report that God is in you of a truth. We will look at these verses in depth in a later chapter. But one thing does need to be said about them. Specifically something needs to be said about one verse in particular.

I Corinthians 14:23 - If therefore the whole church be come together into one place, and all speak with tongues, and there come in those that are unlearned, or unbelievers, will they not say that ye are mad? Paul already referred to those that were unlearned in verse 16. It is interesting the Greek word for the "unlearned" in verse 16 is the same Greek word used for "unlearned" in this verse as well meaning that Paul is referring to the same people. When he refers to the unlearned, he is referring to those that do not understand what is being spoken in tongues. Someone who is unlearned that doesn't believe in the spiritual gifts may come into a service. If they heard everyone else speak in tongues, then they will believe that they were insane. Too many times this is the case in Pentecostal and Charismatic churches. Paul is not encouraging this type of behavior. He is not encouraging everyone to speak in tongues all at the same time. Paul is actually speaking against this type of use of the gift of tongues. He has spoken about it throughout the whole chapter about being understood when speaking in tongues. Again, Paul speaks against this use of the gift of tongues. It is not according to the guidelines given in the Word of God. If I went to a Spanish speaking church where everyone there only speaks Spanish, then I would not be able to understand anyone there. Let's just say that at any given point in time all the people there started speaking in

Spanish to no one in particular. Let's just say that they started speaking slowly and quietly but eventually started speaking faster and louder. Eventually everyone was speaking in Spanish ecstatically. Some people might be moving around energetically while others have their eyes rolled in the back of their head. I would say that they were crazy. That probably isn't going to happen. This is just an analogy. I'm not against Spanish-speaking people. I'm not speaking against Spanish as a language. It is a wonderful language, and Spanish-speaking people are wonderful people. They are fearfully and wonderfully made. In fact, they are made in the image of God, and they are precious because of it! I'm simply using this as an example. The problem that people have with tongues is not necessarily the tongues themselves, but the way that tongues are used. Tongues is a language. In any given church service, we should be able to have a Spanish-speaking person give a testimony thanking God for what He has done in their lives while someone interprets. Then right after that we should be able to have someone speaking in tongues giving thanks to God as someone else interprets what they are saying. Comparing the two, there really shouldn't be that much difference. If we just stick with the Word of God, then everything will work the way it was intended to. With that being said, let's look at what the Word of God says in the next several verses.

I Corinthians 14:26 - How is it then, brethren? when ye come together, every one of you hath a psalm, hath a doctrine, hath a tongue, hath a revelation, hath an interpretation. Let all things be done unto edifying. Paul asks them a question. How is it that they all had a psalm, a doctrine, a tongue, a revelation, and an interpretation? Then he said let all things be done for edification. This tells me that when they all had a psalm, a doctrine, a tongue, a revelation, and an interpretation, it wasn't for the purpose of edification. Paul had to correct many things in this first epistle to them. The Corinthian church was a carnal church. Paul had flat out told them that in *I Corinthians 3:3 - For ye are yet carnal: for whereas there is among you envying, and strife, and divisions, are ye not carnal, and walk as men?* These people were carnal. They probably wanted to be heard so they all had a psalm, a doctrine, a tongue, a revelation, and an interpretation. Even if it wasn't for this reason, Paul still writes that everything was to be done for the purpose of edification. Paul doesn't correct their actions, but rather he corrects their attitudes and motivations. He doesn't want them to stop sharing in a church service. He just wanted them to stop doing it for any other motivation than for edification. This verse also indicates that there should be congregational participation. The congregation should be involved in church services and in serving in the local church. I don't need to belabor that point. We already talked about it in chapter 1.

I Corinthians 14:27-28 - If any man speak in an unknown tongue, let it be by two, or at the most by three, and that by course; and let one interpret. 28 But if there be no interpreter, let him keep silence in the church; and let him speak to himself, and to God. This is the guidelines that God gives concerning the gift of tongues. This is the Biblical way of using the gift of tongues. There can only be two or at most three that speak in tongues in any given service. They also must only speak one at a time. There also must be an interpreter. Why does it have to be done this way? Because speaking in tongues is supposed to be done to edify the church! If more than three people are speaking in tongues then it will draw time away from other edifying things in the church service such as preaching, praying, and singing. If more than one person is speaking at a time, it will draw the attention of people in two places. The people won't be able to focus on both of them, and they won't be edified. None of the people are really communicating in a way that leads to edification. If there is no interpreter, then no one will understand. If no one understands, then no one will be edified. If there is no one to interpret, then speaking in tongues should not be done. If these regulation are not met and someone still wants to speak in tongues, he needs to speak silently to himself and God so as not to distract anyone else from being edified by something else that is happening in the church.

I am not against speaking in tongues in a given church service. In fact, I do it all the time, but because of these guidelines I do it silently and I'm speaking to the Lord. I did not write the guidelines, I just read them, believe them, and I am going to obey them.

I Corinthians 14:29-30 - Let the prophets speak two or three and let the other judge. 30 If any thing be revealed to another that sitteth by, let the first hold his peace. 31 For ye may all prophesy one by one, that all may learn, and all may be comforted. There are similar guidelines for prophesying that there is for speaking in tongues. There can only be two or three prophesying in any given service. While they are prophesying there needs to be another person that is to be discerning what they are saying. The person that is sitting by judging what is said should be very knowledgeable in the Word of God, and probably should be someone that has the gift of discerning of spirits. The Spirit of God isn't going to give a prophecy that is contrary to the Word of God. If something is revealed to the person sitting by judging about the veracity of that prophecy, then the person that is giving the prophecy should remain silent. He then encourages them to prophesy. They all could prophesy, one by one, that they could all learn. I thought that they could only prophesy two or three at any given service. Well, it could be that Paul is talking about in general and not at one service. Over a period of time they could all prophesy. If someone receives a prophecy in a given service, they may have an opportunity to pray about it, and talk to the leadership about it. If it is urgent, then they should still talk to the leadership of the church out of respect for them. If they will not hear it, then it fault is on them.

I thought only the people that had the gift of prophesy could prophesy. This is not necessarily true. Remember, someone that has the gift of prophecy was supposed to regularly function in that position in the church as part of the body. That does not mean that the Spirit would never give a prophecy to someone in the congregation that didn't have the gift of prophecy. The result is that they would learn what God's heart for them was, and they would be comforted. Why because prophecy is given for the purpose of exhortation, edification, and comfort.

I Corinthians 14:32-33 - And the spirits of the prophets are subject to the prophets. 33 For God is not the author of confusion, but of peace, as in all churches of the saints. Paul said that the spirits of the prophets are subject to the prophets. What does that mean? It means that the prophets are in control of their own spirits. Many times, in charismatic churches some bizarre things happen. When I say bizarre, I mean things that aren't described in Scripture. Some of these things are actually done in the name of the Spirit which are against what the Scriptures say. That should never happen. The Spirit will not lead us to do something contrary to the Scriptures.

With that being said, he may consistently lead us in a way that is contrary to our understanding of the Scriptures, and in those instances, we need to make sure that it is the Lord, and simply trust Him and obey.

Honestly, I don't mind when things happen that the Scripture doesn't speak about. Sunday School is something that the Scripture doesn't speak about, but we still do that. God will act according to the Scripture as it is recorded. But some things are not recorded. For example, the Bible says in *John 21:25 - And there are also many other things which Jesus did, the* which, if they should be written every one, I suppose that even the world itself could not contain the books that should be written. Amen.* There are things that Jesus did which are not recorded in the Scripture which implies that though God will never do something which is unBiblical, he is perfectly fine with doing things that are aBiblical. The Scripture does not explain in perfect detail what happens when a person is truly touched and anointed by God. Since the Scripture doesn't describe this in perfect details then He is free to do whatever He wants to do. The truth is that dignity is not one of the fruits of the Spirit. In fact I can think of three examples of godly men that had an encounter with God. The first is Isaiah. *Isaiah 6:1-5 - In the year that king Uzziah died I saw also the Lord sitting upon a throne, high and lifted up, and his train filled the temple. 2 Above it stood the seraphims: each one had six wings; with twain he covered his face, and with twain he covered his feet, and with twain he did fly. 3 And one cried unto another, and said, Holy, holy, holy, is the Lord of hosts: the whole earth is full of his glory. 4 And the posts of the door moved at the voice of him that cried, and the house was filled with smoke. 5 Then said I, Woe is me! for I am undone; because I am a man of unclean lips, and I dwell in the midst of a people of unclean lips: for mine eyes have seen the King, the Lord of hosts.* This is an amazing passage of Scripture because it gives us a description of the Lord, and what goes on in heaven. I don't need to get into this description of the Lord. That's for another time and another situation. I do want to focus on what Isaiah said as a result of seeing the Lord. He said, "Woe is me! For I am undone". The Hebrew word for "undone" is דָּמָה dâmâh, daw-mam'; a primitive root; to be dumb or silent; hence, to fail or perish; trans. to destroy:—cease, be cut down (off), destroy, be brought to silence, be undone, × utterly. It could mean that he was dumb or silent, or it could mean to perish, to be destroyed, or to be cut down. In his own words, he said that he was undone. I don't know what happened to Isaiah after he saw the Lord, but I do believe that it was pretty significant. Another example is the apostle John. *Revelation 1:10-16 - I was in the Spirit on the Lord's day, and heard behind me a great voice, as of a trumpet, 11 saying, I am Alpha and Omega, the first and the last: and, What thou seest, write in a book, and send it unto the seven churches which are in Asia; unto Ephesus, and unto Smyrna, and unto Pergamos, and unto Thyatira, and unto Sardis, and unto Philadelphia, and unto Laodicea. 12 And I turned to see the voice that spake with me. And being turned, I saw seven golden candlesticks; 13 and in the midst of the seven candlesticks* *one like unto the Son of man, clothed with a garment down to the foot, and girt about the paps with a golden girdle. 14 His head and his hairs were white like wool, as white as snow; and his eyes were as a flame of fire; 15 and his feet like unto fine brass, as if they burned in a furnace; and his voice as the sound of many waters. 16 And he had in his right hand seven stars: and out of his mouth went a sharp twoedged sword: and his countenance was as the sun shineth in his strength.* This is a pretty intense vision of the Lord. It is very descriptive. We don't have to go into detail about the vision. That is for another time under other circumstances. What is interesting is what happened to him as a result. *Revelation 1:17 - And when I saw him, I fell at his feet as dead. And he laid his right hand upon me, saying unto me, Fear not; I am the first and the last:* In John's own words he said, "When I saw him, I fell at his feet as dead". Many have criticized the charismatic movement because there have been occurrences of people being supernaturally touched laying on the ground. But the same thing happened to one of the godliest men that ever lived. He was a man that was one of the twelve hand-picked disciples of the Lord Jesus Christ. He walked and with him and followed him for three and half years. He wrote five books of the New Testament. But when he saw the same Lord in his glory, he "fell at his feet as dead." I don't know what happened to him, but this was not a voluntary response. It would be easy to fall on the ground voluntary in an act of worship after seeing the Lord Jesus Christ. But to fall on the ground "as dead" is not a voluntary response. No one can make their own body "as dead" in an instance. A "dead" body doesn't move. He was laying on the ground, but he could not move. It was just his body's natural reaction to what just happened. Probably the greatest example that I can think of is Daniel. Daniel sees a vision of the Lord in *Daniel 10:4-8 - And in the four and twentieth day of the first month, as I was by the side of the great river, which is Hiddekel; 5 then I lifted up mine eyes, and looked, and behold a certain man clothed in linen, whose loins were girded with fine gold of Uphaz: 6 his body also was like the beryl, and his face as the appearance of lightning, and his eyes as lamps of fire, and his arms and his feet like in colour to polished brass, and the voice of his words like the voice of a multitude. 7 And I Daniel alone saw the vision: for the men that were with me saw not the vision; but a great quaking fell upon them, so that they fled to hide themselves. 8 Therefore I was left alone, and saw this great vision, and there remained no strength in me: for my comeliness was turned in me into corruption, and I retained no strength. 9*

Yet heard I the voice of his words: and when I heard the voice of his words, then was I in a deep sleep on my face, and my face toward the ground. Daniel saw an amazing vision of the Lord and it was such a powerful experience the men that were with him started shaking and ran away. As a result, he had "no strength" in him. He said so twice. And he said that his comeliness was turned into corruption. The Hebrew word for comeliness is הוֹד hôwd, hode; from an unused root; grandeur (i.e. an imposing form and appearance):—beauty, comeliness, excellency, glorious, glory, goodly, honour, majesty. His comeliness basically deals with his countenance. The Hebrew word for corruption is מַשְׁחִית mashchîyth, mash-kheeth'; destructive, i.e. (as noun) destruction, literally (specifically a snare) or figuratively (corruption):—corruption, (to) destroy(-ing), destruction, trap, × utterly.

Daniel's beauty, comeliness, excellency, glory, and his honor was turned into destruction. I don't know what happened, but I'm pretty sure by the way that it sounds, it wasn't pretty. Furthermore, he said that he was in a "deep sleep on my face, and my face on the ground". This gives the picture that he was laying on the ground. Daniel was one of the godliest men that ever lived. Who, when he was carried away as a captive to Babylon, purposed in his heart that he would not defile himself. By the end of his life he said *...innocency was found in me... - Daniel 6:22.* Imagine that. A man that purposed in his heart at the beginning of his life and lived 70 years in this foreign country where idolatry was rapant and corruption was common. By the end of his life he said that innocency was found in him! That is amazing. This means his purpose never died out. Every single day he purposed in his heart. This man had a testimony among the Babylonians which very likely influenced two world leaders to turn to the one true God in repentance. All the while he wrote a book of the Bible. That is amazing! This man had an encounter with God and his comeliness was turned into corruption. His comeliness was turned into corruption. His beauty, comeliness, excellency, glory, and his honor was turned into destruction. Later on in the chapter it gives us more of a description. *Daniel 10:10-17 - And, behold, an hand touched me, which set me upon my knees and upon the palms of my hands. 11 And he said unto me, O Daniel, a man greatly beloved, understand the words that I speak unto thee, and stand upright: for unto thee am I now sent. And when he had spoken this word unto me, I stood trembling. 12 Then said he unto me, Fear not, Daniel: for from the first day that thou didst set thine heart to understand, and to* *chasten thyself before thy God, thy words were heard, and I am come for thy words. 13 But the prince of the kingdom of Persia withstood me one and twenty days: but, lo, Michael, one of the chief princes, came to help me; and I remained there with the kings of Persia. 14 Now I am come to make thee understand what shall befall thy people in the latter days: for yet the vision is for many days. 15 And when he had spoken such words unto me, I set my face toward the ground, and I became dumb. 16 And, behold, one like the similitude of the sons of men touched my lips: then I opened my mouth, and spake, and said unto him that stood before me, O my lord, by the vision my sorrows are turned upon me, and I have retained no strength. 17 For how can the servant of this my lord talk with this my lord? for as for me, straightway there remained no strength in me, neither is there breath left in me.* Time and time again the text indicates that Daniel experienced physical effects from this spiritual encounter. In verse 10 says that he was on his "knees and upon the palms of his hands". In verse 11 Daniel said that he "stood trembling". In verse 16, he literally said that it was the vision that he had made him have no strength left. He specifically said, "by the vision my sorrows are turned upon me, and I have retained no strength." In the very next verse he said it again. He said, "there remained no strength in me, neither is there breath left in me." Whatever happened to Daniel, it was pretty significant. It was significant enough to turn his corruption into comeliness, to make him lay down on his face in a deep sleep, to put him on his hands and knees, to make him stand trembling, to make him retain no strength or his breath. All three of these men were very godly men. All three of them were prophets, and all three of them had true encounters with the Lord. I thought the Bible said that "the spirits of the prophets are subject to the prophets." It does, but that does not mean their bodies are. All three of these godly men and involuntary physical responses to their vision of the Lord. And yet, all three of these men were right with God. They responded with the right spiritual response. They were all in control of their spirits, as they all responded in humility. All three of these men were very godly men. All three of these men had visions of the Lord. All three of these men had involuntary physical reactions to their visions. And all three of these men were in control of their spirits as evidenced by the way that they responded to the vision that they received of the Lord.

Why did these three godly men react in such a way when they saw the Lord's glory? Moses asked the Lord if he could see his glory, and the Lord told him this in *Exodus 33:20 - Moses asked to see the Lord's glory in*

Exodus 33:20 - And he said, Thou canst not see my face: for there shall no man see me, and live. If we can't see his face and live. As human beings, we can't even see his face, and live, so what do you think is going to happen when we encounter Him? Isaiah became undone, John fell down as dead, and Daniel had a variety of physical effects from encountering the Lord, and his angels. These physical reactions are just the body's natural reaction when encountering God.

Some people point to these physical reactions as demonic seeing that those who involve themselves in voodoo, witchcraft, and other pagan religions experience the same kind of experiencing. I would say that is because in both cases the body is reacting to a reality that is higher than our own. The truth is that God is spirit, and demons are as well. We are spiritual beings living in physical bodies, and our physical bodies cannot handle that kind of spiritual reality. Whether we are encountering evil spirits, or the Holy Spirit, that fact remains the same. As Reinhard Bonnke spoke about concerning the gift of tongues, just because there are counterfeits doesn't mean that there isn't something real to these encounters with God. Just because some people experience physical effects when encountering an evil spirit, that doesn't mean that everyone experiencing those same physical effects is encountering an evil spirit.

Others might respond by quoting *Galatians 5:22-23 - But the fruit of the Spirit is love, joy, peace, longsuffering, gentleness, goodness, faith, 23 meekness, temperance: against such there is no law.* The fruit of the Spirit is temperance, or self-control. Those who oppose the charismatic movement often quote this verse as a source of their opposition. I agree that the fruit of the Spirit is self-control. Since I grew up on a farm, and our family had an orchard, I can tell you a couple of things about fruit. First of all, fruit isn't always grown. It takes all year long to be able to grow an apple in its season. The Bible acknowledges this in *Psalm 1:1-2 - But his delight is in the law of the Lord; and in his law doth he meditate day and night. 3 And he shall be like a tree planted by the rivers of water, that bringeth forth his fruit in his season; his leaf also shall not wither; and whatsoever he doeth shall prosper.* The Bible says that the blessed man who meditates in the Word of God day and night brings forth fruit in his season. Second of all, fruit is produced by a tree for a specific purpose. That purpose is to reproduce itself. Each apple contains seeds that could possibly grow into other apple trees, and many times when the apples fall to the ground, they do. In other words, fruit is produced at a specific time for a specific purpose. The Holy Spirit will produce fruit in us, as a specific time, to reproduce Christ's image in other people. He may overwhelm us with love for unbelievers or fellow Christians so that we pray for them in their time of need so they can either come to Him for salvation or grow in Him in his time of need. Just because he will produce self-control in us for a given season for a specific purpose, that doesn't mean that he will always produce self-control in us, one hundred percent of the time.

Why would God deal with his people in such a way? If this is the body's involuntary physical response to having a true encounter with the Lord, then why would God work this way? I think the answer lies in John's vision of the Lord. *Revelation 1:10-17 - I was in the Spirit on the Lord's day, and heard behind me a great voice, as of a trumpet, 11 saying, I am Alpha and Omega, the first and the last: and, What thou seest, write in a book, and send it unto the seven churches which are in Asia; unto Ephesus, and unto Smyrna, and unto Pergamos, and unto Thyatira, and unto Sardis, and unto Philadelphia, and unto Laodicea. 12 And I turned to see the voice that spake with me. And being turned, I saw seven golden candlesticks; 13 and in the midst of the seven candlesticks one like unto the Son of man, clothed with a garment down to the foot, and girt about the paps with a golden girdle. 14 His head and his hairs were white like wool, as white as snow; and his eyes were as a flame of fire; 15 and his feet like unto fine brass, as if they burned in a furnace; and his voice as the sound of many waters. 16 And he had in his right hand seven stars: and out of his mouth went a sharp twoedged sword: and his countenance was as the sun shineth in his strength. 17 And when I saw him, I fell at his feet as dead. And he laid his right hand upon me, saying unto me, Fear not; I am the first and the last:* Look again at how similar this vision of the Lord is to Daniel's vision of the Lord. They both speak of the Lord clothed with a linen garment wearing a girdle. They both speak of the Lord having eyes as fire, and feet as brass. They both speak of Him as having a very loud voice. John is seeing a very similar vision to the vision that Daniel had. In fact John refers to Christ as being "one like unto the Son of man". Daniel also had another vision of the Lord that is recorded in His book. *Daniel 7:9-14 - I beheld till the thrones were cast down, and the Ancient of days did sit, whose garment was white as snow, and the hair of his head like the pure wool: his throne was like the fiery flame, and his wheels as burning fire. 10 A fiery stream issued and came forth from before him: thousand thousands ministered unto him, and ten thousand times ten thousand stood before him: the judgment was set, and the books were opened. 11 I beheld then because of the voice of the great words which the horn spake: I beheld even till the beast was slain, and his body destroyed, and given to the burning flame. 12 As concerning the rest of the beasts, they had their dominion taken away: yet their lives were prolonged for a season and time. 13 I saw in the night visions, and, behold, one like the Son of man came with the clouds of heaven, and came to the Ancient of days, and they brought him near before him. 14 And there was given him dominion, and glory, and a kingdom, that all people, nations, and languages, should serve him: his dominion is an everlasting dominion, which shall not pass away, and his kingdom that which shall not be destroyed.* Again, we see the same imagery. There a throne where the Ancient of Days sat, his garment that was pure white. Fire shot forth from his throne. In that vision Daniel sees "one like the Son of man". To this Son of Man was crowned King of Kings and Lord of lords. Don't you think that John could've thought about Daniel's vision when he had his own vision? Don't you think that John knew that this "Son of man" was Jesus? Don't you think that he recalled how many times Jesus referred to himself as the "Son of Man"? I believe that he did. I believe at this moment, John realized that the same Jesus that he walked around with for three and half years was this Son of man. I believe that John remembered Jesus breaking the loaves and the fishes and feeding the multitudes and feeding thousands of people. I believe that John realized for the first time that his beloved Master, the same one that he laid his head on at the last supper was the same Son of Man that he was seeing before him with eyes of fire, with hair as white as wool, and feet as brass. What's this mean? This means that God encounters man in such a way as to cause involuntary physical reactions to reveal himself in a literal breathtaking experience to reveal himself in a very intimate way to man.

I don't necessarily have a problem when things happen in the church that the Bible doesn't describe. The Bible doesn't reveal every single detail of how God interacts with His people. This includes when people have a real encounter with the Lord. But I do have a problem when things happen that are contrary to the Scripture. As we have seen, God has designed a special order, and has given specific guidelines for the use of the gift of tongues and prophecy. If these guidelines aren't followed then there will be confusion.

I Corinthians 14:33 - For God is not the author of confusion, but of peace, as in all churches of the saints. When confusion arises, God is not the author of it. The confusion doesn't arise because of the gifts themselves, but because the guidelines that God clearly has laid out aren't being followed. Unfortunately, there are a number of charismatic churches that do not follow these guidelines. I encourage those same churches to read and to study the Scripture in order to see how these gifts are supposed to be used. If we would follow the guidelines given by Paul, then maybe more non-charismatic Christians would be more sympathetic. With that being said, some take this verse and swing the pendulum in the other direction. They recognize that some charismatic churches do not follow the guidelines given by the Lord for the use of the gifts which ultimately produces confusion. As a result they do not want to use the gifts at all. They also might even go as far to say that the gifts are not in the church today because of the confusion. It is pointed out that God is not the author of confusion. Since many times there is confusion in charismatic churches when the gifts are used, therefore the gifts are not of God. No, the gifts are given by God. It is not the gifts that are the issue. Again, God is not the author of confusion. Confusion does not arise from the use of the gifts, it arises from the abuse of the gifts. The confusion arises when we don't follow the Scripture. This is true whenever the Scriptures are not obeyed. Disobedience to the Word of God always leads to confusion. Sin always clouds reality. It can be complicated issues such as dysfunctional families or in areas such as the spiritual gifts. Disobedience leads to confusion. On one extreme side of the argument, there are Christians that don't believe in the spiritual gifts. As a result, the only answer they have in dealing with the Scriptures that do deal with the spiritual gifts is to say that don't apply to us today. Virtually everything else in the Scripture applies to us today, just not the spiritual gifts. In doing so they are denying the Scriptures that they hold so dear, and disobeying God's commands concerning these gifts. The other extreme is to abuse the spiritual gifts by disregarding the guidelines that Paul gives concerning the use of them. As a result, there tends to be doctrines in Pentecostal churches that aren't Scriptural. Such as if a person doesn't speak in tongues, then they aren't saved. That is found nowhere in the Bible. Only people that are saved can speak in tongues, but that does not mean that speaking in tongues is a seal of their salvation. Again, confusion arises because of disobedience to the Scriptures. God is not the author of confusion. He is the author of the Scriptures. If we would just stick with the Scriptures and obey them, then the issues, confusion, and problems would not arise.

I Corinthians 14:34-35 - Let your women keep silence in the churches: for it is not permitted unto them to speak; but they are commanded to be under obedience, as also saith the law. 35 And if they will learn any thing, let them ask their husbands at home: for it is a shame for women to speak in the church. This passage deals with the role of women in the church. That is a touchy subject. It is another subject for another time, for it is not the subject matter we are talking about.

I Corinthians 14:36 - What? came the word of God out from you? or came it unto you only? Paul mentions that the Word of God came out from them. He then asks them if they were the only ones that received the word of God. This is not speaking about the Scriptures. If it was speaking about the Scriptures, then what person in the Corinthian church wrote one the books that are in our cannon of Scripture? Is their other books written by the Corinthians that should be part of the Scripture? Furthermore, Paul asks them it the word of God came to them only. In other words the Word of God came to others. If this is talking about the Scriptures, then there could possibly be other books written by other people that we do not know about. In context, Paul is not writing about the Scriptures, he is writing about the gift of tongues and prophecy. He is saying that God is the one that speaks the prophecy to the one prophesying. When there is someone speaking in tongues, God is speaking through them. When there is an interpretation of tongues, God is the one that gives the interpretation. If God is the one giving the prophecies, then we should probably receive prophecies as such. *I Thessalonians 5:20 - Despise not prophesyings.* If an utterance of tongues, and interpretation of tongues is given by God, then we should probably receive them and treat them as such as well.

I Corinthians 14:37-38 - If any man think himself to be a prophet, or spiritual, let him acknowledge that the things that I write unto you are the commandments of the Lord. 38 But if any man be ignorant, let him be ignorant. Paul tells the Corinthian believers that the guidelines that he wrote were the commandments of God. That is what the text says. If anyone believes that they are spiritual, or if they are a prophet, then they must obey the commands of God. Anyone that functions in the gifts, but does not obey the Scriptures is not spiritual. The Corinthian church was zealous of the spiritual gifts, and yet Paul said they were carnal disobeying the commandments of God. This should not be so in any church of God. It is not wrong to be zealous of the spiritual gifts as long as the rest of the Word of God is being obeyed as well. Exercising spiritual gifts does not make someone spiritually mature. Being spiritually mature is marked by obeying His commandments and knowing Him. That does not mean that we should not exercise our God-given spiritual gifts. It does mean, however, that we should be pursuing Him, and seeking to obey his commands.

Since these guidelines are the commandments of God themselves, then it seems to me like God expects us to function with the gifts as part of our lives. It also means that the greater priority should be placed on walking with God, obeying Him, knowing Him, and loving Him. In verse 38, Paul is not saying that he desires people to be ignorant of the spiritual gifts. He expressed his desire that they wouldn't be ignorant of the spiritual gifts in *I Corinthians 12:1 - Now concerning spiritual gifts, brethren, I would not have you ignorant.* In context he is speaking of the commandments of God concerning spiritual gifts. The spiritual man and the prophet were to acknowledge those commands as from the Lord. The Greek word for "ignorant" is ἀγνοέω agnoéō, ag-no-eh'-o; not to know (through lack of information or intelligence); by implication, to ignore (through disinclination):—(be) ignorant(-ly), not know, not understand, unknown. It can mean to ignore, and in this context, I believe that it does. If someone ignores and refuses to obey the commands of God after being shown the Scripture, then we are to let him remain in such a state. We are to let God work in their life through the conviction of the Holy Spirit. This is good advice concerning any of the commands of God. If we show the Scriptures to someone and they refuse to obey them, the only thing we can do is pray for them. At that point we need to let the Holy Spirit use the Scriptures to convict them.

I Corinthians 14:39-40 - Wherefore, brethren, covet to prophesy, and forbid not to speak with tongues. 40 Let all things be done decently and in order. Concerning this verse, Cate writes, "Since we believed that tongues have ceased, some would like to know why Paul said in I Corinthians 14:39, 'Forbid not to speak with tongues.' This is while the nine gifts were still in effect."[16] The truth is that statement is based completely on a presupposition that states that the gifts are not still in effect today. He even says that they believe that they have ceased. At best he is explaining away the Scriptures to fit his presupposition. At worst, he is denying the Scriptures at face value. Do you see how much power a presupposition can have? It can lead someone that is very intelligent, and very well learned in the Scriptures to the say that they believe that tongues have ceased, when the Bible clearly says "forbid not to speak with tongues." I am not trying to tear Cate down. In fact, I think that his knowledge of the Scriptures is admirable. It just seems as though he was led by his presupposition when he was interpreting this verse. Wherefore means for this cause. What reason is Paul talking about? He just got done referring to the commands of God. Since God has given commandments concerning spiritual gifts he expects His church to be functioning in them. The words "covet" and "forbid" are both in the imperative mood in the Greek. The imperative mood is the mood in which commands are expressed, but it can also be used to entreat. Paul may be commanding them, or entreating them but either way, the will of God is expressed. "Covet to prophesy, and forbid not to speak in tongues."

In context, I do believe that Paul is giving a command when he says "forbid not to speak in tongues." This seems to be a problem in the body of Christ. Some have seen the abuse of the gift of tongues and as a result they forbid speaking in tongues altogether. Paul commands that we don't forbid speaking in tongues. Paul then says, "Let all things be done decently and in order." Many have used this verse to prove that the spiritual gifts are not to be exercised. Why? Because many times the spiritual gifts are used in a way that is decently and in order. It doesn't mean that they are not supposed to be used, but that they are supposed to be used according to the guidelines of Scripture. To the people that use this verse to support their beliefs concerning this topic, I would like to remind them of the context of this verse. The contexts commands us to "forbid not to speak with tongues". So when he says, "Let all things be done decently and in order" Obviously he is talking about speaking in tongues and prophesying. This means this verse in it's context is actually supporting the use of the gift of tongues in the right context, and the right way. Paul does write that things were to be done "decently and in order", but he also said "let all things be done". In other words prophesying and speaking in tongues should be done in the church according to the commands of Scripture.

I hope you can see that this verse really is the summary of this chapter. Paul does want all things to be done, but he also wants them done decently and in order. This whole chapter Paul has been talking about understanding what is said during their times of gathering together so they can all be edified. He speaks specifically about the gift of prophecy and the gift of tongues and their functions. He gives some guidelines for how they are used. He exhorts the Corinthians to remain zealous for spiritual gifts just so long as they exercise them to edify the church in a manner that is decently and in order according to the commands of God.

Chapter 4

The Gift of Prophecy

Cate's whole argument against the spiritual gifts rests on the belief that the gift of prophecy was given in the early church for the purpose of revealing the Scriptures. I hope you have already seen that it wasn't. That is how someone can interpret "we know in part, and we prophesy in part" to mean the Word of God in *I Corinthians 13:8-10* when the context is clearly speaking about love. In this chapter we'll see the justification that some people have for doing this, and why it is wrong to do so. *I Corinthians 14:29-37 - Let the prophets speak two or three, and let the other judge. 30 If any thing be revealed to another that sitteth by, let the first hold his peace. 31 For ye may all prophesy one by one, that all may learn, and all may be comforted. 32 And the spirits of the prophets are subject to the prophets. 33 For God is not the author of confusion, but of peace, as in all churches of the saints. 34 Let your women keep silence in the churches: for it is not permitted unto them to speak; but they are commanded to be under obedience, as also saith the law. 35 And if they will learn any thing, let them ask their husbands at home: for it is a shame for women to speak in the church. 36 What? came the word of God out from you? or came it unto you only? 37 If any man think himself to be a prophet, or spiritual, let him acknowledge that the things that I write unto you are the commandments of the Lord.* This is the passage that B.F. Cate used to prove that prophecy was the tool that God used to reveal His word to the church. He states,

> Paul, in telling the Corinthian church how the gifts of tongues and prophecy were to be controlled while they were in effect, said concerning those who had the gift of prophecy, "Let the PROPHETS speak two or three, and let the others judge. For if anything be REVEALED to another that sitteth by, let the first hold his peace. For all may PROPHESY one by one, that all may learn, and all may be comforted… What came THE WORD OF GOD out from you? Or

came it unto you only? If any man think himself to be a PROPHET, or spiritual, let him acknowledge that the things that I write unto you are the commandments of the Lord" (I Corinthians 14:29-31, 36, 37). Thus we see, THOSE WHO HAD THE GIFT OF PROPHECY WERE PROPHETS. The prophets in the early church did not get their messages by studying, like preachers do today (II Timothy 2:15), because they did not at that time have the New Testament. Their messages were REVEALED to them while they were sitting in the service. Read again verse 30. It was because those prophets received only a little New Testament truth at a time that Paul said in chapter 13, "We know in PART, and we prophesy in PART." Therefore it was necessary for the early churches to have prophets until the time of the New Testament was given in permanent form. Paul made it very clear that those who had the gift of prophecy received the Word of God direct from God, when he said to them, "What? came the Word of God OUT FROM YOU? or CAME IT UNTO YOU only?" Thus it is clear that those who had the gift of prophecy not only gave out the Word of God, but they also received the Word of God by divine revelation. This gift had to cease when the New Testament was completed, because John said, as he finished the book of Revelation, "I testify unto every man that heareth the words of the PROPHECY of this book. [You see, John had the gift of prophecy], if any man ADD UNTO THESE THINGS, God shall add to him the plagues that are written in this book." In other words, he is saying that this completes the writings of the New Testament. Hence there is no longer a place for the gift of prophecy in the church.[17]

First of all in this quote of Scripture, Cate leaves out five verses of the Scripture to prove his point. But for sake of argument, let's overlook that. Let's assume that he's right. Cate writes, "The prophets in the early church did not get their messages by studying, like preachers do today (II Timothy 2:15), because they did not at that time have the New Testament. Their messages were REVEALED to them while they were sitting in the service. Read again verse 30."[18] This statement is problematic for a couple of reasons. First, it wasn't the prophet that was sitting in the service that was receiving the revelation. It was someone else in the service. *I Corinthians*

14:29 - Let the prophets speak two or three, and let the other judge. The prophets are speaking, but the others are standing by judging. The other problem with this statement is that the revelation was not a sermon given from God. It was a message from God to either confirm the word that was being spoken by the prophet, or to warn them that the prophet was giving a false prophecy. It wasn't giving the Word of God, it was the confirmation or the warning of the word spoken by the prophet. That is why Paul writes "let the other judge". Cates states, "It was because those prophets received only a little New Testament truth at a time that Paul said in chapter 13, "We know in PART, and we prophesy in PART." Therefore it was necessary for the early churches to have prophets until the time of the New Testament was given in permanent form." [19] We have already looked at this passage in *I Corinthians 13*, when Paul said "we know in part", he wasn't saying that we know the Word of God in part until it was completed. He was saying that they only knew Christ in part until he came back and they would know him as he knows them. When he says that "we prophesy in part", he is not saying that they were going to receive the Word of God by prophecy until it was completed then it would be done away. He was saying that they were going to prophesy (speaking words of exhortation, edification, and comfort) until Jesus comes, then He would speak those words to His saints personally. Cate states,

> Paul made it very clear that those who had the gift of prophecy received the Word of God direct from God, when he said to them, "What? came the Word of God OUT FROM YOU? or CAME IT UNTO YOU only?" Thus it is clear that those who had the gift of prophecy not only gave out the Word of God, but they also received the Word of God by divine revelation.[20]

I will admit that Paul said that the Word of God came to them. I will admit that in context he was referring to the gift of prophecy. But he was also speaking of the interpretation of tongues. If prophecy was the method that God used to reveal his word, then the Corinthians must have written a book of Scripture. What book did they write then? It simply means that the words that were spoken through prophecy were spoken by God. Paul already told us the purpose of the gift of prophecy in *I Corinthians 14:3 - But he that prophesieth speaketh unto men to edification, and exhortation, and comfort.* The audience of prophecy was individual men. It was a very personal word spoken by God through the New Testament prophets to individuals. What were they speaking? They speak words of edification, exhortation, and comfort. A good example of this is *Acts 15:32 - And Judas and Silas, being prophets also themselves, exhorted the brethren with many words, and confirmed them.* Judas and Silas were prophets. What did they do? They exhorted the brethren! The best way to illustrate this gift at work is by looking at the prophet Agabus and his ministry in Paul's life. *Acts 21:10-11 - And as we tarried there many days, there came down from Judæa a certain prophet, named Agabus. 11 And when he was come unto us, he took Paul's girdle, and bound his own hands and feet, and said, Thus saith the Holy Ghost, So shall the Jews at Jerusalem bind the man that owneth this girdle, and shall deliver him into the hands of the Gentiles.* Agabus was a prophet. God used him to speak his word directly to Paul. The Holy Ghost is God, is He not? Agabus was speaking the words that the Holy Ghost revealed to him to speak to Paul, hence the word of God. He operated according to his office. He was a prophet. The Greek word for "prophet" in *Acts 21:10* is προφήτης prophḗtēs, prof-ay'-tace; a foreteller ("prophet"); by analogy, an inspired speaker; by extension, a poet:— prophet. He was an inspired speaker that spoke of future events as a foreteller. I looked up every reference in the book of *Acts* that dealt with the New Testament prophets, prophecy, and prophesying. *Acts 2:17-18 - And it shall come to pass in the last days, saith God, I will pour out of my Spirit upon all flesh: and your sons and your daughters shall prophesy, and your young men shall see visions, and your old men shall dream dreams: 18 and on my servants and on my handmaidens I will pour out in those days of my Spirit; and they shall prophesy:* This is a prophecy about prophecy. It happens after the baptism of the Spirit. Notice who God pours His Spirit upon. He is pouring out his Spirit "upon" his "servants" and "handmaidens". This is another good example of the baptism of the Spirit. God pours out his Spirit "upon" individuals to empower them to serve Him. We will deal this passage in depth later on. *Acts 11:27-28 - And in these days came prophets from Jerusalem unto Antioch. 28 And there stood up one of them named Agabus, and signified by the Spirit that there should be great dearth throughout all the world: which came to pass in the days of Claudius Cæsar.* Agabus was prophesying. He was acting according to his office as he spoke the word of the Lord about what was to happen in the world. *Acts 13:1-2 - Now there were in the church that was at Antioch certain prophets and teachers; as Barnabas, and Simeon that was called*

Niger, and Lucius of Cyrene, and Manaen, which had been brought up with Herod the tetrarch, and Saul. 2 As they ministered to the Lord, and fasted, the Holy Ghost said, Separate me Barnabas and Saul for the work whereunto I have called them. It seems as though the same thing could be happening here as what happened in *Acts 21:10-11*. It doesn't have to be. It could've been that the Holy Spirit just spoke to one of them, and they obeyed his voice. It is interesting that this verse speaks of teachers and prophets in the same verse as two different offices. It may have been that they all held both offices, or it could've been that some were prophets and some were teachers. *Acts 15:32 - And Judas and Silas, being prophets also themselves, exhorted the brethren with many words, and confirmed them.* Judas and Silas were prophets. Again, they acted according to their office by exhorting the brethren! *Acts 19:6 - And when Paul had laid his hands upon them, the Holy Ghost came on them; and they spake with tongues, and prophesied.* This was the baptism of the Spirit. Paul had laid his hands upon them, and the Holy Spirit "came on" them. They prophesied as a result. *Acts 21:8-9 - And the next day we that were of Paul's company departed, and came unto Cæsarea: and we entered into the house of Philip the evangelist, which was one of the seven; and abode with him. 9 And the same man had four daughters, virgins, which did prophesy.* Apparently women could prophesy as long as it was according to the guidelines given in *I Corinthians 14. Acts 21:10-11 - And as we tarried there many days, there came down from Judæa a certain prophet, named Agabus. 11 And when he was come unto us, he took Paul's girdle, and bound his own hands and feet, and said, Thus saith the Holy Ghost, So shall the Jews at Jerusalem bind the man that owneth this girdle, and shall deliver him into the hands of the Gentiles.* We have already talked about this passage of Scripture. Needless to say Agabus was a prophet, and this was an example of prophecy. All of these passages deal with prophets, prophecies, or prophesying. None of these passages deal with the inspiration of Scripture. If prophecy was the tool that God used to reveal his Scripture to his church, then what book did Agabus write? What about Silas? What about Barnabas, Simeon, Lucius of Cyrene, Manaen? Did the daughters of Philip write any books? I'm not trying to be mean but I am trying to make a point. Prophesy was not what God used to inspire Scripture, it was and is one of God's methods to speak edification, exhortation, and comfort to individuals concerning the secrets of their hearts. This have seen this before, but revelation is the tool that God used to inspire the Scripture. *Ephesians 3:3-*

6 - how that by revelation he made known unto me the mystery; (as I wrote afore in few words, 4 whereby, when ye read, ye may understand my knowledge in the mystery of Christ) 5 which in other ages was not made known unto the sons of men, as it is now revealed unto his holy apostles and prophets by the Spirit; 6 that the Gentiles should be fellowheirs, and of the same body, and partakers of his promise in Christ by the gospel: As we have seen before. Paul says in verse 3 that God used revelation to inspire his truth to his people that the Gentiles could be saved and enjoy the benefits of that salvation. To say that the gift of prophecy was the means that God used to inspire his Word is an assumption at best that cannot be proved. Cate states,

> This gift had to cease when the New Testament was completed, because John said, as he finished the book of Revelation, "I testify unto every man that heareth the words of the PROPHECY of this book. [You see, John had the gift of prophecy], if any man ADD UNTO THESE THINGS, God shall add to him the plagues that are written in this book." In other words, he is saying that this completes the writings of the New Testament. Hence there is no longer a place for the gift of prophecy in the church.[21]

We have already seen that prophecy was not used in the giving of Scripture. In the Greek the words "prophecy" and "book" are both in the ablative case. Particularly they are partitive ablatives. A partitive ablative is a bigger category of something which the noun it refers to is part of. The partitive ablative is the whole, whereas the noun it refers to is part of the whole. Basically all this means is that the words are part of prophecy, and the prophecy is part of this book. There are more words than prophetic words in this book, but there certainly are prophetic words in this book. This makes sense. The prophecy is written on the pages of Scripture, and the words make up the prophecy. The word "book" is also a partitive ablative. That means that the prophecy is part of the book. The book is the whole, while the prophecy is part of the whole. In other words, the whole book is not prophetic. Prophecy certainly is part of the book, but it is not the whole book. This can be seen by looking at the first three chapters of the book of *Revelation*. The first three chapters deal with certain things such as the vision that John has of the Lord Jesus Christ, and His message to the seven churches. Remember if someone uses the gift of prophecy they are not adding to the Scripture because the Bible tells us in *I Corinthians 14:3 - But he that prophesieth speaketh unto men to edification, and exhortation, and comfort.*

Cate writes,

> Why should it be difficult to see that we have no prophets today? The same thing occurred before. Between Malachi and John the Baptist there were about 400 years during which Israel received no messages from the Lord. They had to depend wholly upon the written Word as their only guide. So it is with us today. The last prophet of the Old Testament foretold the coming of the next prophet (Malachi 3:1), which was John the Baptist (Matthew 11:10). John the apostle, the last prophet of the New Testament, foretold the coming of the next prophets who will be the two witnesses in the tribulation period.[22]

It is difficult to see that we have no prophets today because the Bible states that we do. *I Corinthians 12:28 - And God hath set some in the church, first apostles, secondarily prophets, thirdly teachers, after that miracles, then gifts of healings, helps, governments, diversities of tongues.* The Bible specifically says that God has set prophets in the church. This is not the only passage of Scripture that says that He has. *Ephesians 4:11 - And he gave some, apostles; and some, prophets; and some, evangelists; and some, pastors and teachers; 12 for the perfecting of the saints, for the work of the ministry, for the edifying of the body of Christ: 13 till we all come in the unity of the faith, and of the knowledge of the Son of God, unto a perfect man, unto the measure of the stature of the fulness of Christ:* The Bible says that God has given some prophets, and some apostles. He gave them for the purpose of edifying the body of Christ. They will continue to edify the body of Christ until we come to the unity of the faith, and of the knowledge of God, unto a perfect man, unto the measure of the stature of the fulness of Christ. As far as I know, we haven't reached that point yet. My question is this. Why is it so hard to believe the simple claims of Scripture concerning prophets? It takes faith to believe that. Notice something here. Claiming that there are no prophets today doesn't require faith, it requires unbelief in these two verses of Scripture. In fact it requires faith that these two verses of Scripture do not apply to us today. Just because there was a time in Israel's history that there were no prophets doesn't mean that there are no prophets today. Israel was the people that

God has used in the past and will use again in the future. Israel and the church are two different entities. To say that John was the last prophet in the New Testament is problematic when God has said that he has set prophets in His church. Not only has He set them in His church, but He has given them to His church for the purpose of edification, and will continue to give them until we come to the unity of faith.

Another argument given by cessationists to prove that there are no apostles and prophets in the church today is found comes from *Ephesians 2:19-21 - Now therefore ye are no more strangers and foreigners, but fellowcitizens with the saints, and of the household of God; 20 and are built upon the foundation of the apostles and prophets, Jesus Christ himself being the chief corner stone; 21 in whom all the building fitly framed together groweth unto an holy temple in the Lord:* The argument teaches that the apostles and the prophets were the foundation of the New Testament because they wrote the Word of God. Writing the Word of God was the duty of their office, and once the Word of God was completed, then their office passed off the scene. It is said by cessationists that there are no apostles or prophets doing exploits like Peter, Paul, or John walking around on the earth in our day and age. Another passage that is quoted to further develop their theory from *Acts 2:20-22 - For it is written in the book of Psalms, Let his habitation be desolate, and let no man dwell therein: and his bishoprick let another take. 21 Wherefore of these men which have companied with us all the time that the Lord Jesus went in and out among us, 22 beginning from the baptism of John, unto that same day that he was taken up from us, must one be ordained to be a witness with us of his resurrection.* This passage is used to prove that the office of an apostle had to be fulfilled by someone who walked with them during Christ's earthly ministry from the time that he was baptized by John until he ascended, and that witnessed his resurrection. Since no one alive today experienced these things, no one can claim to have the office of an apostle.

I have several problems with this interpretation of Scripture. First of all, notice how the Scriptures say "and his bishoprick let another take". Whose bishoprick? Judas' bishoprick. For someone to take his bishoprick, or his place as an apostle, they would have had to experience all of those things. They would have had to experience walking with Jesus from the time of his baptism until he ascended. They would have had to experience witnessing his resurrection. Why? Because Judas was his disciple, and Jesus taught his disciples through these circumstances. God's will is going to be accomplished one way or another. It will be accomplished whether his chosen vessels are willing or not. How do I know? *Esther 4:13-14 - Then Mordecai commanded to answer Esther, Think not with thyself that thou shalt escape in the king's house, more than all the Jews. 14 For if thou altogether holdest thy peace at this time, then shall there enlargement and deliverance arise to the Jews from another place; but thou and thy father's house shall be destroyed: and who knoweth whether thou art come to the kingdom for such a time as this?* Mordecai told Esther that she may have become queen in order to deliver the Jews from Haman's wicked schemes, but if she held her peace, or remained quiet, then she and her father's house would be destroyed. But, God would raise up another deliverer in another way, in another place.

Second, I know that all these qualifications do not apply to all apostles, but simply to Judas' office because Paul did not experience all these things. He was a Pharisee while Jesus was on earth, not to mention that Barnabas is mentioned as an apostle as well, and we have no idea according to the Scriptures whether he experienced these things or not. *Acts 14:14 - Which when the apostles, Barnabas and Paul, heard of, they rent their clothes, and ran in among the people, crying out.*

Third, the duty of the office of an apostle, or prophet for that matter, did not include writing the Scripture. How do I know? Because if it did, then what book did Bartholomew, Thomas, or Andrew write? What book did Agabus, or any other prophet write? There is a difference between the will of God for someone's life, and the office that they fulfill. The Greek word for "apostle" is ἀπόστολος apóstolos; a delegate; specially, an ambassador of the Gospel; officially a commissioner of Christ ("apostle") (with miraculous powers):—apostle, messenger, he that is sent. It specifically means an ambassador of the Gospel. Proof of this can be found in *I Corinthians 9:2 - If I be not an apostle unto others, yet doubtless I am to you: for the seal of mine apostleship are ye in the Lord.* He specifically said that the seal of his apostleship was not the Scriptures which he left behind, but the believers which he led to the Lord. More proof is in the fact that Barnabas was referred to as an apostle on a missionary journey. *Acts 14:14 - Which when the apostles, Barnabas and Paul, heard of, they rent their clothes, and ran in among the people, crying out,* Yet another proof that apostles are simply ambassadors of the gospel is found in *Romans 1:5 - by whom we have received grace and apostleship, for obedience to the faith among all nations, for his name:* The Greek word for "obedience" is an accusative of purpose meaning that the purpose for which they were given the apostleship for the purpose of sharing the gospel so that the people from all nations would be obedient to the faith. It is interesting that Paul does not mention any co-authors of this book, nor does he mention any of the other apostles, yet he still uses the word "we" meaning that he is including the Roman believers in this apostleship. Why? Because apostleship involves being ambassadors of the gospel which is something that every Christian should be if they want to carry our the Great Commission. The reason why they had miraculous powers is because they were sent out to preach the gospel. The same gospel in which the Lord confirms with signs following. They weren't anyone special to have these miraculous powers, but it was a definite sign of their ministry because they were used to preach the gospel. Since the office of the apostle was to be an ambassador of the gospel, then part of the will of God for each, and every one of the apostles was to preach the gospel in one way, shape, or form. Yet, God had a specific will for each and every one of their lives as well. He ordained some like Peter, Paul, and John to write books of the New Testament, and others he used in different ways. It is no different today. There are many pastors today that write books, and yet, there are many others who don't. Yet they are still fulfilling the will of God for their lives.

Ephesians 2:19-21 - Now therefore ye are no more strangers and foreigners, but fellowcitizens with the saints, and of the household of God; 20 and are built upon the foundation of the apostles and prophets, Jesus Christ himself being the chief corner stone; 21 in whom all the building fitly framed together groweth unto an holy temple in the Lord: When Paul writes of the "foundation of the apostles and prophets" he is not saying that the apostles and prophets were the foundation of the church. He is saying that they laid the foundation. How do I know? *I Corinthians 3:9-11 - For we are labourers together with God: ye are God's husbandry, ye are God's building. 10 According to the grace of God which is given unto me, as a wise masterbuilder, I have laid the foundation, and another buildeth thereon. But let every man take heed how he buildeth thereupon. 11 For other foundation can no man lay than that is laid, which is Jesus Christ.* This is definitely speaking about the same subject. Paul specifically referred to the church as the building of God in both passages. In this passage though, Paul makes an interesting statement. He says that there is no other foundation than that which is laid which is Jesus Christ. In other words, Jesus Christ is the only foundation which the church is founded upon. The church needs to be founded on a relationship with Christ. Referring to himself Jesus said in *Matthew 16:18 - And I say also unto thee, That thou art Peter, and upon this rock I will build my church; and the gates of hell shall not prevail against it.* Jesus is the rock upon which he builds his church. Just as David said, the Lord is my rock! That isn't a theological concept, that is real. It is every day life. Everything we do needs to go back to the Lord. When we are in the middle of a crisis, and everything around us is stirring, we need to turn to the Lord for help. We need to turn to the Lord for answers. When we need wisdom as to the way we should live life, or for clarity in certain decision, we need to turn to the Lord for those things. It is in our relationship with the Lord that we must be founded upon. I understand that we need the Scriptures, but they testify to us of him. At the end of the day, we need practical help, and we need the Lord to move, because if he doesn't move, then nothing will change. But if he is going to move, then he must be our rock. He is the rock and foundation of every single person in the church individually, and he is the rock and foundation for the church collectively. In those storms, and challenges we don't turn to apostles and prophets, we don't even look to the Scriptures solely. We must look to the Lord of whom the Scriptures testify. "For other foundation can no man lay than that is laid, which is Jesus Christ."

Now that I've had my say, I do want to emphasize that Jesus is the only foundation. What is interesting is that Paul talks about laying the foundation of Christ. How can you lay the foundation of the church, if the foundation is Christ? Before any building exists, the foundation must be laid. In other words, the church doesn't exist in the way that it was intended to without the foundation. What is the church? It is a called-out assembly of believers. Before there can be a called-out assembly of believers, individuals must choose to believe the gospel. In other words, sharing the gospel of Jesus Christ is how the foundation of Christ is laid. I know this because of what Paul wrote in *Romans 15:18-20 -For I will not dare to speak of any of those things which Christ hath not wrought by me, to make the Gentiles obedient, by word and deed, 19 through mighty signs and wonders, by the power of the Spirit of God; so that from Jerusalem, and round about unto Illyricum, I have fully preached the gospel of Christ. 20 Yea, so have I strived to preach the gospel, not where Christ was named, lest I should build upon another man's foundation:* Paul wrote that he preached the gospel to the Gentiles through signs and wonders where he was not name, so that he wouldn't build on the foundation that another man had already built. What does this all mean? First, it means that the foundation that the apostles built for the church was to preach the gospel, not to write the Scriptures. It is inherent to the office of an apostle as an ambassador of the gospel. It is clearly seen in all three of these passages, especially seeing that the Greek word for "foundation" is the same Greek word. If that is the case then how did the prophets lay the foundation. They didn't, they just strengthened the church's relationship with the foundation, who is Christ, by speaking words of edification, exhortation, and comfort directly from Him to his church.

Second, it means that the foundation of Christ is still being laid all over the world. There are unreached people groups that need to hear the gospel, and if Paul is the pattern for us who believe on him, then we should be using signs, and wonders to fully preach the gospel to those who are lost. This argument that there are no more apostles or prophets in the church today by claiming that their duty has been fulfilled misunderstands the role of the apostle, and prophet, as well as the qualities required to be one. *Ephesians 2:20* is one of the main passages which cessationists use to prove that apostles, prophets, and the sign gifts are all a glorious memory of the past, when in reality, it wonderfully shows the necessity of the apostle, prophet, and the sign gifts to preach the gospel!

Some might object by asking whether or not I believe that there are apostles or prophets walking around in the earth today that rival the caliber of Peter, and Paul. First, Peter and Paul weren't great men because they were apostles. They were great men because they walked with Christ. Judas was chosen to be an apostle, but he betrayed his Lord, after walking with Him for three and half years. Second, if Peter and Paul were great men because they walked so intimately with the Lord, then yes, I do believe that we can still walk intimately with the Lord today, even to the extent that Peter and Paul walked with Him. It would require a great cost, as they both suffered tremendously being beaten by the religious leaders, but I am sure that there are Christians now a days in Muslim, and Communist countries who walk with the Lord so very intimately because of their suffering as well.

Then Cates writes,

> That there are no prophets in the church today is also seen in II Peter 2:1, "But there were false PROPHETS also among the PEOPLE, even

as there shall be false TEACHERS among YOU" (in the churches). Looking backward he called them prophets. Looking forward he called them teachers. This was because there were to be no prophets in the church after the New Testament was completed.[23]

The verse that he is referring to is *II Peter 2:1 - But there were false prophets also among the people, even as there shall be false teachers among you, who privily shall bring in damnable heresies, even denying the Lord that bought them, and bring upon themselves swift destruction.* Cate didn't quote the whole verse. He is not stating that there will be no more prophets in the church. He is comparing the false prophets of the past to the false teachers in the New Testament. Both of them claimed to be speaking for the Lord, but in reality they were speaking blasphemy. If we look a couple pages over in our Bibles. The Bible tells us in *I John 4:1 - Beloved, believe not every spirit, but try the spirits whether they are of God: because many false prophets are gone out into the world.* This first epistle of John was written several years after Peter penned his second epistle. John wrote that there were false prophets that were gone out into the world in his day proving that Peter was not trying to say that there were no more prophets in the church. In fact, you don't counterfeit something that isn't real. No one tries to counterfeit $25 bills. Why? Because everyone would know that it would be fake. It would stick out. If there were false prophets, then there must have been real prophets of the Lord just as Paul said there would be. The Bible clearly says in *I Corinthians 12:28 - And God hath set some in the church, first apostles, secondarily prophets, thirdly teachers, after that miracles, then gifts of healings, helps, governments, diversities of tongues.* The Bible clearly says that God has set prophets in the church. That's why there could be false prophets counterfeiting them. Let's just stick with what the Bible says and we'll be okay.

I hope you can see that there is no Scriptural evidence for saying that prophecy was the gift that God has used to reveal his Scriptures. To say that there are no prophets in the church today is deny what the Scriptures clearly teach in *I Corinthians 12:28* and *Ephesians 4:11-12*. This is the central argument of Cate who claims that all the spiritual gifts are not to be exercised in the church today. As a result, drastic measures have to be taken to prove this belief, even to the point of denying the Scriptures. Let's just take the Scriptures at face value, and believe what they say!

Chapter 5

The Gift of Healing

Some have claimed that the gift of healing is not in the church today. Others have taught problematic beliefs based on the experiences of people that are not healed when they are prayed for. We'll see what the Scriptures teach about this topic instead of other's beliefs or opinions. Before we get to the Scriptures, let's see what B.F. Cate says. He writes,

> While Christ was offering Himself to Israel as their promised Messiah, the miracles He performed proved Him to be such. Compare Isaiah 35:5, 6 with Matthew 11:2-6. But Israel rejected Him, and during the transition period (following the Lord's resurrection and before a WRITTEN revelation, the New Testament was given to the church) miracles were still performed in the early church to confirm the Word (Mark 16:17-20).[24]

Cate refers to the period of church history when the church was in infancy as the "transition period". Granted, it probably was a transition. God used to work through Israel, but after the resurrection God began working through the church. But the fact of the matter is the concept of a "transition period" is foreign to Scripture. *Hebrews 13:7-9 - Remember them which have the rule over you, who have spoken unto you the word of God: whose faith follow, considering the end of their conversation. 8 Jesus Christ the same yesterday, and to day, and for ever. 9 Be not carried about with divers and strange doctrines. For it is a good thing that the heart be established with grace; not with meats, which have not profited them that have been occupied therein.* In context, the Bible is speaking about the way of salvation when it refers to Jesus Christ as the "same yesterday, and to day, and for ever". Believers weren't supposed to have their hearts established with meats, but with grace. The meats probably is a reference to the sacrificial system as opposed to the grace of God that sufficiently saves us without works today as it did in the Old Testament. The sacrificial system was the way in which the Old Testament saints kept themselves right in their relationship with God, whereas today God's grace sufficiently saves us, sanctified us, and keeps us right with him. How do we know all of this? Because of the "word of God". The writer of Hebrews exhorts these Jewish believers to remember those that had the rule over them. Those same people spoke the "word of God" to them. We know that Jesus is the Savior of the world yesterday, to day, and for ever" because of the Word of God. Since he is the same yesterday, to day, and for ever", he is immutable. He doesn't change. Since immutable, he also is faithful. Since he is faithful, he acts according to His Word "yesterday, to day, and for ever." This is true for every part of the "word of God". If it isn't then we have some issues as believers. He also acts according to the "word of God" today as he did yesterday in regards to healing, the baptism of the Spirit, and all the sign gifts for that matter. Whenever the Bible teaches us about healing, the sign gifts, or the baptism of the Spirit, it is as true for us today as it was in the days of the apostles. If this was not the case then we have some major issues in our Christianity today. This proves that there was no transition period. I challenge you as the reader to do a simple search of the Scripture. On any Bible search engine, just type in the words "transition", "transitional", and "normative". You'll find that none of these words are actually in the Bible. People have used the words "transition" and "transitional" to refer to the period of church history when they were still waiting for the completed New Testament in order to fit their own theological ideologies. As a result another term was created. That term is "normative". It is used to teach that none of the sign gifts are to be exercised as a normal way of life today. All of these terms originated with man to accommodate his doctrine. Cate continues on by writing,

> Now let us read Matthew 11:2-6, and we will see that the purpose of the miracles of Christ was to aid people to believe in Him. "Now when John had heard in prison the works of Christ, he sent two of his disciples, and said unto Him. Art thou he that should come, or do we look for another? Jesus answered and said unto them, Go and shew John AGAIN those things which you do hear and see: The blind receive their sight, and the lame walk, the lepers are cleansed, and the deaf hear, the dead are raised up, and the poor have the gospel preached to them. And blessed is he,

whosoever shall not be offended in me." Here we see that John in prison was in DOUBT concerning Christ, and wanted to know if He was the one that should come as promised in the Old Testament. To help John BELIEVE that He was, He referred to the miracles that He was performing, which Isaiah said He would perform when He came. Christ's referring to His miracles as He did is proof that His miracles were to aid people to believe in Him. Some think the Lord performed His miracles of mercy just because He loved people. If this were true it would show that He loves some more than others, because many Christians have had brothers die, but He did not raise them from the dead as He did the brother of Mary and Martha.[25]

If truth be told, Cate is right. He is right that the miracles that Jesus performed were to confirm the word that he was preaching. His miracles confirmed His identity as the only begotten Son of God. That was something that the scribes and Pharisees couldn't do. They never told the lame man to pick up his bed and walk. They never raised the dead. They never cleansed any lepers. This proved that Jesus had an actual connection to God as His Son, and they didn't. But that doesn't mean that Jesus didn't heal people out of compassion. In fact there is a passage that tells us that he did. *Matthew 9:35-39 - And Jesus went about all the cities and villages, teaching in their synagogues, and preaching the gospel of the kingdom, and healing every sickness and every disease among the people. 36 But when he saw the multitudes, he was moved with compassion on them, because they fainted, and were scattered abroad, as sheep having no shepherd. 37 Then saith he unto his disciples, The harvest truly is plenteous, but the labourers are few; 38 pray ye therefore the Lord of the harvest, that he will send forth labourers into his harvest.* Notice in this passage that Jesus healed "every sickness and every disease among the people." But as he did so, he accompanied the miracles which he performed with the preaching of the gospel. Why did he do this? He both healed their physical bodies, and preached the gospel to them because "he was moved with compassion on them". But he knew that their greatest need was the salvation of their souls. Is it possible that Jesus healed those who came to him because he wanted them to further exercise their faith in order to be saved? There are so many examples of this. *Mark 10:51-52 - And Jesus answered and said unto him, What wilt thou that I should do unto thee?*

The blind man said unto him, Lord, that I might receive my sight. 52 And Jesus said unto him, Go thy way; thy faith hath made thee whole. And immediately he received his sight, and followed Jesus in the way. Jesus is speaking to Blind Bartimaeus who came to Jesus to receive his sight. Jesus responded by saying your faith has made you whole. The Greek word for "whole" is σώζω sōzō, sode'-zo; from a primary σῶς sōs (contraction for obsolete σάος sáos, "safe"); to save, i.e. deliver or protect (literally or figuratively):—heal, preserve, save (self), do well, be (make) whole. This same word is the Greek word that is commonly used to refer to salvation. Another example of this is that of the Canaanite woman. *Matthew 15:21-28 - Then Jesus went thence, and departed into the coasts of Tyre and Sidon. 22 And, behold, a woman of Canaan came out of the same coasts, and cried unto him, saying, Have mercy on me, O Lord, thou son of David; my daughter is grievously vexed with a devil. 23 But he answered her not a word. And his disciples came and besought him, saying, Send her away; for she crieth after us. 24 But he answered and said, I am not sent but unto the lost sheep of the house of Israel. 25 Then came she and worshipped him, saying, Lord, help me. 26 But he answered and said, It is not meet to take the children's bread, and to cast it to dogs. 27 And she said, Truth, Lord: yet the dogs eat of the crumbs which fall from their masters' table. 28 Then Jesus answered and said unto her, O woman, great is thy faith: be it unto thee even as thou wilt. And her daughter was made whole from that very hour.* She came to Jesus because her daughter was possessed by a devil. At first he didn't respond. He wasn't insensitive to her. He just keep responding to her in a way that would make her faith soar. Notice how he didn't heal her daughter until she exercised her faith to the point that Jesus himself said, "O woman, great is thy faith." It is very true that Jesus had compassion on people which caused him to preach the gospel to them so that their souls could be saved, but it is also true that he had compassion on them to heal them of their diseases. To say that he healed them solely to prove that he was the Messiah, takes away the heart from Jesus.

  To say that Jesus loved some more than others is because he healed some and not others is absolutely wrong. As we have already said, the greatest show of his compassion on people was the salvation of their souls. The truth is the Bible says in *Romans 2:4 - Or despisest thou the riches of his goodness and forbearance and longsuffering; not knowing that the goodness of God leadeth thee to repentance?* It is the goodness of God that leads us to repentance, but what that goodness looks like may vary depending on our reaction to Him. The goodness of God may manifest itself in mercy like when Jesus healed, every disease, and every sickness among the people. But, it may also look like his severity as well. He also tries to extend his mercy towards an individual first, but if they don't respond in repentance, then after he has been patient with them, he will extend his severity towards them to bring them to a place of surrender. How do I know this? Because I regularly work with the homeless. Those that are homeless have a lot of needs. Originally I was laying down my life for them constantly, but there was no change in their life. Then God spoke to me, and said that if I provided for their physical needs, without providing for their spiritual needs, then I was just making their life a little bit better, but ultimately enabling them to stay the same. He later spoke to me and said that if people start expecting something from me, then at that point, I just became their God. He doesn't want anyone to look to any one of us as their God, He wants to be their God. I learned that the goal in helping others that are homeless is to help them establish their own relationship with God, and the only way that happens is through surrender. Once they surrender to Him, then he can start working in their hearts in order to change their lives. At that point, then you can provide for their physical needs, but not until they surrender. Why? Because God may be using that hardship to bring them to a place of surrender to him. The Bible says in *Hosea 6:1 -Come, and let us return unto the Lord: for he hath torn, and he will heal us; he hath smitten, and he will bind us up.* Let's apply these principles to Jesus. This is exactly why he healed some, and not others by not healing them. It is exactly why the Bible says in *John 2:24-25 - But Jesus did not commit himself unto them, because he knew all men, 25 and needed not that any should testify of man: for he knew what was in man.*, and it is why he healed all those who came to him to be healed. His ultimate goal was the salvation of their souls. He had compassion on everyone by desiring that they be saved. Out of compassion, he healed some to bring them to repentance, and out of compassion he didn't to bring them to repentance.

Cate continues to write,

> Now let us read Mark 16:17-20, and see that miracles performed during the Acts of the Apostles were to aid people to believe the message concerning the Son of God. "And these SIGNS shall follow them that believe; In my name shall they cast out devils; they shall speak with new tongues; they shall take up serpents; and if they drink any deadly thing,

it shall not hurt them; they shall lay hands on the sick, and they shall recover. So then after the Lord had spoken unto them, He was received up into heaven, and sat on the right hand of God. And they went forth, and preached everywhere, the Lord working with them, and CONFIRMING THE WORD WITH SIGNS FOLLOWING." Notice, those signs were to confirm the Word. Now that the New Testament has been confirmed and completed we no longer need the signs. Some insist that those signs were to follow believers for all time. If this were true it would prove too much. Because there are no believers today who can "take up serpents," and "drink any deadly thing," without being "hurt." It is evident, therefore that those signs were ONLY for the confirming of the Word, until the New Testament was completed.[26]

Let's look at the context of the verses that Cate is referring to. *Mark 16:15-20 - And he said unto them, Go ye into all the world, and preach the gospel to every creature. 16 He that believeth and is baptized shall be saved; but he that believeth not shall be damned. 17 And these signs shall follow them that believe; In my name shall they cast out devils; they shall speak with new tongues; 18 they shall take up serpents; and if they drink any deadly thing, it shall not hurt them; they shall lay hands on the sick, and they shall recover. 19 So then after the Lord had spoken unto them, he was received up into heaven, and sat on the right hand of God. 20 And they went forth, and preached every where, the Lord working with them, and confirming the word with signs following. Amen.* The context of verses 17-20 is referring to the gospel. Look at verse 15 again. *Mark 16:15 - And he said unto them, Go ye into all the world, and preach the gospel to every creature.* The word "preach" is in the imperative mood in the Greek. The Lord Jesus was commanding his disciples to preach the gospel. The words "them that believe " are all one word in the Greek. It is a participle. A participle is a verbal adjective. This means that when the Bible says "them that believe" it is an adjective. These people are the people that believe. What do they believe? First, in context when he said "these signs shall follow them that believe" he is referring to those that believe the gospel. This tells me that signs were not something that was only to be done by the apostles. This is why Steven and Philip both could perform signs. This also tells me that this is available to us today. It is available to anyone that believes the gospel. Second, "them that believe" refers to something else.

Remember "them that believe" is a participle or a verbal adjective. It is describing the people. These are the people that believe. In context it also means that they have the faith to perform miracles. Nowhere in this context does the Bible mention the gift of healing. It does, however, mention faith. This is evidenced by the fact that the first sign on the list is casting out devils. When Jesus came down from the mount of transfiguration, there was a man whose son was possessed by a devil. His disciples had tried to cast it out, but they couldn't. Jesus then casts it out, and his disciples ask why they were unable to do so. Do you remember how Jesus replied? *Matthew 17:19-20 - Then came the disciples to Jesus apart, and said, Why could not we cast him out? 20 And Jesus said unto them, Because of your unbelief: for verily I say unto you, If ye have faith as a grain of mustard seed, ye shall say unto this mountain, Remove hence to yonder place; and it shall remove; and nothing shall be impossible unto you.* He told his disciples that the reason that they could not cast out the demon was because of their own unbelief. In fact, right in the context, he said that if they had "faith as a grain of a mustard seed" then nothing would be impossible to them. The parallel passage Jesus told the man who came to him in *Mark 9:23 - Jesus said unto him, If thou canst believe, all things are possible to him that believeth.* If all things are possible to him that believeth, then nothing is impossible to him that believeth. Faith allows the impossible to become possible. Jesus also said in *John 14:12 - Verily, verily, I say unto you, He that believeth on me, the works that I do shall he do also; and greater works than these shall he do; because I go unto my Father.* The words "he that believeth" is also a participle in the Greek. This is for anyone who is saved, but it also requires them to have faith in Christ to perform miracles. Jesus said that the one that believes on him would do the same works that he did. He even said that he would do greater works than He did. That is amazing! This tells me that faith is required to cast out a devil. This also tells me that everything else on the list in *Mark 16:17-18* is also done through faith. The reason why believers don't drink any deadly thing, or take up serpents today is because they don't have the faith to do so. I don't know about you, but I just don't have the faith to drink antifreeze, and I don't have the faith to be playing around with cobras. I'd rather just thank God for the safety that he does provide. The disciples were exercising faith when "they went forth, and preached every where, the Lord working with them, and confirming the word with signs following." This is why the Lord worked with them. The Bible says, "These signs shall follow them that believe". The Lord was working with them, "confirming the word with signs following." This proves that the Lord confirmed the word with signs because the disciples had the faith to step out, and believe. It wasn't because they had the spiritual gift, or because they were apostles.

What word was being confirmed? In context, it wasn't the New Testament. Some have said that it was the New Testament that was being confirmed when the signs were performed. The logic behind it goes like this. The Word was being revealed to them as they were preaching the gospel. This was something brand new. The church was brand new. The New Testament was the brand new Scriptures that were still being revealed. On the other side of the coin, Israel was the instrument that God used for thousands of years. They had the completed Old Testament for four hundred years. Therefore the signs were used by God to confirm the Word until the New Testament was completed. They were God's stamp of approval on the new church, and on the brand new Scriptures being revealed. Once the New Testament was revealed, the signs served their purpose and weren't used anymore. God stopped giving the gifts. Granted, the signs were God's stamp of approval on the word. He was confirming the word with signs following. The problem with all that logic was that it was not the New Testament being confirmed, it was the gospel. In verse 15, Jesus commanded his disciples to "preach the gospel to every creature." In verse 20, the disciples "went forth, and preached everywhere." What were they preaching? It was the gospel. They were obeying the Lord's command to "preach the gospel to every creature." The Lord responded by "confirming the word with signs following".

Why did the gospel need confirming? Because Jesus had just spent three and half years preaching that he was the Messiah and the Jews rejected Him. The Pharisees, Sadducees, scribes, lawyers, and the chief priests all condemned him as a heretic and a blasphemer. As a result they crucified Him. At the same time the Gentiles saw him being crucified between two thieves. He was crucified by the Roman centurions just like the two thieves. The Jews saw Him as a blasphemer, and the Gentiles saw Him as a criminal. The gospel needed to be confirmed by the signs to break what people previously thought about Jesus. The same happens today when people experience a miracle. It breaks all their preconceptions, and presuppositions about Jesus, and confronts them with the truth.

Paul preached the gospel with the aid of these signs and wonders. *Romans 15:18-19 - For I will not dare to speak of any of those things which*

Christ hath not wrought by me, to make the Gentiles obedient, by word and deed, 19 through mighty signs and wonders, by the power of the Spirit of God; so that from Jerusalem, and round about unto Illyricum, I have fully preached the gospel of Christ. Paul said that signs and wonders were an active part of his ministry to the Gentiles. The signs and wonders were done by Paul in his ministry to the "Gentiles". The signs and wonders weren't just used to preach the gospel to the Jews in the so-called "transition period". They weren't used just used by God to authenticate the message of the gospel to the Jews until the New Testament was completed. Paul said that he used signs and wonders to preach to the Gentiles. How could these signs and wonders be used to preach the gospel to the Gentiles? Jesus and Paul both said that it was the Jews that were looking for a sign. From the time of Moses, God used signs to confirm his Word to the Jews when they were in Egypt. He turned Moses' staff into a serpent, Moses' hand leprous and back again, and he turned water to blood. Throughout Israel's history, God used signs and wonders when dealing with His people Israel. How did the signs and wonders confirm the gospel to the Gentiles? When Moses smote the dust of the earth and it became lice, even the pagan magicians of Egypt said, "This is the finger of God"! When God wants to show his power, he can confirm his Word to the Jews and the Gentiles if He pleases to. A miracle cannot be denied. The only option is to either choose to accept it from God, or reject the message altogether. That's why God used signs and wonders to confirm the gospel to the Gentiles.

Here's my question. If the sign gifts were used to confirm the gospel in the first century, why wouldn't they be used to confirm the gospel today? Let's be honest, many people have preconceptions, and presuppositions about Jesus. But, if they are touched by the power of God, and they get healed from a terminal disease, then that would break all those presuppositions and preconceptions at once. What would happen if an unbeliever was touched so much by the power of God that they were healed of cancer? What if that same person was given the gospel at that very moment? There's a good chance that they might get saved. If we don't believe that's possible then look at the text again. *Mark 16:19 - So then after the Lord had spoken unto them, he was received up into heaven, and sat on the right hand of God.* The Lord was in heaven, but he was still working with them. What is happening here? When they believed, heaven responded. It is true for us as well. When we believe, then heaven responds. When we say that the sign gifts are not for today, it just proves that we don't believe. That is not meant to be condemning, but it is meant to be challenging. Take that for what it was meant to be and be better for it. Cate states,

> Now concerning the prayer of faith. James said, "The prayer of faith SHALL SAVE THE SICK, and the Lord SHALL raise him UP." There are a few things we must get straight if we want to find the meaning of this verse. To "save the sick" means he shall be saved from sickness and DEATH, because James said, "the Lord shall raise him UP." But notice that this healing is contingent upon the prayer of faith. The prayer of faith can be prayed when medicine is used if the medicine is applied "in the name of the Lord." Hezekiah prayed the prayer of faith and the Lord healed him, but He did it with medicine (II Kings 20:1-7). When the prayer of faith is prayed for a sick person he is sure to be healed as there is a God in Heaven, because "the Lord shall raise him UP." But here is where the catch comes. The prayer of faith cannot always be prayed. Before we prove this with Scripture, let us prove it with a simple illustration. A man gets sick at the age of 50, the prayer of faith is prayed, and he is raised UP. He gets sick again at age 100, the prayer of faith is prayed, and he is raised UP. He gets sick again at 125, the prayer of faith is prayed (?), and he is raised UP (?) He gets sick again at 150, the prayer of faith is prayed (?), and he is raised UP (?). He gets sick at 200, the prayer of faith is prayed (?), and he is raised UP (?). When speaking of healing, the faith healers always emphasize the POWER of God and His ABILITY to heal. (This is to trap the non-thinking person.) If it were only a matter of his ability, and not a matter of his will, couldn't he heal a person at 200 years of age as well as He could at 50? Therefore if the prayer of faith could always be prayed, we would never need to die. Just keep on praying the prayer of faith and keep on being raised UP. It is not difficult to see that it is not always God's will to raise His children UP, because, "It is appointed unto man once to die" (Hebrews 9:27). "Oh yes," you say, "everybody has to die." Not if the prayer of faith can always be prayed. Perhaps you have not yet seen what James said. He said, "The prayer of faith shall save the sick, and the Lord shall raise him UP." Dead people are not UP, they

are DOWN. So as long as a person can stay UP, he is not dead. Therefore, James teaches that the prayer of faith will heal a person and save him from DEATH. How can we harmonize this with Hebrews 9:27? The will of God must be brought into the matter.[27]

The passage that Cate is referring to is *James 5:14-15 - Is any sick among you? let him call for the elders of the church; and let them pray over him, anointing him with oil in the name of the Lord: 15 and the prayer of faith shall save the sick, and the Lord shall raise him up; and if he have committed sins, they shall be forgiven him.* Cate states,

> Now concerning the prayer of faith. James said, "The prayer of faith SHALL SAVE THE SICK, and the Lord SHALL raise him UP." There are a few things we must get straight if we want to find the meaning of this verse.[28]

It is interesting that Cate says that there are a few things that we must get straight before we interpret this verse. The plain reading of the verse will not do. That is not a proper interpretation. If I put as much effort into disproving the plain interpretation of the Great Commission as Cate does with this verse, then I could prove that the Great Commission is not something that should happen today either. Notice Cate goes into depth trying to disprove the plain reading of the text. This is not a position of faith, but of unbelief. I am not trying to tear down B.F. Cate in any way. I am just trying to point out an error for others to avoid. One thing that I would like to note is that Cate is right when he says that the gift of healing is not mentioned. He is absolutely right. Because it is not about the gift of healing. It is about faith. Need I remind us of *Mark 16:17 - And these signs shall follow them that believe; In my name shall they cast out devils; they shall speak with new tongues; 18 they shall take up serpents; and if they drink any deadly thing, it shall not hurt them; they shall lay hands on the sick, and they shall recover.* "These signs shall follow them that believe...they shall lay hands on the sick, and they shall recover." It is not a matter of having the gift or not. It is a matter of faith or unbelief. It is not the prayer of unbelief that heals the sick. It is the prayer of faith. If a prayer of unbelief was prayed, then the person being prayed for wouldn't be healed. So it is today that many prayers have been prayed for people to be healed then and there but they weren't healed. Why? Because they were made in unbelief. I will not go as far to say that it is the only reason why people aren't healed, but it certainly is one of them. I will be the first to admit that I have prayed many of these prayers and can speak from experience. Cate goes on to write,

> To "save the sick" means he shall be saved from sickness and DEATH, because James said, "the Lord shall raise him UP." But notice that this healing is contingent upon the prayer of faith. The prayer of faith can be prayed when medicine is used if the medicine is applied "in the name of the Lord." Hezekiah prayed the prayer of faith and the Lord healed him, but He did it with medicine (II Kings 20:1-7). When the prayer of faith is prayed for a sick person he is sure to be healed as there is a God in Heaven, because "the Lord shall raise him UP."[29]

There is no indication that being raised up means being saved from death. Just because it says that he will be raised up, it does not mean that they are being saved from death. Death is inevitable. It is a consequence of sin. Everyone has sinned, and therefore everyone must face death.

> But here is where the catch comes. The prayer of faith cannot always be prayed. Before we prove this with Scripture, let us prove it with a simple illustration. A man gets sick at the age of 50, the prayer of faith is prayed, and he is raised UP. He gets sick again at age 125, the prayer of faith is prayed, and he is raised UP. He gets sick again at 100, the prayer of faith is prayed, and he is raised UP. He gets sick again at 125, the prayer of faith is prayed (?), and he is raised UP (?) He gets sick again at 150, the prayer of faith is prayed (?), and he is raised UP (?). He gets sick at 200, the prayer of faith is prayed (?), and he is raised UP (?). When speaking of healing, the faith healers always emphasize the POWER of God and His ABILITY to heal. (This is to trap the non-thinking person.) If it were only a matter of his ability, and not a matter of his will, couldn't he heal a person at 200 years of age as well as He could at 50? Therefore if the prayer of faith could always be prayed, we would never need to die. Just keep on praying the prayer of faith and keep on being raised UP. It is not difficult to see that it is not always God's will to raise His children UP, because, "It is appointed unto man once to die" (Hebrews 9:27).

"Oh yes," you say, "everybody has to die." Not if the prayer of faith can always be prayed. Perhaps you have not yet seen what James said. He said, "The prayer of faith shall save the sick, and the Lord shall raise him UP." Dead people are not UP, they are DOWN. So as long as a person can stay UP, he is not dead. Therefore, James teaches that the prayer of faith will heal a person and save him from DEATH. How can we harmonize this with Hebrews 9:27? The will of God must be brought into the matter.[30]

Cate writes that the will of God must be considered. That's right, it should be! I really am not trying to condemn him or anyone else that holds to his position, but I do have a question. Do you really think that God's will is always accomplished? Nowhere do the Scriptures teach that. I understand that we say that God is in control, and I agree. He is in control. But that does not mean He controls everything that happens. This is now a much deeper matter than just the spiritual gifts. This touches the very character and heart of God. Though Cate didn't explicitly say that death was the will of God, he did get dangerously close to saying it. It was implied in his statements. I am not attacking Cate here, but I am attacking the idea that death is the will of God. The belief that God wills death impugns the very heart and character of our Heavenly Father. The same Heavenly Father who loves us so dearly that He willingly gave up His own Son to die in our place to pay the penalty for our sins so that we wouldn't have to face death. God would rather send Jesus to die in our place, then to let us suffer and die. It should be obvious that God's will is not death! In fact the Bible refers to death as an enemy in *I Corinthians 15:26 - The last enemy that shall be destroyed is death.* It should be obvious that death is not the will of God. But to further illustrate this point, let's look at the Lord's Prayer. *Matthew 6:9-13 - After this manner therefore pray ye: Our Father which art in heaven, Hallowed be thy name. 10 Thy kingdom come. Thy will be done in earth, as it is in heaven. 11 Give us this day our daily bread. 12 And forgive us our debts, as we forgive our debtors. 13 And lead us not into temptation, but deliver us from evil: For thine is the kingdom, and the power, and the glory, for ever. Amen.* This is the entirety of what is known as the Lord's Prayer. First of all the prayer in this passage is what Jesus told his disciples to pray. It would logically make sense that if He tells them what to pray, then everything in this prayer is the will of God. We're going to specifically focus on verse 10. The very fact that Jesus told us to pray that that His will would be done points to the fact that it is not always done. If God's will was always done, then why would we have to pray anyway? His will would be done whether we prayed or not. The basic reason for why His will is not always done is sin. We sin and miss the mark of God perfect will. What is God's perfect will? He desires that his will would be done in earth, as it is in heaven. His will for the earth is that the things in it are the same way that things are in heaven. Some might say that this is referring to His will being completely obeyed in earth as it is in heaven. Even if that was the case, it wouldn't make much difference. If God's will was completely obeyed in earth as it is in heaven, then the earth would become heavenly. Either way, he specifically says that we are to pray that God's will be done in earth as it is in heaven. How is it in heaven? Is there any sickness in heaven? What about sin? Is there any sin in heaven? Is there any death or suffering in heaven? *Revelation 21:4 - And God shall wipe away all tears from their eyes; and there shall be no more death, neither sorrow, nor crying, neither shall there be any more pain: for the former things are passed away.* I understand that this is the new heaven, but do you think these things exist in the current heaven? If they do, then it is very minimal. I know for a fact that there is no death in the current heaven. It is God's will that there will be no more tears, death, sorrow, crying, or pain on earth. It is not God's will that these things should be in the earth, and when these things happen on the earth then it is not God's will. To say that he doesn't is to contradict *Matthew 6:10* and is in the very least a misunderstanding of the heart of God. To say that these things are His will would be to impugn the very will, nature, heart, and character of God. To someone who believes that everything that happens is God's will, I would ask them this question. Is sin ever God's will? Is the growing problem of human trafficking God's will? What about gang violence? Is that God's will? Are broken homes and dysfunctional families God's will? Is drug addiction God's will? What about rape and other violent crimes? The obvious answer is no. I have gone into the local juvenile detention center for about four years now, and I have heard many stories of all these things. I cannot believe that these horrendous things are God's will. I have talked to prostitutes out on the streets trying to win them to Christ by handing out tracts. I have found that many of them have PTSD levels that rival that of soldiers because of all the abuse that they have been through. I cannot believe that any of these things happen because it is God's will. I personally have had an immediate family member die. I wish I was closer to them, but I'll have all of eternity to spend with them in heaven. I understand that it can be very offensive and hurtful thought to believe that death is God's will especially when death hits home in our families. B.F Cate didn't specifically say that death was God's will, but it was implied. I have a hard time believing that, and it was a little bit offensive when I read it. But it's okay because there is now no condemnation to them which are in Christ Jesus. God may allow these thing to happen to mold us into the image of Christ, or to call an unbeliever to repentance, but from the beginning it was not so. God designed a paradise in the beginning with Adam and Eve, but they were the ones that sinned and messed it up. Adam was the one that brought death into the world, not God. *Romans 5:12 - Wherefore, as by one man sin entered into the world, and death by sin; and so death passed upon all men, for that all have sinned:* Adam sinned and because of his sin, death was brought into the world. Death is a result of sin, not the will or desire of God. *Romans 6:23 - For the wages of sin is death; but the gift of God is eternal life through Jesus Christ our Lord.* Some may say that this is speaking of spiritual death. I agree, but is it only spiritual death? How many people have died because of a drug overdose? How many people have died because of an STD? How many have died from a result of violence? It should be obvious that sin results in physical death as well. When we sin, we are actually working for death. It is true, the Bible does teach us that God has our lives in His hand. Daniel told Belshazzar that God had his breath in His hand. *Daniel 5:22-23 - And thou his son, O Belshazzar, hast not humbled thine heart, though thou knewest all this; 23 but hast lifted up thyself against the Lord of heaven; and they have brought the vessels of his house before thee, and thou, and thy lords, thy wives, and thy concubines, have drunk wine in them; and thou hast praised the gods of silver, and gold, of brass, iron, wood, and stone, which see not, nor hear, nor know: and the God in whose hand thy breath is, and whose are all thy ways, hast thou not glorified:* Doesn't that show God's longsuffering? This whole time that we sin, God could've easily and justly extinguished our lives. But He doesn't because He is gracious, merciful, and longsuffering. If God does extinguish someone's life it is a result of sin. Because "the wages of sin is death". Even if it wasn't a result of their own sin, we still are paying as a result of Adam's sin. That is why he allows a loved one to pass away. He is holy, and though he doesn't will death, he may allow it because "the wages of sin is death". Instead of questioning why someone has passed away, it would be a much better response to be thankful for the fact that God allowed that person to live as long as they did. The real question is not, "Why did God allow them to die?" The real question is, "Why did God allow us to remain alive?" The answer to that question is simple though it may not be easy to swallow. The answer to that question is that we would be conformed to the image of Christ.

Hebrews 9:27 - And as it is appointed unto men once to die, but after this the judgment: The Greek word for appointed is ἀπόκειμαι apókeimai, ap-ok'-i-mahee; to be reserved; figuratively, to await:—be appointed, (be) laid up. I really don't believe that God is doing the appointing in this verse. God would be laying up death for every man. God would be reserving death for every man. As we have seen that thought is ridiculous both when we look at the Scriptures, and also when we consider the heart and nature of God. We could substitute the words "laid up" or "reserved" in this verse for "is appointed". "And as it is laid up unto man once to die". Or we could read the verse like this "And as it is reserved unto man once to die". Both of these are valid translations. The Greek word for "is appointed" is in the present tense and passive voice. The present tense in the Greek refers to a continuous action. It keeps on going. This appointing is not a one-time action. It is a continuous action. If it was God that was doing the appointing it would make sense that it would be aorist tense. The aorist tense in the Greek indicates an undefined action in the Greek. He would be appointing death for every man sometime in the past, but we wouldn't know when. The problem is that this verb is not in the aorist tense. It is in the present tense. It is a continuous ongoing action. This verb is also in the passive voice not in the active. The active voice in the Greek is an active action. That makes sense. The noun it refers to is doing the action. The passive voice in the Greek is a passive action. The noun that it refers to is being acted on. Let me give an example. This is an example of an active voice verb in a sentence. "I am taking my dog to the veterinarian." I am doing the action of taking my dog to the veterinarian. Now a passive voice verb would look like this. "My dog is being taken to the veterinarian." My dog is being acted on. She is being taken to the vet. In this verse the word "is appointed" is not in the active voice, but in the passive. If God was the one appointing, then it would make sense that it would be an active voice verb seeing that he would be the one actively appointing. If it was God doing the appointing it would make sense that this verb would be in the aorist tense. It would make sense in the aorist because aorist is an undefined action. God would have actively appointed this sometime in the past, but we don't know when. The problem is this verb is neither. This verb is in the present tense and passive voice. It is in the present tense which indicates a continuous, ongoing action. It is in the present tense, because man is continually sinning. He is continually sinning and continually reaping the wages for sin which is death. It is also in the passive voice because man is passively and indirectly being reserved to death because of his own sin. This verse does not prove that death is God's will at all. That interpretation would not fit in the rest of the Bible. All it means is that man has to die because of his sin. However, this verse does not say how or when. When James says that "the prayer of faith shall save the sick" he is not talking about death, he is talking about suffering. The prayer of faith shall save the sick from suffering, and the Lord shall raise them up out of the bed of afflictions.

Hebrews 9:27 does not tell us how or when we must die, just that we will die. Praying that prayer of faith can save someone from a premature death, and suffering on the way there. *James 5:14-15* also does not teach that the prayer of faith shall save the sick from death. To conclude that the prayer of faith saves the sick from death is not Biblical. Why do we have to oppose the plain reading of the Scriptures? Why do we go to great lengths to argue with them? Why can't we just accept the plain reading of the Scriptures at face value? It would cause less confusion, and would lead to faith.

This passage is most likely referring to supernatural healing. How do I know? The next verse states this in *James 5:16 - Confess your faults one to another, and pray one for another, that ye may be healed. The effectual fervent prayer of a righteous man availeth much.* The Greek word for "healed" is ἰάομαι iáomai, ee-ah'-om-ahee; to cure (literally or figuratively):—heal, make whole. This Greek word is commonly used to refer to supernatural healings in the New Testament. Here are a couple of examples. *Luke 6:19 - And the whole multitude sought to touch him: for there went virtue out of him, and healed them all.* This is obviously referring to a supernatural healing. *Luke 22:51 - And Jesus answered and said, Suffer ye thus far. And he touched his ear, and healed him.* This is when Peter cuts off the ear of Malchus, and Jesus heals him. Here is one of my favorites. *Acts 10:38 - How God anointed Jesus of Nazareth with the Holy Ghost and with power: who went about doing good, and healing all that were oppressed of the devil; for God was with him.* Jesus went forth healing all that were oppressed of the devil. Praise God! I understand this word does sometimes refer to a spiritual or emotional healing, and in this context it could refer to a spiritual healing. Personally I believe that it refers to both given the context. It seems as though James is specifically speaking of sickness which is caused by sin. That is why he tells them to call for the elders, and tells them to confess their faults. Once they do so, they could experience spiritual healing from their sins, and be restored to a right relationship with God. This is why I believe that James specifically writes "if he have committed any sins, they shall be forgiven him." At that point, the elders could anoint them with oil, which is a symbol of the Holy Spirit, in order to pray the prayer of faith so they could experience physical healing.

Cate also states,

> That miracles were performed during the Acts of the Apostles to aid people to believe the message of the Son of God, is seen in the way God worked through Paul. In Acts 19:11, 12 we read, "And God wrought SPECIAL miracles by the hands of Paul: So that from his body were brought unto the sick handkerchiefs or aprons, and the diseases departed from them, and the evil spirits went out of them." Now let us notice that Paul didn't use any SPECIAL miracles to heal his coworkers who were firm believers in Christ. He said to Timothy, "Drink no longer water, but use a little wine for thy stomach's sake and thine often infirmities" (I Timothy 5:23). Timothy was already a firm believer in Christ and didn't in Christ and didn't need any SPECIAL miracles for him to believe the message of Christ. Therefore Paul didn't send him a handkerchief to heal him, but told him to take medicine for his sickness. Neither did Trophimus need any SPECIAL miracles, therefore Paul left him at Miletum sick (II Timothy 4:20). Epaphroditus was a believer and God didn't use any handkerchiefs from Paul, or the laying on of his hands, to raise him up. He did get well but there is no evidence about anything spectacular about it (Philippians 2:25-30). All three of these men were co-workers with Paul, yet they all suffered sickness like the average Christian does today. It is evident, therefore that God allowed these to suffer as the average Christians do today, that we might not see that THE GIFT OF HEALING WAS NOT FOR THE PURPOSE OF HEALING THE SAVED, but was to aid people to believe in Christ,

during the transition period, before the New Testament was completed.[31]

The passage that Cate is referring to is *Acts 19:8-12 - And he went into the synagogue, and spake boldly for the space of three months, disputing and persuading the things concerning the kingdom of God. 9 But when divers were hardened, and believed not, but spake evil of that way before the multitude, he departed from them, and separated the disciples, disputing daily in the school of one Tyrannus. 10 And this continued by the space of two years; so that all they which dwelt in Asia heard the word of the Lord Jesus, both Jews and Greeks. 11 And God wrought special miracles by the hands of Paul: 12 so that from his body were brought unto the sick handkerchiefs or aprons, and the diseases departed from them, and the evil spirits went out of them.* Paul preached the gospel, and taught about the kingdom of God. The Jews were hardened like they usually were and so he left them. As a response, Paul preached there for two years. It was during this two year time span that the special miracles were being done. The Bible doesn't specify whether the people that were healed were believers or unbelievers. It just specifically states that they were sick, and possessed by devils. He could've very well healed both believers and unbelievers during this time. We don't know, it is not unreasonable to believe that he did heal both believer and unbelievers during this time. Cate argues that the special miracles that were done in this time period by Paul, were not duplicated when his fellow workers needed healing. Let's look at *James 5:14-15 - Is any sick among you? let him call for the elders of the church; and let them pray over him, anointing him with oil in the name of the Lord: 15 and the prayer of faith shall save the sick, and the Lord shall raise him up; and if he have committed sins, they shall be forgiven him.* If there were any sick among them they were to call for elders. The elders were the ones that were supposed to pray the prayer of faith. I understand that this passage most likely refers to sickness which was caused by a sin, but it could apply to any kind of sickness. The reason why Paul didn't heal Timothy, Epaphroditus, and Trophimus was because it wasn't his job. They were to call for the elders of the church. The Greek word for elders is πρεσβυτέρους. It is commonly used in the New Testament to refer to those that are pastors. The pastors were to pray the prayer of faith. This makes perfect sense. It is the pastor's job to care for his flock. It is therefore the pastor's job to pray the prayer of faith to heal the sick. Never once is Paul referred to as a pastor. He certainly may have served as a pastor at different points in time, but he is never referred to as a pastor. *Romans 15:20 - Yea, so have I strived to preach the gospel, not where Christ was named, lest I should build upon another man's foundation:* Paul was careful not to preach the gospel in a city where Christ was not named, lest he built on another man's foundation, let alone functioning in another man's role as pastor over his congregation. The care of Epaphroditus, Trophimus, and Timothy was to be done by the pastors of the church of the cities that they were dwelling in. Even if Epaphroditus, Trophimus, or Timothy were pastors themselves or at the very least serving as pastors, most likely there were more pastors in that city which could tend to them in a pastoral manner. Even if Epaphroditus, Trophimus, and Timothy were functioning as pastors, and there weren't anyone other pastors in the cities in which they were dwelling, there would have been at least one person who had the gift of healing in those same cities. Let me ask the pastors reading this book a question. Is it important to you who cares for your congregation? Are you willing to let someone else care for your congregation? Even if it is only temporarily, are you willing to let someone else care for your people?

    Another problem is that it would've contradicted everything of what he had written in *I Corinthians 12* about the body of Christ. Every single person has a part to play. Every single person serves a function in the body of Christ. It was in the pastor's responsibility to pray the prayer of faith that healed them. In the very least it was the person's responsibility who had the gift of healing. If Paul decided to pray the prayer of faith for Trophimus, Epaphroditus, and Timothy, then he would've been contradicting his own teaching instead of having faith in it. He would be taking someone else's job in the body of Christ, and function as a part of the body that he wasn't intended by God to be. To this same church just a chapter before he discusses the spiritual gifts and the body of Christ, he said in *I Corinthians 11:1 - Be ye followers of me, even as I also am of Christ.* If Paul would have violated the principles in *I Corinthians 12*, by functioning as a part of the body that he was never intended to be, then he may have caused chaos in the Corinthian church. He already told them in *I Corinthian 14:12 - Even so ye, forasmuch as ye are zealous of spiritual gifts, seek that ye may excel to the edifying of the church.* They were zealous of the spiritual gifts in a very unhealthy way, so he responds by encouraging them to use them in a healthy manner. If he functioned as part of the body that he wasn't intended by God to be, and commanded them to follow him as he followed Christ, then the problem would have been made much worse. He would have set a bad example, and would have been living in hypocrisy. Cate writes,

> It is evident, therefore that God allowed these to suffer as the average Christians do today, that we might not see that THE GIFT OF HEALING WAS NOT FOR THE PURPOSE OF HEALING THE SAVED, but was to aid people to believe in Christ, during the transition period, before the New Testament was completed.[32]

It is true that God miraculously healed, and still does, to confirm the gospel to unbelievers. Anyone who had faith to step out and believe in the Lord could lay their hands on unbelievers to confirm the Word to them. The Bible says in *Mark 16:17-18 - And these signs shall follow them that believe; In my name shall they cast out devils; they shall speak with new tongues; 18 they shall take up serpents; and if they drink any deadly thing, it shall not hurt them; they shall lay hands on the sick, and they shall recover.* These signs did not only follow those who had the gift of healing, but all those who believed. On the other hand, the prayer of faith is to be done by believers for believers. It is specifically to be done by the pastor to care for his congregation. *James 5:14-15 - Is any sick among you? let him call for the elders of the church; and let them pray over him, anointing him with oil in the name of the Lord: 15 and the prayer of faith shall save the sick, and the Lord shall raise him up; and if he have committed sins, they shall be forgiven him.* Not to mention that there were certain individuals who were given the gift of healing for the purpose of being profitable to the church. The literal purpose of the gift of healing was to benefit the body of Christ. *I Corinthians 12:7 - But the manifestation of the Spirit is given to every man to profit withal.* To say that the gift of healing was not for the purpose to edify the church is at best ignorance of the spiritual gifts and what the Scripture teaches about them, and at worst it is a straight up denial of Scripture.

Cate writes,

> It is evident, therefore that God allowed these to suffer as the average Christians do today, that we might not see that THE GIFT OF HEALING WAS NOT FOR THE PURPOSE OF HEALING THE SAVED, but was to aid people to believe in Christ, during the transition period, before the New Testament was completed.[33]

Again, do a search. If you look up the words "transition" "transitional" and "normative" in a Bible search engine, you will find that none of those words are actually in the Bible. In fact I would venture as far to say that there is no passage in the Bible that even alludes to the concepts of a "transition period". If there is a passage that speaks of a "transition period", then I would like to see it.

Chapter 6

Passages that Prove the Gifts are for Today

There are some passages that people misuse to prove that gifts are not to be used today. The same passages that B.F. Cate uses to prove that the spiritual gifts are not for today are the same passages that prove all the gifts are to be exercised today. There are other passages that prove the gifts are for today.

Let's look at *Hebrews 13:7-9 - Remember them which have the rule over you, who have spoken unto you the word of God: whose faith follow, considering the end of their conversation. 8 Jesus Christ the same yesterday, and to day, and for ever. 9 Be not carried about with divers and strange doctrines. For it is a good thing that the heart be established with grace; not with meats, which have not profited them that have been occupied therein.* Cate writes,

> The professed believers among the Christians among the Christian Hebrews were constantly warned against giving up their professed faith in Christ and returning to temple worship in Jerusalem. In verses 10-17 of this same chapter they are exhorted to have real faith in Jesus Christ and forget about the law. Verse 8 speaks of the past, present, and future. Verse 7 speaks of the PAST, in that they are told to REMEMBER their former teachers and follow their FAITH. Verse 9 speaks of the FUTURE, in that they are told, "BE NOT [from now on] carried about with divers and strange doctrines. For it is a good thing that the heart be ESTABLISHED with GRACE; and not with MEATS" of the LAW. But verse 8 comes between verse 7 and 9 and was a PRESENT exhortation for those Hebrews. Therefore, verse 8 means that faith in Christ saved "yesterday," faith in Christ will save "today," faith in

Christ will save "forever." Therefore they didn't need Judaism any more. Those in the healing movements quote verse 8 and insist that Christ will heal today as He did during His last few years on earth. But remember, there is nothing in this Scripture about healing. It has to do with salvation.[34]

I whole-hearted agree with Cate on this interpretation of the passage. I really couldn't add much of anything to this interpretation of this passage. The writer of Hebrews said that they were to remember them that had the rule over them. He is referring to the pastors by saying that. They spoke unto these Jews the "word of God". In verse 9, the writer exhorts the Jews not to be children carried about by every wind of doctrine. They were not to be eating the meats of the law from the sacrifices in the sacrificial system of Judaism. Instead they were to be established with grace. Where is grace found? *John 1:17 - For the law was given by Moses, but grace and truth came by Jesus Christ.* They were to leave the law behind, and embrace the grace that Christ has to offer. This is speaking of the salvation of souls. Jesus Christ is the same yesterday, today, and forever. He is the Savior yesterday today and forever. How did they know that He is the Savior? They knew because of the elders which "have spoken unto you the word of God". They knew that He is the Savior from hearing the word of God. His Word tells us that He is the Savior. This is true yesterday, today, and forever because he doesn't change. This means his character remains the same. Since he is faithful, he acts according to His Word "yesterday, today, and forever." The interpretation of the passage has to do with salvation, but an application can be made for the sign gifts. I understand that Jesus supersedes His word for example the Bible tells us in *Matthew 5:27 - Ye have heard that it was said by them of old time, Thou shalt not commit adultery: 28 but I say unto you, That whosoever looketh on a woman to lust after her hath committed adultery with her already in his heart.* Though Jesus supersedes his Word, he simply explained his Word. He neither changed it, nor abolished it. In fact, from His own mouth from this same chapter he said in *Matthew 5:17-18 - Think not that I am come to destroy the law, or the prophets: I am not come to destroy, but to fulfil. 18 For verily I say unto you, Till heaven and earth pass, one jot or one tittle shall in no wise pass from the law, till all be fulfilled.* He did not abolish the

Word, he came to fulfill it. In fact he says that it cannot be changed till heaven and earth pass away, and until all be fulfilled. He neither changed his word, nor did he abolish it, but lived perfectly according to it while he was on earth. In fact, when Jesus was on earth the Bible says of him in *Matthew 8:16 - When the even was come, they brought unto him many that were possessed with devils: and he cast out the spirits with his word, and healed all that were sick.* Jesus cast devils out of the possessed with his word. What does that mean? It means that if the Word doesn't empower us to do the miraculous, then we are probably using it wrong.

Cessationists are forced to believe that either he does not act according to his Word "yesterday, and to day, and forever", or that his Word has changed. The Bible says in *Mark 16:17-18, 20 - And these signs shall follow them that believe; In my name shall they cast out devils; they shall speak with new tongues; 18 they shall take up serpents; and if they drink any deadly thing, it shall not hurt them; they shall lay hands on the sick, and they shall recover. 20 And they went forth, and preached every where, the Lord working with them, and confirming the word with signs following. Amen.* When the Bible says in this passage, "these signs shall follow them that believe" it is true yesterday, today, and forever because God acts according to His word and will confirm "the word with signs following" today as he did with the apostles. The Bible says in *Ephesians 1:13 - in whom ye also trusted, after that ye heard the word of truth, the gospel of your salvation: in whom also after that ye believed, ye were sealed with that holy Spirit of promise.* The Bible tells us that we were "sealed" with that holy Spirit of promise "after that ye believed." We are sealed with the Holy Spirit, after we believed. This means in the book of *Acts* when the disciples received the Holy Spirit after they had hands laid on them, this was not the sealing of the Holy Spirit. This is when the Holy Spirit came "upon" them which is the baptism of the Spirit. The Bible tells us in *I Corinthians 12:28 - And God hath set some in the church, first apostles, secondarily prophets, thirdly teachers, after that miracles, then gifts of healings, helps, governments, diversities of tongues.* The Bible also tells us in *Ephesians 4:11-12 - And he gave some, apostles; and some, prophets; and some, evangelists; and some, pastors and teachers; 12 for the perfecting of the saints, for the work of the ministry, for the edifying of the body of Christ:* The Bible clearly tell us that God has set apostles, prophets, those that work miracles, those that have the gift of healing, and those that have the gift of tongues in his church. All of those have been denied by those that oppose the charismatic movement. The Bible clearly tells us that God gave apostles, and prophets to his church for their edification. Many have denied that Scriptures as well saying that there are no prophets and apostles today. If God acts according to his Word yesterday, today, and forever, then that means that there should be apostles and prophets in the church today. The Bible tells us in *I Corinthians 12:7-11 - But the manifestation of the Spirit is given to every man to profit withal. 8 For to one is given by the Spirit the word of wisdom; to another the word of knowledge by the same Spirit; 9 to another faith by the same Spirit; to another the gifts of healing by the same Spirit; 10 to another the working of miracles; to another prophecy; to another discerning of spirits; to another divers kinds of tongues; to another the interpretation of tongues: 11 but all these worketh that one and the selfsame Spirit, dividing to every man severally as he will.* The Bible clearly tells us that God gives all these gifts to those that are members of his church. If God acts according to his Word yesterday, today, and forever, then He still gives these gifts today. In other words, if God acts according to His word yesterday, today, and forever, then there never was a so called "transition period". This means in the early days of the church God was not acting differently back then in the "transition period" than He does today. He was just simply acting according to His Word, and He acts the same way today. If God does not act according to His Word yesterday, today, and forever, then we should probably eat, drink, and be merry for tomorrow we die. If God does not act according to His Word yesterday, today, and forever, then how can we trust His Word? How can we know anything the Bible says is true? Let's just believe that He does act according to His word today as He did in those days. We can trust God, and we can trust His word because He does act according to it yesterday, today, and forever.

There are a couple passages that relate to each other that deal with healing. One of those passages were found in *I Peter 2:24-25 - who his own self bare our sins in his own body on the tree, that we, being dead to sins, should live unto righteousness: by whose stripes ye were healed. 25 For ye were as sheep going astray; but are now returned unto the Shepherd and Bishop of your souls.* Cate writes,

> This passage of Scripture is the fulfillment of Isaiah 53:5, 6. There is another passage in Matthew 8:16, 17 which reads, "He...healed all that

were sick: That it might be fulfilled which was spoken of by Esaias the prophet, saying, Himself took our infirmities, and bare our sickness." This passage is the fulfillment of Isaiah 53:4. By comparing Isaiah 53:4 with Matthew 8:16, 17 it is clearly seen that these passages have to do with physical healing, which Christ did in His earthly ministry. But Isaiah 53:5, 6 and I Peter 2:24, 25 have to do with spiritual healing, which Christ does in saving sinners. Let us place the corresponding Scriptures side by side to see this truth clearly.

MATTHEW	ISAIAH
"He...healed all that were sick: That it might be FULFILLED which was spoken by Esaias the prophet, saying, Himself took our infirmities, and bare our sickness" (Matthew 8:16-17).	"Surely he hath borne our griefs, and carried our sorrows: yet we did esteem him stricken, smitten of God, and afflicted." (Isaiah 53:4)

Matthew makes it clear that Isaiah 53:4 was FULFILLED in the healing ministry of Christ before He went to the cross. He took their infirmities and bare their sicknesses in order to aid them to believe in Him (as we have seen before). "Yet," in spite of that, says Isaiah, "we [those present when Christ went to the cross] did esteem Him stricken, smitten of God," for His OWN sins.

ISAIAH	
"But [says Isaiah] he was wounded for OUR transgressions, he was bruised for OUR iniquities: the chastisement of OUR peace was upon him; and with is stripes we are HEALED [of "OUR TRANSGRESSIONS"]. All we like SHEEP have gone ASTRAY; we have	turned every one to his own way; and the Lord hath laid on him the iniquity of us ALL" (Isaiah 53:5, 6).
	PETER
	"Who his own self bare OUR sins in his own body on the tree, that we, being DEAD TO SINS, should LIVE UNTO

RIGHTEOUSNESS: by whose stripes ye WERE HEALED [of UNRIGHTEOUS LIVING]. For ye WERE as SHEEP going ASTRAY; but are NOW RETURNED [healed of "going astray"] unto the Shepherd and Bishop of your souls" (I Peter 2:24, 25)

In speaking of physical healing, Matthew did not use the phrase "by whose stripes ye were healed"; because that phrase is not in Isaiah 53:4, to which he was referring. But Peter used the phrase; because it is in Isaiah 53:5, 6, to which he was referring which has to do with spiritual healing. The fact that Isaiah and Peter used the word "healed" doesn't mean that they were talking about physical healing. This same terminology is used many times in referring to spiritual healing. The Lord said, "I will HEAL their backsliding" (Hosea 14:4). Jesus said, "They that are whole have no need of the physician, but they that are SICK [the sinners]: I came not to call the righteous, but SINNERS [the SICK] to repentance," and thus HEAL them of their sinning. (Mark 2:17) The above comparison should help the reader to see that Isaiah and Matthew were talking about physical healing, which Christ did in His earthly healing, which Christ does in saving sinners. Therefore, to say that "by whose stripes ye were healed means physical healing, is another good example of not "rightly dividing the Word" (II Timothy 2:15).[35]

These passages prove that Jesus' role as the Messiah included healing. If we just put things in the right context, then we can see this clearly. Cate states,

> By comparing Isaiah 53:4 with Matthew 8:16, 17 it is clearly seen that these passages have to do with physical healing, which Christ did in His earthly ministry. But Isaiah 53:5, 6 and I Peter 2:24, 25 have to do with spiritual healing, which Christ does in saving sinners. Let us place the corresponding Scriptures side by side to see this truth clearly.[36]

There isn't a basis to say that these Scriptures don't deal with physical healing. In fact if we do look at these Scriptures, then we will see that they truly do deal with healing. He goes on to states,

> Matthew makes it clear that Isaiah 53:4 was FULFILLED in the healing ministry of Christ before He went to the cross. He took their infirmities and bare their sicknesses in order to aid them to believe in Him (as we have seen before). "Yet," in spite of that, says Isaiah, "we [those present when Christ went to the cross] did esteem Him stricken, smitten of God," for His OWN sins.[37]

If truth be truth be told, Cate is right. *Matthew 8:16-17 - When the even was come, they brought unto him many that were possessed with devils: and he cast out the spirits with his word, and healed all that were sick: 17 that it might be fulfilled which was spoken by Esaias the prophet, saying, Himself took our infirmities, and bare our sicknesses.* The passage was fulfilled in Jesus' healing ministry before He died on the cross. But, this means that if *Matthew 8:16-17* tells us that *Isaiah 53:4* was fulfilled in Jesus' healing ministry, then the context of *Isaiah 53:5-6* is healing. Cate writes,

> In speaking of physical healing, Matthew did not use the phrase "by whose stripes ye were healed"; because that phrase is not in Isaiah 53:4, to which he was referring. But Peter used the phrase; because it is in Isaiah 53:5, 6, to which he was referring which has to do with spiritual healing.[38]

Just because this same phrase wasn't used in *Isaiah 53:4*, it doesn't mean that *Isaiah 53:5-6* doesn't deal with physical healing. *Isaiah 53:4 - Surely he hath borne our griefs, and carried our sorrows: yet we did esteem him stricken, smitten of God, and afflicted.* The Hebrew word for griefs is חֳלִי chŏlîy, khol-ee'; malady, anxiety, calamity:—disease, grief, (is) sick(-ness). The Hebrew word for "griefs" literally means diseases, griefs, and sicknesses. The Hebrew word for "sorrows" is מַכְאֹב mak'ôb, mak-obe'; sometimes מַכְאוֹב mak'ôwb; also (feminine Isaiah 53:3) מַכְאֹבָה mak'ôbâh; anguish or (figuratively) affliction:—grief, pain, sorrow. He carried our afflictions, grief, pain, and sorrow. Why did he even have this sorrow? We had sorrows because we had sickness, griefs, and diseases. Have you ever seen someone get healed from cancer? Do you know how much pain that cancer has caused? Do you know how much relief it brings when someone is supernaturally healed from it? What about HIV? Do you know how much pain is caused from that, and the relief that comes from being supernaturally healed of it? Why would you want to stop that? Why do we try to fight against that? Why do we want to try to take away that physical and emotional relief away from someone else? The context of *Isaiah 53:5-6* is verse 4, which literally speaks of physical healing. Cate writes,

> The fact that Isaiah and Peter used the word "healed" doesn't mean that they were talking about physical healing. This same terminology is used many times in referring to spiritual healing. The Lord said, "I will HEAL their backsliding" (Hosea 14:4). Jesus said, "They that are whole have no need of the physician, but they that are SICK [the sinners]: I came not to call the righteous, but SINNERS [the SICK] to repentance," and thus HEAL them of their sinning. (Mark 2:17). [39]

It also doesn't mean that it isn't talking about physical healing. In fact let's take a look at this passage. *Isaiah 53:5 - But he was wounded for our transgressions, he was bruised for our iniquities: the chastisement of our peace was upon him; and with his stripes we are healed. 6 All we like sheep have gone astray; we have turned every one to his own way; and the Lord hath laid on him the iniquity of us all.* The Hebrew word for "healed" is רָפָא râphâ', raw-faw'; or רָפָה râphâh; a primitive root; properly, to mend (by stitching), i.e. (figuratively) to cure:—cure, (cause to) heal, physician, repair, × thoroughly, make whole. It is the same word is *Psalm 103:2-3 - Bless the Lord, O my soul, and forget not all his benefits: 3 who forgiveth all thine iniquities; who healeth all thy diseases;* The psalmist says that we are supposed to bless the Lord, and remember what he does for us. He forgives all our iniquities, and heals our sins. This means that physical healing and spiritual healing are connected. That's why *Isaiah 53:5* also deals with the forgiveness of sin. In the same verse, the psalmist says the Lord "forgiveth all thine iniquities", and "healeth all thy diseases". Who's the person he's talking to in this verse? He's talking to himself. The Lord heals our diseases. It is true that the Bible does talk about spiritual healing. It is true that Jesus came to give spiritual healing. But in this context he is talking about physical healing. *Isaiah 53:4* literally speaks of physical healing. The word for "healed" in *Isaiah 53:5* is the same word used in

Psalm 103:2-3 which connects physical healing and the forgiveness of sins. *I Peter 2:24-25 - who his own self bare our sins in his own body on the tree, that we, being dead to sins, should live unto righteousness: by whose stripes ye were healed. 25 For ye were as sheep going astray; but are now returned unto the Shepherd and Bishop of your souls.* In this context is healing and the forgiveness of sins. How do I know that this verse includes physical healing? I know because of the Greek word for "healed". This Greek word is ἰάομαι iáomai; to cure (literally or figuratively):—heal, make whole. I will admit that it can refer to spiritual and emotional healing, but this same word is more commonly used in the New Testament to refer to supernatural physical healings. This makes perfect sense since Peter is quoting from *Isaiah 53:5-6*. The Bible clearly connects the forgiveness of sins with physical healing in *Psalm 103:2-3*. As we said at the beginning, this means Christ's role as Messiah includes physical healing.

More proof of this fact includes the man who was let down through the roof when he was preaching. There was a crowd that gathered around Jesus when he was preaching, and in that crowd was Pharisees. This man was let down through the roof of the house by his friends. Jesus tells the man who was sick of the palsy that his sins were forgiven. The Pharisees reasons that he was blaspheming, because no one could forgive sins but God. They were right in that, but they didn't realize that Jesus was God. Jesus then asked them a question. The Bible says in *Mark 2:9-12 - Whether is it easier to say to the sick of the palsy, Thy sins be forgiven thee; or to say, Arise, and take up thy bed, and walk? 10 But that ye may know that the Son of man hath power on earth to forgive sins, (he saith to the sick of the palsy,) 11 I say unto thee, Arise, and take up thy bed, and go thy way into thine house. 12 And immediately he arose, took up the bed, and went forth before them all; insomuch that they were all amazed, and glorified God, saying, We never saw it on this fashion.* The proof that Jesus could forgive sin was the fact that he could heal the man sick of the palsy. What does this mean? It means that physical healing is connected with salvation.

More proof of this is in *James 5:14-15 - Is any sick among you? let him call for the elders of the church; and let them pray over him, anointing him with oil in the name of the Lord: 15 and the prayer of faith shall save the sick, and the Lord shall raise him up; and if he have committed sins, they shall be forgiven him.* What is interesting about this verse is that the Greek word for "shall save" in this verse is σώζω sṓzō, sode'-zo; from a primary σῶς sōs (contraction for obsolete σάος sáos, "safe"); to save, i.e.

deliver or protect (literally or figuratively):—heal, preserve, save (self), do well, be (make) whole. This is the same word used for "thou shalt be saved" in *Romans 10:9 - that if thou shalt confess with thy mouth the Lord Jesus, and shalt believe in thine heart that God hath raised him from the dead, thou shalt be saved.* The same word that refers to the salvation of someone's soul, also refers to the salvation of the body. What's this mean? It means that physical healing comes as part of the package of salvation.

One last proof that I will use is the serpent on the pole in the wilderness. This story is found in *Numbers 21:4-9 - And they journeyed from mount Hor by the way of the Red sea, to compass the land of Edom: and the soul of the people was much discouraged because of the way. 5 And the people spake against God, and against Moses, Wherefore have ye brought us up out of Egypt to die in the wilderness? for there is no bread, neither is there any water; and our soul loatheth this light bread. 6 And the Lord sent fiery serpents among the people, and they bit the people; and much people of Israel died. 7 Therefore the people came to Moses, and said, We have sinned, for we have spoken against the Lord, and against thee; pray unto the Lord, that he take away the serpents from us. And Moses prayed for the people. 8 And the Lord said unto Moses, Make thee a fiery serpent, and set it upon a pole: and it shall come to pass, that every one that is bitten, when he looketh upon it, shall live. 9 And Moses made a serpent of brass, and put it upon a pole, and it came to pass, that if a serpent had bitten any man, when he beheld the serpent of brass, he lived.* The people spoke against God, and against Moses. In response the Lord sent fiery serpents to them in judgement. These serpents bit the people, and they died. Then the people cried out to Moses admitting that they had sinned. Moses goes to the Lord for direction, and the Lord tells him to make another fiery serpent to put it on a pole. The people who would look at the serpent would be healed, and would live. This is very interesting. God commands Moses to make a fiery serpent of brass for the people to look to in order to be healed. He commanded Moses to make the very thing that was killing them to ensure their physical healing. Jesus said in *John 3:14-15 - And as Moses lifted up the serpent in the wilderness, even so must the Son of man be lifted up: 15 that whosoever believeth in him should not perish, but have eternal life.* Jesus was to be lifted up just like the way the serpent was lifted up in the wilderness. In what way? The Bible says in *Romans 6:23 - For the wages of sin is death; but the gift of God is eternal life through Jesus Christ our Lord.* Sin was literally killing us, and Jesus became the very thing that was killing us. *II Corinthians 5:21 - For he hath made him to be sin for us, who knew no sin; that we might be made the righteousness of God in him.* Jesus became sin for us so that we could look to him and be saved. Through his death on the cross, Jesus gave us spiritual healing, but as the serpent healed the Israelites in the wilderness so too did the cross of Christ ensure our physical healing as well.

Acts 2:16-21 - But this is that which was spoken by the prophet Joel; 17 And it shall come to pass in the last days, saith God, I will pour out of my Spirit upon all flesh: and your sons and your daughters shall prophesy, and your young men shall see visions, and your old men shall dream dreams: 18 and on my servants and on my handmaidens I will pour out in those days of my Spirit; and they shall prophesy: 19 and I will shew wonders in heaven above, and signs in the earth beneath; blood, and fire, and vapour of smoke: 20 the sun shall be turned into darkness, and the moon into blood, before that great and notable day of the Lord come: 21 and it shall come to pass, that whosoever shall call on the name of the Lord shall be saved. This is another confusing passage of Scripture. B.F. Cate does a great job writing about the prophecy surrounding this passage. He writes,

> Because of this Scripture many think prophets should be in the church today. To understand this Scripture we must find out what Peter meant by the last days. Christ said in Luke 21:24, "Jerusalem shall be trodden down of the Gentiles, UNTIL the times of the Gentiles be fulfilled." Old Jerusalem is still under Gentile dominion, and will be UNTIL the times of the Gentiles be fulfilled. The last days mentioned by Peter in verse 17 refers to "the times of the Gentiles," which extend the fall of Jerusalem, about 606 B.C unto the coming of Christ, who shall deliver Jerusalem from the hands of the Gentiles. At this time "the times of the Gentiles" will be fulfilled. When Peter quoted Joel's prophecy, it was as though they were in the last of "the times of the Gentiles"; because it was just after the Messiah was cut off (see Scofield's notes on Daniel 9:24-27), and it was only seven years until Messiah COULD have come (Acts 3:19-20) and delivered Jerusalem from Gentile dominion. But there was something which God had not revealed to Peter or any Old Testament prophet. It was this present church age. So the last seven years of Israel's history, as spoken by Daniel, will not come until the

church is taken out. Then the last seven years of Israel's history will be will be fulfilled in what is generally known as the seven years' tribulation period. When Paul referred to the last days in II Timothy 3:1-8, he referred to the last days of the church age; but Peter referred to the last days of Israel, with regard to Jerusalem, under Gentile dominion. See Scofield's notes on Acts 2:17. As we have seen, prophesying referred to in Acts 2:17, 18 was fulfilled in the early days of the church has ceased. But the signs of verses 19, and 20 will not be fulfilled until the end of the tribulation period – the very last moments of Israel's history under Gentile rule (Matthew 24:21-31). This is why Peter did not use the word "fulfilled" in referring to Joel's prophecy. He said, when Joel's prophecy BEGAN to come to pass, "THIS IS that which was spoken by the prophet Joel." The only thing is, all of "THAT" has not YET come. Therefore since the last days referred to by Peter have reference to Israel, It does not mean that we are to have prophets in the last days of the church age. To point to Joel's prophecy in Acts 2:17, 18 as proof that we should have prophets in the church today, makes it contradict I Corinthians 13:8-13; II Peter 2:1 and Revelation 22:18. This is a good example of not "rightly dividing the Word" (II Timothy 2:15).[40]

Let's start by looking at the passage again. *Acts 2:16-21 - But this is that which was spoken by the prophet Joel; 17 And it shall come to pass in the last days, saith God, I will pour out of my Spirit upon all flesh: and your sons and your daughters shall prophesy, and your young men shall see visions, and your old men shall dream dreams: 18 and on my servants and on my handmaidens I will pour out in those days of my Spirit; and they shall prophesy: 19 and I will shew wonders in heaven above, and signs in the earth beneath; blood, and fire, and vapour of smoke: 20 the sun shall be turned into darkness, and the moon into blood, before that great and notable day of the Lord come: 21 and it shall come to pass, that whosoever shall call on the name of the Lord shall be saved.* Peter is speaking here and he is quoting from Joel. To prove this let's look at that passage. *Joel 2:28-32 - And it shall come to pass afterward, that I will pour out my spirit upon all flesh; and your sons and your daughters shall prophesy, your old men shall dream dreams, your young men shall see visions: 29 and also upon the servants and upon the handmaids in those days will I pour out my* spirit. *30 And I will shew wonders in the heavens and in the earth, blood, and fire, and pillars of smoke. 31 The sun shall be turned into darkness, and the moon into blood, before the great and the terrible day of the Lord come. 32 And it shall come to pass, that whosoever shall call on the name of the Lord shall be delivered: for in mount Zion and in Jerusalem shall be deliverance, as the Lord hath said, and in the remnant whom the Lord shall call.* In this chapter, Joel starts prophesying about the day of the Lord. He prophesied about the horrible judgement of the tribulation. Then he turns to the people and tells them to repent. *Joel 2:12 - Therefore also now, saith the Lord, turn ye even to me with all your heart, and with fasting, and with weeping, and with mourning:* The coming judgement was to be motivation to them to repent. He then tells them the amazing blessing that would arise if they would just turn back to him. *Joel 2:19 - Yea, the Lord will answer and say unto his people, Behold, I will send you corn, and wine, and oil, and ye shall be satisfied therewith:* This is simply the blessings that they would receive from the covenant they had with God. *Deuteronomy 28:9-14 - The Lord shall establish thee an holy people unto himself, as he hath sworn unto thee, if thou shalt keep the commandments of the Lord thy God, and walk in his ways. 10 And all people of the earth shall see that thou art called by the name of the Lord; and they shall be afraid of thee. 11 And the Lord shall make thee plenteous in goods, in the fruit of thy body, and in the fruit of thy cattle, and in the fruit of thy ground, in the land which the Lord sware unto thy fathers to give thee. 12 The Lord shall open unto thee his good treasure, the heaven to give the rain unto thy land in his season, and to bless all the work of thine hand: and thou shalt lend unto many nations, and thou shalt not borrow. 13 And the Lord shall make thee the head, and not the tail; and thou shalt be above only, and thou shalt not be beneath; if that thou hearken unto the commandments of the Lord thy God, which I command thee this day, to observe and to do them: 14 and thou shalt not go aside from any of the words which I command thee this day, to the right hand, or to the left, to go after other gods to serve them.* Simply put, God would bless them as they would walk with them. Joel flashes ahead to the future and he explains the deliverance that would come. The day of the Lord was coming, but so would deliverance come right in the midst of it. After all the suffering that is going to happen to the Jews in the tribulation then God would pour out his Spirit. The Bible tells us in *Joel 2:28-29 - And it shall come to pass afterward, that I will pour out my spirit upon all flesh; and your sons and your daughters shall prophesy, your old men shall dream dreams, your young men shall see visions: 29 and also upon the servants and upon the handmaids in those days will I pour out my spirit.* He would pour out his spirit on the Jews after the great trouble of the tribulation when they turn back to him in repentance. He says that as a result they would prophesy, dream dreams, and see visions. The Bible gives us additional information in *Zechariah 12:9-10 - And it shall come to pass in that day, that I will seek to destroy all the nations that come against Jerusalem. 10 And I will pour upon the house of David, and upon the inhabitants of Jerusalem, the spirit of grace and of supplications: and they shall look upon me whom they have pierced, and they shall mourn for him, as one mourneth for his only son, and shall be in bitterness for him, as one that is in bitterness for his firstborn.* There will be nations that come against Jerusalem but the Lord will protect them and destroy them at the end of the tribulation. When will he come to save them? Jesus said to the Jews in *Matthew 23:39 - For I say unto you, Ye shall not see me henceforth, till ye shall say, Blessed is he that cometh in the name of the Lord.* He would not come back till they repented, changed their minds about Jesus, and said "blessed is he that cometh in the name of the Lord." Before they thought he was a blasphemer, but at this point in time they will say that he is blessed. Before he comes back there will be "wonders in the heavens and in the earth, blood, and fire, and pillars of smoke. The sun shall be turned into darkness, and the moon into blood." These announce his presence as he comes back. Jesus said this in *Matthew 24:29-30 - Immediately after the tribulation of those days shall the sun be darkened, and the moon shall not give her light, and the stars shall fall from heaven, and the powers of the heavens shall be shaken: 30 and then shall appear the sign of the Son of man in heaven: and then shall all the tribes of the earth mourn, and they shall see the Son of man coming in the clouds of heaven with power and great glory.* Jesus said right before he comes back "shall the sun be darkened", the "moon shall not give her light", the "stars shall fall from heaven" and the "powers of the heavens shall be shaken". This sounds like what is happening in *Joel 2:31*. That is when Jesus comes back and "all the tribes earth shall mourn" when "they shall see the Son of man coming in the clouds of heaven with power and great glory". This is exactly what Zechariah said would happen. He said that "they shall mourn for him, as one mourneth for his only son, and shall be in bitterness for him, as one that is in bitterness for his firstborn." When the Jews realize that Jesus is their Messiah, and they finally cry out to him to save them, then he comes back to make war with all the nations that are gathered round against them. The Bible tells us in *Revelation 19:11-15 - And I saw heaven opened, and behold a white horse; and he that sat upon him was called Faithful and True, and in righteousness he doth judge and make war. 12 His eyes were as a flame of fire, and on his head were many crowns; and he had a name written, that no man knew, but he himself. 13 And he was clothed with a vesture dipped in blood: and his name is called The Word of God. 14 And the armies which were in heaven followed him upon white horses, clothed in fine linen, white and clean. 15 And out of his mouth goeth a sharp sword, that with it he should smite the nations: and he shall rule them with a rod of iron: and he treadeth the winepress of the fierceness and wrath of Almighty God.* There's a lot going on in this passage but basically Jesus himself is coming out of heaven, and He is coming against the "nations" that have turned against the Jews to judge them. Once the wrath of God is thoroughly poured out, that's when Christ will set up his kingdom with the Jews that have turned to him. *Revelation 20:4 - And I saw thrones, and they sat upon them, and judgment was given unto them: and I saw the souls of them that were beheaded for the witness of Jesus, and for the word of God, and which had not worshipped the beast, neither his image, neither had received his mark upon their foreheads, or in their hands; and they lived and reigned with Christ a thousand years.* This is when revival breaks out, and he turns away the false prophets away. *Zechariah 13:1-2 - In that day there shall be a fountain opened to the house of David and to the inhabitants of Jerusalem for sin and for uncleanness. 2 And it shall come to pass in that day, saith the Lord of hosts, that I will cut off the names of the idols out of the land, and they shall no more be remembered: and also I will cause the prophets and the unclean spirit to pass out of the land.* Some might point to this passage saying that he will cause the prophets to pass out of the land. Look at the context. These are false prophets. He will cut the idols out of the land. He will also make the unclean spirits to pass out of the land. Jesus is cleansing the land of idolatry, false prophets, and sin. This is also when Jesus will establish the new covenant with Israel. *Romans 11:25-27 - For I would not, brethren, that ye should be ignorant of this mystery, lest ye should be wise in your own conceits; that blindness in part is happened to Israel, until the fulness of the Gentiles be come in. 26 And so all Israel shall be saved: as it is written, There shall come out of Sion the Deliverer, and shall turn away ungodliness from Jacob: 27 for this is my covenant unto them, when I shall take away their sins.* Right now

Israel is nationally blinded to the truth of the gospel until the "fullness of the Gentiles be come in." This is speaking of a national revival in Israel when all of Israel will turn to God. Jesus the Deliverer will come to Sion and save the Jews when they repent and turn to him. He saves them from their enemies and from their sin. This is just what Joel said would happen in *Joel 2:32*. The Israelites who do not turn to him in repentance will be judged, and the only Isrealites left alive will be saved. Joel said that "And it shall come to pass, that whosoever shall call on the name of the Lord shall be delivered: for in mount Zion and in Jerusalem shall be deliverance". Once he does this, he sets up his kingdom in Israel and establishes His New Covenant with them that He promised in *Jeremiah 31:31-34 - Behold, the days come, saith the Lord, that I will make a new covenant with the house of Israel, and with the house of Judah: 32 not according to the covenant that I made with their fathers in the day that I took them by the hand to bring them out of the land of Egypt; which my covenant they brake, although I was an husband unto them, saith the Lord: 33 but this shall be the covenant that I will make with the house of Israel; After those days, saith the Lord, I will put my law in their inward parts, and write it in their hearts; and will be their God, and they shall be my people. 34 And they shall teach no more every man his neighbour, and every man his brother, saying, Know the Lord: for they shall all know me, from the least of them unto the greatest of them, saith the Lord: for I will forgive their iniquity, and I will remember their sin no more.* Israel will be under the leadership of Jesus as their king for a thousand years. Do you get the picture yet? The Jews will be persecuted in the tribulation period as the nation of the earth come against them. They cry out to Jesus to save them, and as a result he pours his spirit upon them. There will be signs in the sky. The moon shall not shine, and the sun shall be darkened. They will repent, and turn to Him to save them. When they do so, He will pour out his Spirit upon them. Then He will be seen in heaven to defend his people. As the Jews see Jesus in heaven, they will be mourning over Him because they had pierced Him, and rejected Him for thousands of years. He will save them, and turn away ungodliness and sin from them. This is when He establishes His covenant with them. After he does so, He will be their king for a thousand years in His millennial kingdom. What does this have anything to do with the spiritual gifts? Cate writes,

When Peter quoted Joel's prophecy, it was as though they were in the last of "the times of the Gentiles"; because it was just after the Messiah was cut off (see Scofield's notes on Daniel 9:24-27), and it was only seven years until Messiah COULD have come (Acts 3:19-20) and delivered Jerusalem from Gentile dominion. But there was something which God had not revealed to Peter or any Old Testament prophet. It was this present church age. So the last seven years of Israel's history, as spoken by Daniel, will not come until the church is taken out. Then the last seven years of Israel's history will be will be fulfilled in what is generally known as the seven years' tribulation period. When Paul referred to the last days in II Timothy 3:1-8, he referred to the last days of the church age; but Peter referred to the last days of Israel, with regard to Jerusalem, under Gentile dominion.[41]

Let's look at our passage again. *Acts 2:16-21 - But this is that which was spoken by the prophet Joel; 17 And it shall come to pass in the last days, saith God, I will pour out of my Spirit upon all flesh: and your sons and your daughters shall prophesy, and your young men shall see visions, and your old men shall dream dreams: 18 and on my servants and on my handmaidens I will pour out in those days of my Spirit; and they shall prophesy: 19 and I will shew wonders in heaven above, and signs in the earth beneath; blood, and fire, and vapour of smoke: 20 the sun shall be turned into darkness, and the moon into blood, before that great and notable day of the Lord come: 21 and it shall come to pass, that whosoever shall call on the name of the Lord shall be saved.* Peter did not say, that is was as though they were in the last of the times of the Gentiles. He said "this is that which was spoken of by the prophet Joel". How could he say that? This is a prophecy to the Jews concerning the second coming of Christ? They will be persecuted in the tribulation period. Finally they will repent, and call upon the name of the Lord. That's when he will pour his Spirit out upon them. That's when they shall prophesy. Well, the Bible also tells us something interesting in *Romans 11:17 - And if some of the branches be broken off, and thou, being a wild olive tree, wert graffed in among them, and with them partakest of the root and fatness of the olive tree;* He is making an analogy. God is the olive tree. The Jews were receiving blessings from God being his chosen people as the branches of the olive tree. The Jews rejected Jesus and were set aside by God. As a result, He chose a brand new entity to work through which is the church. The church now receives the blessings of Israel. Some might object saying that the prophecy in *Acts 2* is specifically to the Jews, and not for the Gentiles. I would agree. That doesn't mean that they will experience all the prophecy of Joel, but they would experience the pouring out of the spirit. They would prophesy, have dreams, and visions. How do I know? Because the church experienced all of it in the book of Acts. The Samaritans experienced the baptism of the Spirit. Agabus prophesied. Peter had a vision of the unclean meats, and Paul had a dream of the Macedonian man. This is why Peter said "this is that which was spoken of by the prophet Joel". This can be said because Joel said this would happen "before that great and notable day of the Lord come". This will happen during the tribulation period when the Jews turn to the Lord and He pours out his Spirit upon them. This will still happen before the "great and notable day of the Lord come". The signs in the heavens, the moon not shining, the sun being darkened will also happen before the "great and notable day of the Lord come." Peter could say that what was happening on the day of Pentecost was the pouring out of the Spirit of God. Why? He could say this for two reasons. First, the church gets to partake of the blessings of Israel. The church is the wild olive branches that were graft into the olive tree. Some may still have a problem with that because the prophecy was specifically to Israel. I would respond by saying so was the promise of the New Covenant. Yet, that is the covenant that we live under today. *Hebrews 8:8-12 - For finding fault with them, he saith, Behold, the days come, saith the Lord, when I will make a new covenant with the house of Israel and with the house of Judah: 9 not according to the covenant that I made with their fathers in the day when I took them by the hand to lead them out of the land of Egypt; because they continued not in my covenant, and I regarded them not, saith the Lord. 10 For this is the covenant that I will make with the house of Israel after those days, saith the Lord; I will put my laws into their mind, and write them in their hearts: and I will be to them a God, and they shall be to me a people: 11 and they shall not teach every man his neighbour, and every man his brother, saying, Know the Lord: for all shall know me, from the least to the greatest. 12 For I will be merciful to their unrighteousness, and their sins and their iniquities will I remember no more.* Look again back at *Jeremiah 31:31-34*. This is the covenant that we live under, and yet twice that this promise was specifically for Israel in this passage and also in *Jeremiah 31:31-34*. The church is the branches that were graft into the olive tree. This explains the New Covenant, and *Acts 2:16-21*. The second reason that Peter could say this was because it was still before the "great and notable day of the Lord come." The truth of the matter is that it is still before the "great and notable day of the Lord come." This passage teaches that the church is still supposed to prophesy, dream dreams, see visions, and experience the outpouring of the Spirit.

Cate writes, "To point to Joel's prophecy in Acts 2:17, 18 as proof that we should have prophets in the church today, makes it contradict I Corinthians 13:8-13; II Peter 2:1 and Revelation 22:18. This is a good example of not "rightly dividing the Word" (II Timothy 2:15)." [42] We have already looked at I Corinthians 13:8-13. It does not teach that the spiritual gifts passed off the scene when the New Testament was completed. It teaches that the gifts will be done away when Jesus comes back in the rapture. II Peter 2:1 doesn't teach that there will be no more prophets in the church. That interpretation conflicts with *I Corinthians 12:28* and *Ephesians 4:11-12*. It compares the false prophets of the past with the false teachers of the present seeing that they both speak blasphemy. Revelation 22:18 doesn't teach that the book of *Revelation* was the last book of the Bible given by prophecy. It teaches that prophecy is a significant part of the book. This can be clearly seen simply by the fact that most of it hasn't happened yet. These passages are used to deny the spiritual gifts because it is believed that prophecy was used in the inspiration of Scripture. That is not taught anywhere. The Bible teaches that the purpose of prophecy. *I Corinthians 14:3 - But he that prophesieth speaketh unto men to edification, and exhortation, and comfort.* The whole argument against the spiritual gifts is teaching doctrines against the Scriptures. Why do we have to argue with Scriptures? Why can't we simply believe the Scriptures for what they clearly teach?

Another passage that has been misused by those that oppose the charismatic movement is *Matthew 3:11-12 - I indeed baptize you with water unto repentance: but he that cometh after me is mightier than I, whose shoes I am not worthy to bear: he shall baptize you with the Holy Ghost, and with fire: 12 whose fan is in his hand, and he will throughly purge his floor, and gather his wheat into the garner; but he will burn up the chaff with unquenchable fire.* Though many in opposition to the charismatic movement have used this passage incorrectly, it is a passage that actually deals with the baptism of the Spirit. John the Baptist is speaking in reference to Jesus. He said that he would baptize them with the

Holy Ghost, and with fire. Some people have said that the baptism with the Holy Ghost refers to the moment salvation. It is said that it refers to what happens to a saint at the moment of salvation when he is baptized into the body of Christ. *I Corinthians 12:12-13 - For as the body is one, and hath many members, and all the members of that one body, being many, are one body: so also is Christ. 13 For by one Spirit are we all baptized into one body, whether we be Jews or Gentiles, whether we be bond or free; and have been all made to drink into one Spirit.* The reasoning behind this belief is based on the Greek word that is translated as the words "with the Holy Spirit". This Greek word is πνεύματι. Many have said that it is an instrumental of agency which means that Christ would be baptizing us into himself through the agency of the Holy Spirit. I believe that this is a poor interpretation of this verse. Let me explain. This same Greek word could very well be a locative of sphere meaning that this word could be translated as "in the Holy Ghost". I believe that this is a better translation. Why? This is a different baptism than the one mentioned in *I Corinthians 12:12-13*. Notice, that in *I Corinthians 12:12-13* the Spirit is baptizing us into the body of Christ, whereas in *Matthew 3:11-12*, Christ is baptizing us into the Spirit. John the Baptist said, "he shall baptize you with the Holy Ghost." Jesus said that He would be baptizing us into the Spirit. Others have recognized that these are two different baptisms. They reconcile them with each other by saying that they happen at the same time. The Holy Spirit baptizes us into Christ at the moment of salvation whereas Jesus baptizes us with the Spirit at the same time. The problem with that is when Jesus himself referred to this verse in *Acts 1:5 - For John truly baptized with water; but ye shall be baptized with the Holy Ghost not many days hence.* The Greek word translated as "with the Holy Spirit" is also πνεύματι. It is the same word translated as "with the Holy Ghost" in *Matthew 3:11-12*. Jesus himself is speaking to his disciples in this verse, but his disciples had already received the Spirit in *John 20:21-22 - Then said Jesus to them again, Peace be unto you: as my Father hath sent me, even so send I you. 22 And when he had said this, he breathed on them, and saith unto them, Receive ye the Holy Ghost:* Jesus sent his disciples as the Father sent Him. John the Baptist gave us a description of the one that God sends. *John 3:34 - For he whom God hath sent speaketh the words of God: for God giveth not the Spirit by measure unto him.* John was referring to Jesus, John the Baptist said that the ones that God sends speaks God's words. This is what is exactly what Jesus sent his disciples to do. In fact, Jesus ordained them to speak God's words. *Mark 3:14 - And he ordained twelve, that they should be with him, and that he might send them forth to preach.* The disciples were definitely sent by Jesus to speak God's words. John the Baptist also said that the ones who God sends are not given the Spirit by measure. In other words, those that He sends are not given a limited amount of the Spirit. Paul referenced the fact that he had a certain amount of the Spirit in *Philippians 1:19 - For I know that this shall turn to my salvation through your prayer, and the supply of the Spirit of Jesus Christ.* Apparently there are different amounts of the Spirit that we can have upon us. The Bible tells us that Jesus sent His disciples in *John 20:21*. In the very next verse, he breathes on them and said "Receive ye, the Holy Ghost". The disciples had already received the Holy Ghost, which means that Jesus was referring to something else other than the sealing of the Holy Ghost in *Acts 1:5 -For John truly baptized with water; but ye shall be baptized with the Holy Ghost not many days hence.* If that is the case, then we know that John the Baptist was not referring to the moment of salvation, but to a specific moment after salvation. Those that oppose the charismatic movement have said that the "unquenchable fire" in *Matthew 3:11-12* refers to the fires of hell. It is said that the wheat refers to believers that have been baptized by the Spirit into the body of Christ at the moment of salvation, while the chaff refers to unbelievers who are cast into the lake of fire. We have already seen that the baptism of the Spirit does not refer to the moment of salvation when He baptizes believers into the body of Christ at the moment of salvation. I will admit, the Scripture does refer to the wicked as chaff, and to believers as wheat in certain passages. But, just because unbelievers are referred to as chaff, and believers are referred to as wheat in other passages of Scripture, that doesn't mean that they do in *Matthew 3:11-12*. The Bible compares the devil to a serpent in different places in the Scripture such as in the Garden of Eden and in *Revelation*, but Jesus also compares himself to a serpent in *John 3:14 - And as Moses lifted up the serpent in the wilderness, even so must the Son of man be lifted up:* Since the baptism of the Spirit doesn't refer to the moment of salvation in this verse, it tips us off to the fact that the fire mentioned in *Matthew 3:11-12* does not refer to hell. Let's look back at the passage in context. *Matthew 3:7-12 - But when he saw many of the Pharisees and Sadducees come to his baptism, he said unto them, O generation of vipers, who hath warned you to flee from the wrath to come? 8 Bring forth therefore fruits meet for repentance: 9 and think not to say within yourselves, We have Abraham to our father: for I say unto you, that God is able of these stones to raise up children unto Abraham. 10 And now also the axe is laid unto the root of the trees: therefore every tree which bringeth not forth good fruit is hewn down, and cast into the fire. 11 I indeed baptize you with water unto repentance: but he that cometh after me is mightier than I, whose shoes I am not worthy to bear: he shall baptize you with the Holy Ghost, and with fire: 12 whose fan is in his hand, and he will throughly purge his floor, and gather his wheat into the garner; but he will burn up the chaff with unquenchable fire.* John is speaking to the Pharisees and Sadducees in this passage. Most of them were unbelievers. That makes sense because he referred to them as the offspring of vipers. That seems to be a definite indication that they weren't saved. He asked them who warned them to flee from the upcoming wrath of God. They didn't need to flee from it. They needed to repent of their sins because The wrath of God would come upon them if they didn't repent. In other words, he is telling them that the only way that anyone escapes the wrath of God is by repenting of their sin. For this reason, John exhorts them to turn from their wickedness. He exhorts them to repent and bring forth good fruit. Good fruit does not replace repentance and faith, but it is a sign of it. John told them don't think that just because they were in the lineage of Abraham, that they wouldn't be spared from the wrath of God. Abraham couldn't save them, only Jesus could. He tells them that the axe is laid to the root of the trees. Every tree that doesn't bring forth fruit would be cut down and thrown into the fire. How many trees are being inspected for fruit? All of them. If a tree did not bring forth fruit it was cut down and thrown into the fire. This certainly is referring to the fires of hell in this verse. Notice something, John has repeatedly spoken of good fruit. He has repeatedly referred to sin, even if he did it indirectly. In context, John is speaking of good fruit. Good fruit is a sign of repentance and faith. John the Baptist said that he baptized them with water, but Jesus would baptize them with the Holy Ghost and with fire. "Repentance" refers to the moment of salvation. When someone repents and believes the gospel they are saved from the fires of hell. This means that John's baptism of repentance had already dealt with the fires of hell. They didn't need to be saved again. John's baptism of repentance was a different baptism than the baptism of the Spirit. John said that Jesus would baptize them in the Holy Ghost, but He said that he would do it in the future. The baptism of the Spirit and John's baptism of repentance were not the same event. This also proves that the baptism of the Spirit does not occur at the moment of salvation. When he speaks of the chaff and the wheat he is speaking of the people there. What exactly is the chaff and the wheat? Well we know what the wheat is. It is actually the fruit of the plant. It is grain that can be used for good purposes, like making bread. What about the chaff? The chaff is the stalk on which the wheat kernels grow, which means that the wheat and the chaff are connected. How do we know? Because he is purging the wheat from the chaff meaning that they are part of the same plant. The wheat refers to the people that are being baptized in the Spirit, while the chaff refers to the useless parts of our lives that are burned up by the fire of God. Though others might find a purpose for the chaff, God sees it as useless as evidenced by the fact that it are thrown into the fire to be burned This is why he is purging. He is purging us from anything that is holding us back from being useful to Him by burning up the unusable parts of our lives with His fire. Some might say that the chaff refer to the tares in the parable of the wheat and the tares. *Matthew 13:24-30 - Another parable put he forth unto them, saying, The kingdom of heaven is likened unto a man which sowed good seed in his field: 25 but while men slept, his enemy came and sowed tares among the wheat, and went his way. 26 But when the blade was sprung up, and brought forth fruit, then appeared the tares also. 27 So the servants of the householder came and said unto him, Sir, didst not thou sow good seed in thy field? from whence then hath it tares? 28 He said unto them, An enemy hath done this. The servants said unto him, Wilt thou then that we go and gather them up? 29 But he said, Nay; lest while ye gather up the tares, ye root up also the wheat with them. 30 Let both grow together until the harvest: and in the time of harvest I will say to the reapers, Gather ye together first the tares, and bind them in bundles to burn them: but gather the wheat into my barn.* Some might say that the wheat and tares refer to the same thing, seeing that they are planted in the same field. They may say that the tares refer to the unbelievers which are living amongst believers that aren't saved. The Greek word for tares in this passage is ζιζάνιον zizánion, dziz-an'-ee-on; darnel or false grain:—tares. The tares are darnels. I looked up what a darnel is, and I found out it is a plant that looks like wheat but produces false grain. Tares are not chaff. They are not the real thing. It is not the chaff which is part of the same plant as the wheat. The tares are completely separate plants that produce false grain. If this passage is not speaking of the baptism of the Spirit which occurs after we are saved, then what was Jesus speaking of when he referred to this same thing in *Acts 1:5 -For John truly baptized with water; but ye shall be baptized with the Holy Ghost not many days hence.* In this verse, Jesus was speaking to his disciples after they had already received the Spirit in *John 20:22* about the baptism of the Spirit when the Holy Spirit comes upon a believer to empower them to serve Him. *Matthew 3:11-12 - I indeed baptize you with water unto repentance: but he that cometh after me is mightier than I, whose shoes I am not worthy to bear: he shall baptize you with the Holy Ghost, and with fire: 12 whose fan is in his hand, and he will throughly purge his floor, and gather his wheat into the garner; but he will burn up the chaff with unquenchable fire.* The chaff represents anything that we need purged from. The chaff prevents the wheat from being used. Before the wheat can be used, it must be harvested and separated from the chaff. As long as it is connected to the stalk it can't be used. John the Baptist said that Jesus would purge his floor. What floor? His threshing floor. It was a place to purge the wheat from the chaff. He will purge his wheat so he can gather it into the garner. The garner is a barn. A barn is where wheat is stored until it can be used for purposes in the future. The wheat was to be purged where it could be stored in the barn for later use while the chaff was to be burned with the fire unquenchable. What is this fire? The Greek word for fire in this context is πῦρ pŷr, poor; a primary word; "fire" (literally or figuratively, specially, lightning):—fiery, fire. The Greek word is also the same Greek word used for "fire" in *Hebrews 12:29 - for our God is a consuming fire.* Our God is a consuming fire that burns up all the chaff in our lives. The fire of God consumes the things that keep us from being used by God. It is this fire that Jesus baptizes us into. The Holy Spirit in particular is pictured as a fire in *I Thessalonians 5:19 - Quench not the Spirit.* He is pictured as a fire that can be quenched. I understand that he said that Jesus said that he would purge (future tense would be nice) us with an unquenchable fire, but His fire is only unquenchable for those "who are baptized into it" "If we choose to reject his baptism, then we will quench the fire of the Spirit in our lives, and we will not experience the purifying effects from his fire. We are the ones that are being baptized in fire to be consumed so the fruit of lives can be used by God to make bread! *Matthew 4:4 - But he answered and said, It is written, Man shall not live by bread alone, but by every word that proceedeth out of the mouth of God.* God compares his spoken words to bread. Just as we need physical bread to live, we also need the spiritual bread of his words to live spiritually. In other words, after God purges us with his fire, then we can produce fruit or "wheat" that can be used by God to speak to others. He will baptize us with the Holy Ghost and with fire so that we can be thoroughly purged and ready for the Master's use! The Greek word for "fire" in *Matthew 3:12* also the same word used for "fire" in *Acts 2:3 - And there appeared unto them cloven tongues like as of fire, and it sat upon each of them.* This proves that the "fire" which Jesus spoke of in *Matthew 3:11-12* does not refer to hell. Why? Because the same believers which are being baptized into the Spirit, are also being baptized into fire. How do I know that this is the right interpretation? Because that is exactly what happened on the day of Pentecost.

Chapter 7

Some Misused Passages and Objections to the Charismatic Movement

There are many passages that are misused by Christians that are opposed to the charismatic movement. Many of these simply need to be put in their proper context, and it can be seen that these passages do not speak against the charismatic movement.

Here is a good example of one of these passages. *Matthew 12:39 - But he answered and said unto them, An evil and adulterous generation seeketh after a sign; and there shall no sign be given to it, but the sign of the prophet Jonas:* This is a passage that is commonly used by those who are in opposition to the charismatic movement. They say that an evil generation seeks after a sign. Let's put this verse in context. *Matthew 12:38-39 - Then certain of the scribes and of the Pharisees answered, saying, Master, we would see a sign from thee. 39 But he answered and said unto them, An evil and adulterous generation seeketh after a sign; and there shall no sign be given to it, but the sign of the prophet Jonas:* This kind of scenario happens more than once in the gospels. The Bible records this same kind of scenario in *Luke 11:29*. We know that it is a parallel passage by the language that is used in it, but we can figure out who Jesus is talking to by looking at *Matthew*'s account. It was the scribes and Pharisees. Apparently they tried again in *Matthew 16:1-4 - The Pharisees also with the Sadducees came, and tempting desired him that he would shew them a sign from heaven. 2 He answered and said unto them, When it is evening, ye say, It will be fair weather: for the sky is red. 3 And in the morning, It will be foul weather to day: for the sky is red and lowring. O ye hypocrites, ye can discern the face of the sky; but can ye not discern the signs of the times? 4 A wicked and adulterous generation seeketh after a sign; and there shall no sign be given unto it, but the sign of the prophet Jonas. And he left them, and departed.* The Pharisees and Sadducees came to see him this time to give them a sign from heaven. Apparently healing wasn't good enough for them. He said that they could discern the weather by looking at the sky. How couldn't they discern that he was the Christ? He gives them a similar response here as he did in *Matthew 12*. The parallel account of this particular scenario is found in *Mark 8:12*. Every single time Jesus responded this way, he was speaking to the scribes, Sadducees, and Pharisees. Were they good role models? I don't think so. The difference between the scribes, Sadducees, and Pharisees and the Charismatic movement is this. The scribes, Sadducees, and Pharisees sought after a sign because they didn't believe. In the Charismatic movement, we seek after signs because we do believe. In fact there is a Biblical precedent to do so. The early church did the same thing. *Acts 4:29-30 - And now, Lord, behold their threatenings: and grant unto thy servants, that with all boldness they may speak thy word, 30 by stretching forth thine hand to heal; and that signs and wonders may be done by the name of thy holy child Jesus.* The early church is praying to God in this passage. It is obvious that they were seeking after signs and wonders. But they were asking God in faith as evidenced by the fact they were praying for them. There is nothing wrong with seeking after signs and wonders in the proper way, and proper context. They certainly aren't the focal point of Christianity, but the early church gives us an example to follow. They sought after signs and wonders, and we should too.

Another passage that is commonly misused is *Matthew 7:21-23 - Not every one that saith unto me, Lord, Lord, shall enter into the kingdom of heaven; but he that doeth the will of my Father which is in heaven. 22 Many will say to me in that day, Lord, Lord, have we not prophesied in thy name? and in thy name have cast out devils? and in thy name done many wonderful works? 23 And then will I profess unto them, I never knew you: depart from me, ye that work iniquity.* Many have used this passage to strengthen their argument against the using the spiritual gifts. It is pointed out that though these people prophesied, cast out devils, and did many wonderful works, yet Jesus still told them to depart from him because they worked iniquity. Let's get something straight right now. Prophesying, casting out devils, and the many wonderful works, was not the iniquity which Jesus was referring to. How do we know? Because Jesus did all of these things. If these things were iniquity then Jesus would have sinned, and that is blasphemy. He is saying that these people were working iniquity while they were prophesying, casting out devils, and doing many wonderful works, and worst of all they didn't have a relationship with him. To get a better understanding of this passage, let's put this passage in context. *Matthew 7:15-23 - Beware of false prophets, which come to you in sheep's clothing, but inwardly they are ravening wolves. 16 Ye shall know them by their fruits. Do men gather grapes of thorns, or figs of thistles? 17 Even so every good tree bringeth forth good fruit; but a corrupt tree bringeth forth evil fruit. 18 A good tree cannot bring forth evil fruit, neither can a corrupt tree bring forth good fruit. 19 Every tree that bringeth not forth good fruit is hewn down, and cast into the fire. 20 Wherefore by their fruits ye shall know them. 21 Not every one that saith unto me, Lord, Lord, shall enter into the kingdom of heaven; but he that doeth the will of my Father which is in heaven. 22 Many will say to me in that day, Lord, Lord, have we not prophesied in thy name? and in thy name have cast out devils? and in thy name done many wonderful works? 23 And then will I profess unto them, I never knew you: depart from me, ye that work iniquity.* Jesus starts by warning the people of "false prophets". These false prophets didn't look like false prophets. They looked like sheep. In reality though they are ravening wolves. The Greek word for ravening is ἅρπαξ hárpax, har'-pax; rapacious:—extortion, ravening. These false prophets are really seeking their own benefit. They were like wolves hunting for the next meal. They are not seeking the benefit of the people, they are seeking their own benefit. Jesus said that they would know these false prophets, by their fruits. He asks a question. Do people gather grapes from thorns? No, of course not. People gather grapes from a grape vine. Do people gather figs from thistles? No, of course not. People gather figs from a fig tree. I have lived on a farm all of my life. I hate thistles. Thistles have tiny needles in them. Care must be taken when pulling them out of the ground. Otherwise, you'll end up with tiny needles in your hands. Those tiny needles stay there and fester. Nothing about thistles produces anything good for mankind, except oxygen! Seriously though, thistles are not going to produce figs, neither are thorns going to produce grapes. A plant, a vine, or a tree is only going to produce the fruit of it. A grape vine produces grapes. Fig tree produces figs. Thorns produce thorns, and so do thistles. When you get close to both thorns and thistles, it hurts. Good fruit is not going to be produced by a bad plant, vine, or tree, nor is bad fruit going to be produced by a good plant, vine, or tree. A tree that doesn't produce good fruit is going to be cut down, and burned. If a tree doesn't produce good fruit, then what good is it? It can be used as firewood. Then Jesus said, you'll know the false prophets by their fruits. Remember false prophets look like sheep, but inwardly are ravening wolves. That's when Jesus says that not everyone that calls him Lord will enter the kingdom of heaven. They may look like they are true sheep by saying that Jesus is Lord, but they are not. They aren't truly confessing that Jesus is Lord. The Bible tells us that no one can confess that Jesus is Lord except by the Spirit of God. *I Corinthians 12:3 - Wherefore I give you to understand, that no man speaking by the Spirit of God calleth Jesus accursed: and that no man can say that Jesus is the Lord, but by the Holy Ghost.* These people don't mean what they say. They are false prophets. They may refer to Jesus as Lord, but they do not mean it. They do not live like He is Lord. They are speaking the language, but not living the life. The one that does the will of God, is the one that will enter the kingdom of God. This person is the good tree producing good fruit. This person has already been born again as a child of God and now is living like it. Jesus said many will call him Lord and say that they had prophesied, cast out devils, and did many wonderful works in His name. How can someone that isn't saved, prophesy, cast out devils, do many wonderful works? Judas did. Judas Iscariot was the man that betrayed Jesus, and yet did miracles. Caiaphas prophesied about Jesus, and yet he plotted to kill him. Neither one was ever saved, but they both could do these same miracles. The Bible says in *Romans 11:29 - For the gifts and calling of God are without repentance.* Apparently someone doesn't need to be saved to flow in the gifts of the Spirit, just as Israel was called by God to be his servants, yet most of them were never saved. Judas was an example of a bad tree that produced bad fruit. He may be one of those people that will say these things. What is interesting is the response of Jesus to these people. Jesus will say, "I never knew you." What does this mean? It means that they never had a relationship with Him. In other words, is not talking about believers. What is he saying in *Matthew 7:23*? They were never saved. Jesus said about these people that they were "to depart" from him. They never were close to Him in their life, why should they be now? These were the false prophets producing bad fruit. In fact Jesus said that they "work iniquity". The Greek word for "work" is ἐργάζομαι ergázomai, er-gad'-zom-ahee; to toil (as a task, occupation, etc.), (by implication) effect, be engaged in or with, etc.:—commit, do, labor for, minister about, trade (by), work. The Greek word for ἀνομία anomía, an-om-ee'-ah; illegality, i.e. violation of law or (genitive case) wickedness:—iniquity, × transgress(-ion of) the law, unrighteousness. Not only were they never saved, but they were also actively transgressing the law of God. This has nothing to do with the fact that they prophesied, cast out devils, and had done many wonderful works. All this means is that works can't save anyone. *Ephesians 2:8-9 - For by grace are ye saved through faith; and that not of yourselves: it is the gift of God: 9 not of works, lest any man should boast.* There's nothing wrong with the works. In fact, works done in the right context, in the right way, they can be pleasing to God. If we want to single out prophecy, casting out devils, and doing many wonderful works, then we should probably look at other works. Giving to the poor, or to the church will not save anyone. But those same acts done with the right attitude, will please God very much. Prophecy, casting out devils, and doing many wonderful works will not save anyone. But all those things done in the right context, in the right way, can please God very much. This passage doesn't have much to do with prophecy, casting out devils, and doing many wonderful works at all. It has more to do with the fruit which is being produced by the life of the person who is doing these things. Why do we expect something good to come out of the life of a false prophet? He is just like the thistle. He is just going to produce bad fruit, and those he prophesies to are just going to experience pain. In the same light, why are we expecting evil to come out of a prophet of God? He is going to produce good fruit, and exhort, edify, and comfort others. In other words, the kind of fruit that is produced, is determined by the identity of the one producing it. Prophets of God produce good fruit, and false prophets produce bad fruit. God is more concerned with the fruit of the Spirit, then he is the gifts of the Spirit, but that does not mean that there is anything wrong with the gifts of the Spirit. It just means that they must be accompanied by the fruits of the Spirit.

Another passage that can be misused is *II Peter 1:19-21 - We have also a more sure word of prophecy; whereunto ye do well that ye take heed, as unto a light that shineth in a dark place, until the day dawn, and the day star arise in your hearts: 20 knowing this first, that no prophecy of the scripture is of any private interpretation. 21 For the prophecy came not in old time by the will of man: but holy men of God spake as they were moved by the Holy Ghost.* This passage could be used to prove that prophecy was used to inspire the Scriptures. In fact, many times verse 21 is quoted as a verse of proof of the inspiration of the Scriptures. Though it is not necessarily used as a proof that prophecy was the method of inspiration, I could see how it could be. This passage does not teach that the Scriptures were given by prophecy. This can clearly be seen, when we just look at the context of this passage. *II Peter 1:16-18 - For we have not followed cunningly devised fables, when we made known unto you the power and coming of our Lord Jesus Christ, but were eyewitnesses of his majesty. 17 For he received from God the Father honour and glory, when there came such a voice to him from the excellent glory, This is my beloved Son, in whom I am well pleased. 18 And this voice which came from heaven we heard, when we were with him in the holy mount.* Peter said that our faith is not based on intelligent fables when he spoke about the power and coming of Jesus. In other words. Jesus really came to earth. He really was a man that came to do the Father's will. Peter was an eyewitness of his majesty on the mount of transfiguration. He said that Jesus received honor and glory from God the Father. When was that? When God said, "This is my beloved Son, in whom I am well pleased". God himself referred to Jesus as his beloved Son, and that he was well pleased with him. Peter heard this voice coming out of heaven when he was with Jesus in the holy mount. In other words, Peter is saying that he wasn't fabricating fairy tales about Jesus, he actually experienced his glory. The context of our passage is Peter testifying about the transfiguration of Jesus. If that wasn't enough, he referenced something that could not be denied as confirmation that Jesus is truly the Messiah. When he said that, "we have a more sure word of prophecy", he was speaking about the prophecies concerning Jesus. There are many prophecies in the Bible that tell us about Jesus being the Messiah with probably the most famous passage being *Isaiah 53*. He then said that, "no prophecy of the Scripture is of any private interpretation." The Greek word for "private" is ἴδιος ídios, id'-ee-os; of uncertain affinity; pertaining to self, i.e. one's own; by implication, private or separate:—X his acquaintance, when they were alone, apart, aside, due, his (own, proper, several), home, (her, our, thine, your) own (business), private(-ly), proper, severally, their (own). This is someone's own interpretation that is separate from the accepted and clear interpretation of the Scripture. Peter said that no prophecy of the Scripture is of anyone's own interpretation of it. There were many people saying many things about Jesus. The Pharisees denied that he was the Christ. The people said all kinds of things about him. In fact, when Jesus asked his disciples in *Matthew 16:13-14 - When Jesus came into the coasts of Cæsarea Philippi, he asked his disciples, saying, Whom do men say that I the Son of man am? 14 And they said, Some say that thou art John the Baptist: some, Elias; and others, Jeremias, or one of the prophets.* They said a lot about him, but none of them were right. Peter's point here is that the prophecies of the Old Testament Scriptures point us to Jesus. Peter is combating those that would misuse the Scriptures to fit their own doctrinal position about the Messiah. He's saying that they can't do that. By doing so, they were wresting (twisting) the Scriptures to prove whatever they wanted (II Peter 3:16). And so it is with the spiritual gifts. People that do not believe in the spiritual gifts have to twist the passages that deal with them to prove that the gifts aren't in the church today. The Scriptures make clear statements like *And these signs shall follow them that believe... - Mark 16:17.* The Scriptures clearly state, *and the prayer of faith shall save the sick... - James 5:14.* The Bible clearly says, *And he gave some, apostles; and some, prophets; and some, evangelists; and some, pastors and teachers; - Ephesians 4:11* It also clearly says, *And God hath set some in the church, first apostles, secondarily prophets, thirdly teachers, after that miracles, then gifts of healings, helps, governments, diversities of tongues. – I Corinthians 12:28.* The Bible clearly tells us in *I Corinthians 12:7-11 - But the manifestation of the Spirit is given to every man to profit withal. 8 For to one is given by the Spirit the word of wisdom; to another the word of knowledge by the same Spirit; 9 to another faith by the same Spirit; to another the gifts of healing by the same Spirit; 10 to another the working of miracles; to another prophecy; to another discerning of spirits; to another divers kinds of tongues; to another the interpretation of tongues: 11 but all these worketh that one and the selfsame Spirit, dividing to every man severally as he will.* Whenever someone who doesn't believe in the spiritual gifts comes across these passages, they have to give some type of explanation other than the clear, plain, reading of the text. Notice that someone who does this is doing so out of unbelief in the clear meaning of the text. I've heard so many explanations for these passages and other passages such as those that deal with the baptism of the Spirit, and yet they are all accepted as accurate interpretations of the Scripture. They are all accepted just so long as in the end, the miraculous is not for today. After every one of them, we all think, "Amen to that brother!" If that isn't a private interpretation, then I don't know what is. Need I remind you that God is not the author of confusion, but of peace? I know the interpretation of this passage doesn't speak of the spiritual gifts, but this passage certainly does apply in this situation. If there is confusion, then God is not the author of it. If there is strife, then God is not the author of it. He is the author of peace. There is only one interpretation to any given passage. There may be many applications to that same passage, but only one interpretation. If that is the case, then which interpretation of the passages that deal with the spiritual gifts is right? If there is more than one interpretation of these passages, and they are all accepted, it sounds like confusion to me. When talking about these passages, many times tensions rise and emotions flare. God is not the author of confusion, nor is he the author of strife between believers. He is the author of peace. Many have pointed to the abuse of the gift of tongues as a source of confusion saying that because God is not the author of confusion, therefore the gift of tongues is not of God. As I have said before, the problem with the gift of tongues is not the use of it, but the abuse of it which causes confusion. But if we are trying to disprove the literal interpretation of a passage, or we are trying to prove that the literal interpretation of Scripture, and especially the epistles, doesn't apply to us, then my question is who is confused? I am not writing this to condemn anyone, but to simply ask some thought provoking questions. Peter finishes this chapter by saying that the holy men of the past who wrote the Scriptures concerning Jesus were inspired by the Holy Ghost to write the Scriptures. Therefore the prophecies concerning Jesus are authoritative. By application, all the Scriptures are authoritative, and therefore should be accepted as such. Why don't we just accept the plain, clear, reading of the Scriptures that deal with the spiritual gifts, instead of arguing against them? The truth is that many times people believe what they have been taught, especially in Christianity. What causes someone to reject the authority of the Scriptures concerning any given topic? Many times it is their own presuppositions about that same topic. Many people already have a presupposition that the spiritual gifts are not for today even before looking at the Scriptures. As a result, when they do look at the Scriptures all they see is their presuppositions concerning the topic that the Scriptures address instead of the very words of the Scriptures themselves. Let me ask an honest question. This is not meant to condemn, but it is meant to help evaluate existing belief systems. When someone speaks about spiritual gifts, is it the Spirit that rises against them, or the flesh? Let's be honest. If someone gives a testimony involving the sign gifts, is the Spirit provoked or the flesh? We hear stories of people having physical responses to an encounter with the Lord that, like the apostle John, makes them fall down on the ground "as dead". Is it our spirit that is provoked or our flesh? I personally believe that it is our flesh. I believe that because our flesh doesn't like the idea of losing dignity, but dignity is not one of the fruit of the fruit of the Spirit. Unfortunately, many times it arises out of pride, and I believe that sometimes we react in an attempt to save face. This is why emotions are high and anger flares when this particular discussion is brought up. On the other hand our spirit under the influence of the Holy Spirit should want to submit to whatever the Scriptures teach. Instead of trying to find reasons why a certain topic in the Scripture doesn't apply to us. Why don't we just submit to whatever the Scripture teaches? I encourage you to accept all the Scriptures at face value as authoritative for faith and practice. That includes the passages that speak about the spiritual gifts just as much as they include the prophecies concerning Jesus.

Another passage verse that can be misused is *Ephesians 1:13 - in whom ye also trusted, after that ye heard the word of truth, the gospel of your salvation: in whom also after that ye believed, ye were sealed with that holy Spirit of promise,* This verse is misused to prove that there is no baptism of the Spirit. After all, the Holy Spirit in this passage is called the Spirit of Promise. In *Acts 2:38-39 - Then Peter said unto them, Repent, and be baptized every one of you in the name of Jesus Christ for the remission of sins, and ye shall receive the gift of the Holy Ghost. 39 For the promise is unto you, and to your children, and to all that are afar off, even as many as the Lord our God shall call.* Peter said they had already received the gift of the Holy Ghost. He refers to the Holy Spirit as the promise. Therefore in *Acts 2,* when the disciples received the Spirit, this was when they were being sealed with the Holy Spirit. There's a problem with that thinking. This verse does not tell us that we do not receive the "holy Spirit of promise" more than once. It just says that we are sealed with Him after we believe. In fact, other sections of Scriptures tell us the opposite. *John 3:34 - For he whom God hath sent speaketh the words of God: for God giveth not the Spirit by measure unto him.* The Greek word for "measure" in this verse is μέτρον métron; a measure ("metre"), literally or figuratively; by implication, a limited portion (degree):—measure. Apparently there are varying degrees, or portions of the Spirit of God. Paul said in *Philippians 1:19 - For I know that this shall turn to my salvation through your prayer, and the supply of the Spirit of Jesus Christ.* The person that God sends speaks the words of God, and He does not give his Spirit by measure to him. In other words, He doesn't give a limited amount of the Spirit to those he sends. This verse is specifically referring to Jesus, but He said in *John 20:21 - Then said Jesus to them again, Peace be unto you: as my Father hath sent me, even so send I you.* He told his disciples that as His Father sent Him that is how he was sending them. How did the Father send him? He sent him with the Spirit. He did not give the Spirit by measure to Him. If God didn't send Jesus with a limited amount of the Spirit, and He said, "as my Father hath sent me, even so send I you", then God wouldn't give his disciples a limited amount of the Spirit either. By application, this principle applies to us as well. The very next verse tells us in *John 20:22 - And when he had said this, he breathed on them, and saith unto them, Receive ye the Holy Ghost:* He sent the Holy Spirit to them once here in *John 20:22*. This is when they were sealed with the Spirit. Then in *Acts 2*, they were baptized in the Spirit. *Acts 1:4-5 - and, being assembled together with them, commanded them that they should not depart from Jerusalem, but wait for the promise of the Father, which, saith he, ye have heard of me. 5 For John truly baptized with water; but ye shall be baptized with the Holy Ghost not many days hence.* Granted they were waiting for the Holy Spirit, which Jesus referred to as the promise of the Father. This does refer to the Holy Spirit. But as already mentioned, *Ephesians 1:13* tells us that they would be sealed with the Spirit of promise. It doesn't mean that they couldn't be baptized into the Spirit. In fact, this is exactly what happened. They were to wait for the promise of the Father. Jesus told his disciples in *Luke 24:49 - And, behold, I send the promise of my Father upon you: but tarry ye in the city of Jerusalem, until ye be endued with power from on high.* Notice, where the Spirit is being sent. The "promise of my Father" was being sent "upon" them, not in them. When the Spirit comes upon an individual, it is referred to as the baptism of the Holy Ghost. Jesus repeats this concept in *Acts 1:8 - But ye shall receive power, after that the Holy Ghost is come upon you: and ye shall be witnesses unto me both in Jerusalem, and in all Judæa, and in Samaria, and unto the uttermost part of the earth.* They would receive "power", but it was only after the Holy Ghost came "upon" them. As you can see, there certainly is more than one sending of the Spirit of God. *Acts 8:14-17 - Now when the apostles which were at Jerusalem heard that Samaria had received the word of God, they sent unto them Peter and John: 15 who, when they were come down, prayed for them, that they might receive the Holy Ghost: 16 (for as yet he was fallen upon none of them: only they were baptized in the name of the Lord Jesus.) 17 Then laid they their hands on them, and they received the Holy Ghost.* The apostles heard that Philip had preached the gospel to the Samaritans. In response, they sent Peter and John to them. When they got there, they prayed for them that they would receive the Holy Ghost. When they laid hands on them, then they received the Holy Ghost. If there wasn't more than one sending of the Spirit of God why did the believers in Samaria have to wait until Peter and John prayed for them and laid their hands on them to receive the Holy Ghost? A similar incident occurred in *Acts 19:1-6 - And it came to pass, that, while Apollos was at Corinth, Paul having passed through the upper coasts came to Ephesus: and finding certain disciples, 2 he said unto them, Have ye received the Holy Ghost since ye believed? And they said unto him, We have not so much as heard whether there be any Holy Ghost. 3 And he said unto them, Unto what then were ye baptized? And they said, Unto John's baptism. 4 Then said Paul, John verily baptized with the baptism of repentance, saying unto the people, that they should believe on him which should come after him, that is, on Christ Jesus. 5 When they heard this, they were baptized in the name of the Lord Jesus. 6 And when Paul had laid his hands upon them, the Holy Ghost came on them; and they spake with tongues, and prophesied.* The context tells us that Paul was in Ephesus. He found twelve disciples of the Lord there. He asks them if they had received the Holy Ghost since they believed. They replied that they hadn't even heard that there was any Holy Ghost. Paul asks them what baptism they had. They replied by saying that they were baptized with John the Baptist's baptism of repentance. Paul then reiterates to them what John's baptism meant. After which, they were all baptized with water baptism. Then Paul lays his hands on these believers, and they received the baptism of the Holy Ghost. To the believers in this very city Paul wrote *Ephesians 1:13 - in whom ye also trusted, after that ye heard the word of truth, the gospel of your salvation: in whom also after that ye believed, ye were sealed with that holy Spirit of promise,* The Bible tells us that we are sealed with the Holy Spirit after we believe. In other words, we have the Holy Spirit living inside of us after we believe. It is not after we have someone lay hands on us. It is not after someone prays for us. It is after we believe. To the believers that were a part of this very church that he wrote *Ephesians 1:13*, Paul also asked them "Have ye received the Holy Ghost since ye believed?" That question is very revealing in itself. If we receive the Spirit when we believe, then why would Paul ask them if they received the Spirit since they believed? I thought we were sealed with the Holy Spirit when we believe, not after we believe. Many times this is explained away by saying that these two incidents were part of the "transition period" of the church. God doesn't really work like that today.

The problem with saying that is that the words "transition", "transitional", and "normative" are not found in the Bible. I encourage you to do a search on a Bible search engine and see for yourself. They are just not in the Bible. The other problem is that God always acts according to His word. He always has, He still does, and He always will. This can be seen in *Hebrews 13:8 - Jesus Christ the same yesterday, and to day, and for ever.* Jesus Christ is the same yesterday, today, and forever. He is the same in character which means that he is faithful and He has acted according to His word yesterday, He does today, and He will in the future. (Refer to the beginning of chapter 6 for a more in depth explanation.) If he acts according to his word yesterday, today, and forever, then how can there be a transition period? When the Lord says "after that ye believed, ye were sealed with that holy Spirit of promise", how can this refer to the same thing when those believers had to wait until someone laid hands on them? I understand that in both of these instances, these believers did receive the Holy Spirit after they believed. But, in both of these instances, none of these newborn believers received the Holy Spirit until after Peter, John, and Paul laid hands on them. Either these passages refer to the baptism of the Holy Spirit, and give us a model for how we receive it, or they are giving us a model for how we are sealed with the Spirit of God because Jesus Christ acts according to his Word, yesterday, to day, and for ever. If there is no baptism of the Spirit then these passages become very confusing. God will seal someone with His spirit when they believe, then they can seek the Lord to send His Spirit "upon" them to empower them to serve Him.

Many people that opposed the charismatic movement often quote *Luke 16:31 - And he said unto him, If they hear not Moses and the prophets, neither will they be persuaded, though one rose from the dead.* Many have used this passage to say that miracles will not convince anyone to get saved. I think that is a pretty hard case to make when it is examined in the light of the rest of Scripture. Do you remember when Jesus raised Lazarus from the dead? Do you remember what Jesus said? Jesus repeatedly said that He allowed Lazarus to die in order that people may believe after He had raised him from the dead. *John 11:14 - Then said Jesus unto them plainly, Lazarus is dead. 15 And I am glad for your sakes that I was not there, to the intent ye may believe; nevertheless let us go unto him.* The disciples were confused when Jesus said that Lazarus was sleeping. They thought that he meant that he was resting. Jesus had to explicitly tell them that He was dead. Jesus said that he was glad for their sakes that he was there and healed him "to the intent ye may believe" Jesus is saying that he purposefully allowed Lazarus to die so that he could raise him from the dead so that they would believe in Him. This proves that miracles do lead people to believe. Later on in this chapter Jesus said in *John 11:41-42 - Then they took away the stone from the place where the dead was laid. And Jesus lifted up his eyes, and said, Father, I thank thee that thou hast heard me. 42 And I knew that thou hearest me always: but because of the people which stand by I said it, that they may believe that thou hast sent me.* After they rolled the stone away from Lazarus' tomb, Jesus lifted up his eyes to heaven and prayed to the Father. He thanked His Father that he had heard his prayers in the past, and that the Father always heard him. But he said that he was praying for the sake of the people who stood by. He was praying this prayer out loud so that the people would "believe" that the Father had sent him. The miracle would have been proof of the fact that the Father did always hear him. Again this proves that miracles do lead people to believe in Christ. A few verses later the Bible says in *John 11:45 - Then many of the Jews which came to Mary, and had seen the things which Jesus did, believed on him.* Jesus allowed Lazarus to die so that people would believe in Him when He raised him from the dead. Jesus then does raise Lazarus from the dead, and people do believe in Him as he desired them to. The Bible says that "many of the Jews" "believed on him." It wasn't just one or two, but many believed on Him. Here are several more examples that prove that miracles aid people to believe in Christ. *John 2:11 - This beginning of miracles did Jesus in Cana of Galilee, and manifested forth his glory; and his disciples believed on him.* Again, miracles manifest the glory of God, and leads people to believe in Him, even if they are His disciples. *John 2:23 - Now when he was in Jerusalem at the passover, in the feast day, many believed in his name, when they saw the miracles which he did.* This verse is self-explanatory. Miracles lead people to "believe in his name". *John 4:48 - Then said Jesus unto him, Except ye see signs and wonders, ye will not believe.* In context, this is when the nobleman came to Jesus and asked him to heal his son that was about to die. Of course Jesus did heal him, but this was his first response. He said that the only way that the people would believe was if they saw signs and wonders. It seems to indicate that some people need to see a miracle so that they believe. *John 7:31 - And many of the people believed on him, and said, When Christ cometh, will he do more miracles than these which this man hath done?* The people recognized that the miracles that Jesus did were proof that he truly was

Christ. *John 10:25 - Jesus answered them, I told you, and ye believed not: the works that I do in my Father's name, they bear witness of me.* In reference to the miracles that He did, Jesus said that they were proof that He truly was who He claimed to be. The miracles were to prove his identity as the Son of God. *John 10:37 - If I do not the works of my Father, believe me not.* Jesus literally tells the Jews not to believe in Him if he didn't perform the miracles. *John 12:37 - But though he had done so many miracles before them, yet they believed not on him:* This verse teaches that the miracles that Jesus did proved that He is the Son of God. This also proves that not everyone responds in the right way. Everyone has to make a choice to believe in Jesus or not. When people are not led to faith by a miracle, the problem isn't with the miracle. The problem is unbelief. *John 14:11 - Believe me that I am in the Father, and the Father in me: or else believe me for the very works' sake.* Jesus told his disciples that at the very least believe in Him for the work's sake, or for the miracles that He had done. *Acts 4:4 - Howbeit many of them which heard the word believed; and the number of the men was about five thousand.* Peter healed the lame man at gate Beautiful. Then he proceeds to preach to the people and as a result, five thousand men were saved. This is pretty clear proof that miracles open the door for people to believe. *Acts 8:5-7 - Then Philip went down to the city of Samaria, and preached Christ unto them. 6 And the people with one accord gave heed unto those things which Philip spake, hearing and seeing the miracles which he did. 7 For unclean spirits, crying with loud voice, came out of many that were possessed with them: and many taken with palsies, and that were lame, were healed.* After the rise of persecution, Philip went down to Samaria and preached to the Samaritans. Notice that they saw and heard the "miracles which he did." "Unclean spirits" were cast out of them that were possessed. What was the result? *Acts 8:12 - But when they believed Philip preaching the things concerning the kingdom of God, and the name of Jesus Christ, they were baptized, both men and women.* The result was that they believed the word which he preached. *Acts 9:36-41 - Now there was at Joppa a certain disciple named Tabitha, which by interpretation is called Dorcas: this woman was full of good works and almsdeeds which she did. 37 And it came to pass in those days, that she was sick, and died: whom when they had washed, they laid her in an upper chamber. 38 And forasmuch as Lydda was nigh to Joppa, and the disciples had heard that Peter was there, they sent unto him two men, desiring him that he would not delay to come to them. 39 Then Peter arose and went* with them. *When he was come, they brought him into the upper chamber: and all the widows stood by him weeping, and shewing the coats and garments which Dorcas made, while she was with them. 40 But Peter put them all forth, and kneeled down, and prayed; and turning him to the body said, Tabitha, arise. And she opened her eyes: and when she saw Peter, she sat up. 41 And he gave her his hand, and lifted her up, and when he had called the saints and widows, presented her alive.* Tabitha is described in this passage as a disciple. She did many good works. As a result, she was remembered and cherished for it. When she passed away, the believers at Joppa sent for Peter. He arrived at the house of them who sent for him. He then prays, and commands the body to arise. She came back to life and was raised from the dead. This passage proves that miracles were not only to be done for unbelievers, but for believers as well. Tabitha is described as a "disciple". She was definitely born again, and yet Peter raises her from the dead. What was the result? *Acts 9:42 - And it was known throughout all Joppa; and many believed in the Lord.* The result was that many heard of this miracle and "believed in the Lord." It is evident once again that miracles do lead people to faith. *Acts 13:8-12 - But Elymas the sorcerer (for so is his name by interpretation) withstood them, seeking to turn away the deputy from the faith. Then Saul, (who also is called Paul,) filled with the Holy Ghost, set his eyes on him, 10 and said, O full of all subtilty and all mischief, thou child of the devil, thou enemy of all righteousness, wilt thou not cease to pervert the right ways of the Lord? 11 And now, behold, the hand of the Lord is upon thee, and thou shalt be blind, not seeing the sun for a season. And immediately there fell on him a mist and a darkness; and he went about seeking some to lead him by the hand. 12 Then the deputy, when he saw what was done, believed, being astonished at the doctrine of the Lord.* In context, Paul and Barnabas are just setting out on their journey. They come to a place where there was a man named Elymas, he was a sorcerer and was trying to turn people away from the faith through his sorceries. Paul describes him as a "child of the devil", as an "enemy of all righteousness." He was not a good man. The hand of the Lord came upon him, and as a result he was blind for a season. The deputy that was with Elymas saw what was done, and he "believed, being astonished at the doctrine of the Lord." Do you think that the deputy would've believed if a miracle didn't take place? I don't know, but my guess is that he wouldn't have. He was associating with a sorcerer who did all kinds of supernatural things. Most likely he needed this miracle to show him the truth. Either way, once again a miracle was done that helped someone to believe the truth. *Acts 16:25-28 - And at midnight Paul and Silas prayed, and sang praises unto God: and the prisoners heard them. 26 And suddenly there was a great earthquake, so that the foundations of the prison were shaken: and immediately all the doors were opened, and every one's bands were loosed. 27 And the keeper of the prison awaking out of his sleep, and seeing the prison doors open, he drew out his sword, and would have killed himself, supposing that the prisoners had been fled. 28 But Paul cried with a loud voice, saying, Do thyself no harm: for we are all here.* Paul and Silas were praying and singing praises at midnight. That is incredible! After being beaten, they decide to pray and sing to the Lord at midnight. That just shows the heart and the faith of Paul and Silas. Then there was a supernatural earthquake so great that all the doors were open and the prison was shaken to its foundation. The Philippian jailor was about to kill himself because if he had let any of the prisoners go, then he would have to face dire consequences at the hands of the government. Immediately Paul stops him from doing so. What do you think was the result? *Acts 16:29-34 - Then he called for a light, and sprang in, and came trembling, and fell down before Paul and Silas, 30 and brought them out, and said, Sirs, what must I do to be saved? 31 And they said, Believe on the Lord Jesus Christ, and thou shalt be saved, and thy house. 32 And they spake unto him the word of the Lord, and to all that were in his house. 33 And he took them the same hour of the night, and washed their stripes; and was baptized, he and all his, straightway. 34 And when he had brought them into his house, he set meat before them, and rejoiced, believing in God with all his house.* The result was that it was the Philippians jailer that actually initiated the conversation, and asked Paul and Silas what he needed to do to be saved. Paul then had the opportunity to preach the gospel to the Philippian jailer, and teach the word of God to his entire house! They took care of him and the Philippian jailor "rejoiced, believing in God with all his house". I understand that the last two examples I used were not examples of spiritual gifts, but they both are examples of the Lord's supernatural intervention, and they both helped someone believe in the one true God. It should be obvious by now that God does use the supernatural to lead someone to belief in Christ. Paul evidently used them to preach the gospel in his ministry to the Gentiles. He said so in *Romans 15:18-19 - For I will not dare to speak of any of those things which Christ hath not wrought by me, to make the Gentiles obedient, by word and deed, 19 through mighty signs and wonders, by the power of the Spirit of God; so that from Jerusalem, and round about unto Illyricum, I have fully preached the gospel of Christ.* The book of Hebrews was written to a Jewish audience. Apparently the gospel can be confirmed to the Jews through signs and wonders as well. The writer said this in *Hebrews 2:3-4 - how shall we escape, if we neglect so great salvation; which at the first began to be spoken by the Lord, and was confirmed unto us by them that heard him; 4 God also bearing them witness, both with signs and wonders, and with divers miracles, and gifts of the Holy Ghost, according to his own will?* Whether the gospel is being preached to Jews or Gentiles, God bears witness "with signs and wonders, and with divers miracles, and gifts of the Holy Ghost". This verse also tells us that it is "his own will" to do so. As the Bible says in *Mark 16:17-18, 20 - And these signs shall follow them that believe; In my name shall they cast out devils; they shall speak with new tongues; 18 they shall take up serpents; and if they drink any deadly thing, it shall not hurt them; they shall lay hands on the sick, and they shall recover. 20 And they went forth, and preached every where, the Lord working with them, and confirming the word with signs following. Amen.* It is obvious that God uses miracles to confirm the gospel message so that people can believe. By saying that he doesn't, we are doing a couple of things. First of all, we are denying the Scriptures. I have presented several Scriptures that prove that he does use miracles to confirm the gospel so that people believe in it. To say that he doesn't is to deny those same Scriptures. Second of all, we are forfeiting the Bible example of Jesus, and the apostles for our lives in this area. If God doesn't use miracles to confirm the gospel then we don't need to follow the example of Jesus and the example of the apostles that did, but if he does then we should follow their example. Finally, we are forfeiting an amazing opportunity to share the gospel. Some people have heard the gospel over and over and over again. We may have presented them with all the evidence in creation, and all of the arguments for Christianity. I am not discounting apologetics or creation science. Some people do need that to believe. But some other people might need a miracle to believe. The truth of the matter is that faith is the evidence of things not seen. When we exercise faith, and God confirms with a miracle what argument can they present against that? They either have to accept the message or reject it. There is no middle ground. What then does this passage mean? *Luke 16:27-31 - Then he said, I pray thee therefore, father, that thou wouldest send him to my father's house: 28 for I have five brethren; that he may testify unto* them, lest they also come into this place of torment. *29 Abraham saith unto him, They have Moses and the prophets; let them hear them. 30 And he said, Nay, father Abraham: but if one went unto them from the dead, they will repent. 31 And he said unto him, If they hear not Moses and the prophets, neither will they be persuaded, though one rose from the dead.* The rich man asked Abraham to send Lazarus back to his brethren so that they could believe. Abraham said that they had Moses and the prophets to listen to. In other words, he is saying that they have the Word of God to witness to them of salvation. The rich man replies that if someone comes back from the dead, then they would repent. Notice how Abraham replies to him. He said "if they hear not Moses and the prophets". He said if they didn't believe the Word of God, then they wouldn't believe even if someone rose from the dead. In the examples that were given above, God used miracles to confirm His word. All of them did believe the Word that was presented to them. If the rich man's brethren would not believe the Word that was given to them, then they wouldn't believe in a miracle. He isn't saying that a resurrection from the dead, or any miracle for that matter wouldn't aid them to believe in Christ. He is saying that they are already expressing unbelief in the Scriptures. If they express unbelief in the Scriptures, then they still wouldn't believe the Word of God. It doesn't matter how much evidence is presented to someone who is living in unbelief, they still won't believe. This really applies to any teaching of the Scriptures. If someone expresses unbelief in the passages that teach us about the spiritual gifts, then there is no evidence strong enough to convince them otherwise. It does not matter how many Scriptures are presented to them, they have chosen not to believe. Some even go as far to use the Word of God to prove that other parts of the Word of God don't apply to us today, but at the core it is unbelief. Again, this is not meant to be condemning, but it is meant to be confronting. We can't just pick and choose what parts of the Bible we want to believe and what parts of the Bible we don't want to believe. We have to believe all of the Word of God, and preach it so that we can say with Paul *For I have not shunned to declare unto you all the counsel of God. – Acts 20:27.*

Another passage that is misused by the opponents of the charismatic movement is *II Corinthians 11:13-14 - For such are false apostles, deceitful workers, transforming themselves into the apostles of Christ. 14 And no marvel; for Satan himself is transformed into an angel of light.* Many have said that people that claim to be apostles today are false apostles. They are not of God because there are no apostles today. It is then pointed out that "Satan himself is transformed into an angel of light." Some, but not all of the opponents of the charismatic movement have even said that these apostles are of the devil because of this passage. I understand that there are false apostles, but does that mean that all are false apostles? The man writing this book was an apostle. It was the apostle Paul that wrote this letter to the Corinthians. Using this verse in this way creates two problems. First of all, the apostle Paul wrote on two different occasions that God has placed apostles in the church. One of those occasions, he was specifically writing to the Corinthians believers. *I Corinthians 12:28 - And God hath set some in the church, first apostles, secondarily prophets, thirdly teachers, after that miracles, then gifts of healings, helps, governments, diversities of tongues.* Paul explicitly says that God has set apostles and prophets in his church. The second problem with making these statements is that it accuses fellow brothers and sisters in Christ of being of the devil. Just think about that for a minute. I understand that there are some false apostles, but to believe that all apostles alive today are false apostles that are of the devil is not discerning, neither is it loving to our brothers and sisters in Christ. Another passage that is usually paired along with this one is *Revelation 19:20 - And the beast was taken, and with him the false prophet that wrought miracles before him, with which he deceived them that had received the mark of the beast, and them that worshipped his image. These both were cast alive into a lake of fire burning with brimstone.* Many people have referenced the false prophet of *Revelation* as an example of Satan's counterfeit. Along with this passage, many have cited *Matthew 24:23 - Then if any man shall say unto you, Lo, here is Christ, or there; believe it not. 24 For there shall arise false Christs, and false prophets, and shall shew great signs and wonders; insomuch that, if it were possible, they shall deceive the very elect.* They have used these references to say that not all miracles are of God. Though not explicitly stated, the implication is that miracles are of the devil. This means that what they are implying is that the miracles that are done in the Charismatic movement are a result of the devil's power. Let me remind you that the Pharisees said the same thing about Jesus. Let me make this clear. I am not calling anyone a Pharisee. I am, however, pointing out the trap that they fell into. I am urging other people not to make the same mistake. If our theology can't explain why miracles are performed in the Charismatic movement, maybe we should look at our theology one more time to check with the Scriptures, instead of accusing other Christians of being of the devil. That is not condemning, but it is confronting. *II Corinthians 12:12 - Truly the signs of an apostle were wrought among you in all patience, in signs, and wonders, and mighty deeds.* The signs of a true apostle were signs, wonders, and mighty deeds. You can't counterfeit something that isn't real. If there are false apostles, and false prophets, then there must be true apostles, and true prophets. Why are miracles the signs of an apostle? The Greek word for "apostle" is ἀπόστολος apóstolos, ap-os'-tol-os; a delegate; specially, an ambassador of the Gospel; officially a commissioner of Christ ("apostle") (with miraculous powers):—apostle, messenger, he that is sent. An apostle is an ambassador of the gospel. Proof that this is the case is found in *I Corinthians 9:2 - If I be not an apostle unto others, yet doubtless I am to you: for the seal of mine apostleship are ye in the Lord.* The seal or proof of Paul's apostleship was not the Scriptures which he left behind, but were the people that he led to the Lord. Barnabas was also referred to as an apostle on a missionary journey in *Acts 14:14 - Which when the apostles, Barnabas and Paul, heard of, they rent their clothes, and ran in among the people, crying out,* Yet another proof is found in *Romans 1:5 - by whom we have received grace and apostleship, for obedience to the faith among all nations, for his name:* The Greek word for "obedience" is an accusative of purpose meaning that Paul is saying that he, and the Roman believers had received apostleship for the purpose of sharing the gospel so that people among all nation would be obedient to the faith. It is interesting that Paul without any co-authors to the book, or any reference to any of the other apostles wrote "we have received grace and apostleship". In the context, he is obviously referring to the Roman believers. If the Roman believers had received apostleship "for obedience to the faith among all nations", by application so have all believers of all time. This is not to say that all believers of all time have been, are, or will be apostles. It does, however, mean that all believers of all times are responsible to carry out the Great Commission which proves that apostles truly are ambassadors of the gospel. *Mark 16:17 - And these signs shall follow them that believe; In my name shall they cast out devils; they shall speak with new tongues; 18 they shall take up serpents; and if they drink any deadly thing, it shall not hurt them; they shall lay hands on the sick, and they shall recover.* What's the context of this verse? The context of this verse is the Great Commission. The Bible says in *Mark 16:15 - And he said unto them, Go ye into all the world, and preach the gospel to every creature.* This means that the Lord will confirm the gospel message when any believer has the faith to step out in faith to believe that God will perform miracles when they do share the gospel. Why are apostles special? Because it is their job to share the gospel. They are ambassadors of the gospel. They are supposed to perform miracles. Please do not say that other Christians are of the devil because they perform miracles. Saying that is neither discerning nor is it loving to our fellow brothers and sisters in Christ. We have the same Father. We are part of the family of God. Please don't turn God's glorious family into a dysfunctional family.

Sometimes those that oppose the charismatic movement quote *Exodus 4:11 - And the Lord said unto him, Who hath made man's mouth? or who maketh the dumb, or deaf, or the seeing, or the blind? have not I the Lord?* Many have said that if the Lord is the one that makes man's mouth, if he makes the mute, if he makes people born deaf, if he is the one that is the one that makes gives them the ability to see, or makes born blind, then He has a reason for it beyond our understanding? If God in his sovereignty makes people like this, then why should we go about to change it? With that kind of logic, we shouldn't seek any medical intervention for any kind of malady, illness, or disability for any person who has been born with it. There is a very good reason to try to change it. First of all it would be helpful to read this verse in the context. *Exodus 4:10-12 - And Moses said unto the Lord, O my Lord, I am not eloquent, neither heretofore, nor since thou hast spoken unto thy servant: but I am slow of speech, and of a slow tongue. 11 And the Lord said unto him, Who hath made man's mouth? or who maketh the dumb, or deaf, or the seeing, or the blind? have not I the Lord? 12 Now therefore go, and I will be with thy mouth, and teach thee what thou shalt say.* In the context, the Lord is calling Moses to be the instrument that He uses to free his people from the Egyptian slavery. Moses responds in unbelief several times, but here he said that he was "not eloquent". He said that he was "slow of speech, and of a slow tongue." In some senses he may have been right seeing that he was in the desert caring for sheep for the last forty years. He probably wasn't doing any type of public speaking. On the other hand, we do know that he had the very best education that Egypt could offer. He lived as royalty in Egypt. To say that he wasn't eloquent probably wasn't true. Either way the Lord replies by saying that he made his mouth. If God made Moses mouth, then He could certainly speak through it. In the very next verse, God said that he would be with his mouth and teach him what he should say. I am not doubting that there are some people that God may allow to have a thorn in their flesh so that they are forced to rely on the Lord. But, to say that God allows a particular physical condition in every person's life would be ridiculous to believe. God is speaking to His chosen man. This man was going to be one of the greatest men in all of the Bible. Even if he truly was "slow of speech, and of a slow tongue", God was still going to use him in a way that he could get glory. On the other hand, there may be people who God allows to be born with physical conditions so that he can touch them. *John 9:1-3 - And as Jesus passed by, he saw a man which was blind from his birth. 2 And his disciples asked him, saying, Master, who did sin, this man, or his parents, that he was born blind? 3 Jesus answered, Neither hath this man sinned, nor his parents: but that the works of God should be made manifest in him.* This man was born blind. There is no question about that. His disciples do question whether or not he sinned, or whether his parents sinned. Jesus responds by saying that neither he nor his parents' sin caused him to be born blind. God may have either allowed him to be born blind, or he purposefully made him to be born blind. But it was for a reason. What was that reason? The reason was that "the works of God should be made manifest in him." *John 9:6-7 - When he had thus spoken, he spat on the ground, and made clay of the spittle, and he anointed the eyes of the blind man with the clay, 7 and said unto him, Go, wash in the pool of Siloam, (which is by interpretation, Sent.) He went his way therefore, and washed, and came seeing.* Jesus spit on the ground, made clay, and anointed the eyes of this blind man with the clay. Once he did so he commanded him to go to the pool of Siloam to wash. Once this blind man washed, he was healed. Notice that at this point in time the blind man still hasn't seen Jesus. When his neighbors realized he was healed, they started to ask some questions. *John 9:13 - They brought to the Pharisees him that aforetime was blind.* They didn't get too many answers so they brought this man to the Pharisees. He and the Pharisees argue over Jesus, and at the end of it all they cast him out of the synagogue. *John 9:34 - They answered and said unto him, Thou wast altogether born in sins, and dost thou teach us? And they cast him out.* At this point in time Jesus comes to this man to talk with him. *John 9:35-37 - Jesus heard that they had cast him out; and when he had found him, he said unto him, Dost thou believe on the Son of God? 36 He answered and said, Who is he, Lord, that I might believe on him? 37 And Jesus said unto him, Thou hast both seen him, and it is he that talketh with thee.* Jesus found this man right where he was at. That's an amazing truth in itself. He asked this man if he believed on the Son of God. The man replied that he didn't know who the Son of God was so that he could believe on him. Jesus replied that the one that is talking with you, and that you see is the Son of God. In other words, Jesus is saying that He is the Son of God. What was this man's response? *John 9:38 - And he said, Lord, I believe. And he worshipped him.* This man's response was to worship him. Notice something. Jesus said the Son of God was the one that was talking with him that the one that he had "seen." This man was born blind. He lived as a blind man all of his life. But when Jesus came into his life, and touched him, then he saw Jesus! The restoration of his physical sight actually resulted in the restoration of his spiritual sight. He saw Jesus for who he really was as the Holy Son of God standing right before him. His response was to worship Him! There are so many people that have physical problems in this world. It may or may not be a result of their parent's sin. Some people simply are born with a specific condition that has no correlation with the pregnancy of their mother while they were still in the womb. On the other hand, the pregnancy of their mother has a direct impact on some children's lives. Our world is becoming increasingly sinful. The results of that sin are all around us. There are many mothers that consume alcohol, ingest pills, smoke some type of drugs, and inject other types of drugs while they are pregnant. It is having a direct impact on their children's lives. Many children are born addicted to drugs because their mothers were taking that particular drug while they were pregnant. Many times they are addicted to some type of substance which is causing them to do so. These mothers need help themselves. I am not condemning these mothers. In fact the Bible says in *John 3:17 - For God sent not his Son into the world to condemn the world; but that the world through him might be saved.* God does not want to condemn them, he wants to save them. Needless to say, the fact remains that sin has consequences. Many children are born with many physical and mental disabilities because of what their mother was doing during their pregnancy. Whether someone is born with a disability, disease, or malady because of their mother's sins, or they are born with a disability, disease, or malady that has no correlation with their mother's behavior during her pregnancy, it doesn't matter. The works of God still need to be made manifest in them! Some people think that someone living with a handicap their entire lives would force them to rely on the Lord. It very well could result in such a dependency on the Lord. At the same time some people might become bitter because they were born that way. Do we honestly think that living with a condition would make them rely on the Lord, grow closer to Him, and be thankful for what he has done in their lives more than being healed from that condition? Whether children are born with a handicap condition because of their parents' sin, or that were born with a handicap that had nothing to do with their parents actions, God allowed many of these people to be born that way because he desires the "works of God should be made manifest" in them. Imagine a child that is born with a handicap, grows up with a handicap, lives with that handicap is miraculously healed and touched by God. What do you think the result would be? The result probably would be that they see Jesus for who he really is and worship Him! Why would you want to take that opportunity away from someone? Why would you want them to forfeit the opportunity of directly being touched by God? Why would you want to take away that reason to worship God from the depths of their heart? Too many times all of this is being forfeited because we either simply don't believe or we are unwilling to believe that God works in this way. If you don't believe in the spiritual gifts, I encourage you to evaluate your beliefs about these gifts again. There may be someone just waiting for you to believe that God will use you so that the "works of God" can be made manifest in them!

Some cessationists oppose the believe that there apostles in the church today by citing *I Corinthians 15:7-8 - After that, he was seen of James; then of all the apostles. 8 And last of all he was seen of me also, as of one born out of due time.* It is said from this verse that Paul was the last apostle that was born out of due time. That is just a bad interpretation of Scripture, as we see when we put it into its context. *I Corinthians 15:3-8 - For I delivered unto you first of all that which I also received, how that Christ died for our sins according to the scriptures; 4 and that he was buried, and that he rose again the third day according to the scriptures: 5 and that he was seen of Cephas, then of the twelve: 6 after that, he was seen of above five hundred brethren at once; of whom the greater part remain unto this present, but some are fallen asleep. 7 After that, he was seen of James; then of all the apostles. 8 And last of all he was seen of me also, as of one born out of due time.* Paul explicitly gives the gospel, and then he writes of the witness of Christ after he rose from the dead. He was seen by Peter, then the twelve, and five hundred brethren at once, and then by James, and all the apostles. It is interesting that he differentiates between "the twelve" and "all the apostles". Then Paul said that "last of all he was seen of me". Whether you look at this verse in context, or out of context, it is still clear that Paul was saying that he was a witness of the resurrected Christ. He was not saying that he was the last apostle.

I've heard cessationists try to prove that there was in fact a "transition period" by by quoting verses like *Acts 13:46 - Then Paul and Barnabas waxed bold, and said, It was necessary that the word of God should first have been spoken to you: but seeing ye put it from you, and judge yourselves unworthy of everlasting life, lo, we turn to the Gentiles.* After the Jews rejected the words which Paul and Barnabas spoke to the point that they blasphemed, they said that they turned to the Gentiles. Another similar verse is found in *Acts 18:6 - And when they opposed themselves, and blasphemed, he shook his raiment, and said unto them, Your blood be upon your own heads; I am clean: from henceforth I will go unto the Gentiles.* Again, Paul testified to them that Jesus was Christ, and they blasphemed so he said that he went to the Gentiles. At the end of the book of *Acts* Paul said in *Acts 28:28 - Be it known therefore unto you, that the salvation of God is sent unto the Gentiles, and that they will hear it.* In the same manner as in these two previous, the Jews were hardened and didn't receive the word of the Lord which was spoken by Paul. As a result, Paul said that the "salvation of God is sent unto the Gentiles". Many times the salvation of Cornelius, and the Jerusalem Council is also cited as proof of a transition that was happening in the church which allowed for the Gentiles to be saved and become part of the church. Paul himself even wrote in *Romans 1:16 - For I am not ashamed of the gospel of Christ: for it is the power of God unto salvation to every one that believeth; to the Jew first, and also to the Greek.* Paul said that the gospel was to the Jew first, and then to the Greek, or the Gentile. It is said that a transition of moving away from Judaism to Christianity is pictured by the fact that Paul warned the Jews three times that the gospel was going to be taken to the Gentiles which was always God's plan for the gospel seeing Paul writes that it was "to the Jews first, and also to the Greek." I do not argue with the fact that there was a transition in the early church. But, what was that transition, and who did this transition primarily affect? This transition was a transition from Judaism to Christianity, and it primarily affected the Jews. Why? Because for many Jews the fabric of their existence was being changed at the core. Many of the Jews' lives revolved around Judaism. To become a Christian would be a major change in their lives, especially in how they related to God. The Gentiles did not experience the same transition. There was a change for the Gentiles in how they were made right with God, but there was no transition for the Gentiles to become right with God. A transition was being made in the church by these incidents, as well as Cornelius' salvation, and the Jerusalem council, but it was a transition in the fact that the church was increasingly including Gentiles into their membership. The problem with quoting these verses to prove that a transition was being made is that there was no transition being made by these Jews. These statements made by Paul don't give proof for a transition period, they are actually proof against it because they were made in response to the Jews' rejection of the gospel, not their acceptance of it. Just because there was a transition in the early church to accept Gentiles as fellow joint-heirs with Christ alongside the Jews, doesn't mean that proves that there was a "transition period" for the Jews in which God used miracles to confirm his Word to them to help them believe it.

Most cessationists teach that the church began in *Acts 2*. One of the passages that is used to prove that is *Acts 11:15 - And as I began to speak, the Holy Ghost fell on them, as on us at the beginning. 16 Then remembered I the word of the Lord, how that he said, John indeed baptized with water; but ye shall be baptized with the Holy Ghost.* In context, Peter is telling his fellow Jewish Christians about his experience with Cornelius. During this conversation, Peter speaks of the Holy Spirit falling on them at the beginning. The question is what beginning? It is proposed that Peter is speaking of the beginning of the church. After all, this is the point in time when Cornelius is saved. How do we know? We know because the Bible says in *Acts 11:17-18 - Forasmuch then as God gave them the like gift as he did unto us, who believed on the Lord Jesus Christ; what was I, that I could withstand God? 18 When they heard these things, they held their peace, and glorified God, saying, Then hath God also to the Gentiles granted repentance unto life.* Cornelius "believed on the Lord Jesus Christ" and "God" "granted" to him "repentance unto life." It is pretty obvious that Cornelius was saved at this time, but he was also baptized in the Spirit. Some might say that this proves that the baptism of the Spirit happens at the same time as the moment of salvation. Some people may also try to use this passage to prove that being baptized with the Holy Ghost truly is the baptism to which Paul was referring to in *I Corinthians 12:12-13 - For as the body is one, and hath many members, and all the members of that one body, being many, are one body: so also is Christ. 13 For by one Spirit are we all baptized into one body, whether we be Jews or Gentiles, whether we be bond or free; and have been all made to drink into one Spirit.* It is taught that the baptism with the Holy Ghost refers to the baptism which occurs at the moment of salvation to place any given individual into the body of Christ. In fact, the Greek words translated as "with the Holy Ghost" in *Acts 11:16* are ἐν πνεύματι ἁγίῳ. In particular, the word πνεύματι could be an instrumental of agency meaning that Jesus would be using the Holy Spirit to baptize believers into the body of Christ. Additionally, these believers received the Holy Spirit in this passage, and were "made to drink into one Spirit" which further proves that the baptism of the Spirit refers to the baptism that occurs at the moment of salvation to place a believer in the body of Christ, and that the church really did occur on the day of Pentecost. First of all, just because these believers were sealed with the Spirit at the moment of salvation, that doesn't mean they couldn't have been baptized into the Spirit at the same moment. The Spirit is compared to wind in *John 3:8 - The wind bloweth where it listeth, and thou hearest the sound thereof, but canst not tell whence it cometh, and whither it goeth: so is every one that is born of the Spirit.* Jesus is not saying that the one who is born of the Spirit goes where he wants to, but you cannot tell where he is coming or where he is going. That sounds more like the world who walk after the imaginations of their own hearts, and who walk in darkness not knowing at what they stumble. They simply do whatever comes into their hearts and minds to do. One that is born of the Spirit obeys the Spirit that blows where he wants to, and you cannot tell where he is going, and where he is coming. Those that are born of the Spirit simply yield to Him. If the Holy Spirit is like wind, why do we try to control Him? We cannot control the wind, and neither should we try to control the Spirit. We should let him be God, and let him act according to His will. If he desires to baptize someone into himself at the moment of salvation, then we should let him. Second of all, the Greek word πνεύματι could be an instrumental of agency, but it could also very well be a locative of sphere meaning that Jesus would be baptizing believers into the Spirit. I believe this is a much better translation because the disciples received the Spirit, and were already baptized into the body of Christ in *John 20:22 - And when he had said this, he breathed on them, and saith unto them, Receive ye the Holy Ghost:* After which time, and Jesus told his disciples directly before his ascension in *Acts 1:5 - For John truly baptized with water; but ye shall be baptized with the Holy Ghost not many days hence.* They were going to be baptized in the Holy Ghost after they had already received him. The reason why I believe that Cornelius received the sealing of the Holy Ghost, and the baptism of the

Holy Ghost at the same time was because God was trying to prove to the Jews that not only were they suitable to be saved, but to serve as well. Since the apostles first received the Spirit and baptized into the body of Christ in *John 20:22*, then that is also when the body of Christ was first formed. In other words, that is when the church started. If that is when the church started, then what was the "beginning" to which Peter was referring to? He was referring to the beginning of the proclamation of the gospel. How do I know? After the disciples had already been sealed the Spirit, Jesus had said in *Acts 1:8 - But ye shall receive power, after that the Holy Ghost is come upon you: and ye shall be witnesses unto me both in Jerusalem, and in all Judæa, and in Samaria, and unto the uttermost part of the earth.* After the Holy Ghost came upon them, they would be his "witnesses" in Jerusalem, Judaea, Samaria, and the uttermost parts of the earth. The disciples were baptized in the Spirit, and immediately afterwards, Peter stands up to preach, and three thousand souls were saved. Praise God! This passage does not prove that the baptism of the Spirit refers to the baptism which occurs at the moment of salvation whereby the Holy Spirit baptizes believers into the body of Christ. Nor does it prove that the church began in *Acts 2*

There have been many people who oppose the charismatic church by quoting *Deuteronomy 18:20-22 - But the prophet, which shall presume to speak a word in my name, which I have not commanded him to speak, or that shall speak in the name of other gods, even that prophet shall die. 21 And if thou say in thine heart, How shall we know the word which the Lord hath not spoken? 22 when a prophet speaketh in the name of the Lord, if the thing follow not, nor come to pass, that is the thing which the Lord hath not spoken, but the prophet hath spoken it presumptuously: thou shalt not be afraid of him.* This passage is used to say that those in the charismatic church who are referred to as prophets, but prophesy with one-hundred percent accuracy for them to be a true prophet of the Lord. It is cited that the words of the prophets did all come to pass in the Old Testament. It is usually then mentioned that the prophet in the Old Testament should have died for having prophesied a word from the Lord that did not come to pass. First of all, let me remind us all of the purpose of the law. *Galatians 3:24 - Wherefore the law was our schoolmaster to bring us unto Christ, that we might be justified by faith.* The purpose of the law was to teach of our need for Christ. How did it do that? *Romans 5:20 - Moreover the law entered, that the offence might abound. But where sin abounded, grace did much more abound:* The law was given so that offence might abound. In other words, humanity was already sinning against God before we received the law, but it was given to point out how much we actually do sin. When we finally come to the point of agreeing with God about our sin, we can receive the grace of God which is found in Jesus Christ. Any, and all of the commands of God were given for this purpose. This is why the law was so severe. That doesn't necessarily mean that every time the law was violated, death was demanded by God for the perpetrator, even if the law explicitly called for it. That same violation may have actually been an opportunity to receive mercy from the Lord. How do I know? The law required death for those who committed adultery. *Leviticus 20:10 - And the man that committeth adultery with another man's wife, even he that committeth adultery with his neighbour's wife, the adulterer and the adulteress shall surely be put to death.* It also required death for a murder. *Numbers 35:30 - Whoso killeth any person, the murderer shall be put to death by the mouth of witnesses: but one witness shall not testify against any person to cause him to die.* David committed both of these sins, yet God still had mercy on him, after he spent months running from the Lord, and then finally repented. Do we not think that if a prophet gets a specific word from the Lord wrong, that he will not be merciful? Why would that prophet be wrong in the word that he gives anyway? If the Lord gave the word, wouldn't it come to pass as it says in *Deuteronomy 18:20-22*? The problem isn't with the Lord. The problem lies with the prophet who seeks to hear the word. The Lord may be giving a perfectly good word, but the person hearing the word may not hear it properly. So it is today in any other relationship we may have. Someone such a parent may give perfectly good instructions to their children, but their children might not respond perfectly to their parents instructions because they didn't hear them. That may very well be determined by how well they are listening, but we can still be gracious and merciful to them! How do I know this? The Bible says in *Luke 8:18 - Take heed therefore how ye hear: for whosoever hath, to him shall be given; and whosoever hath not, from him shall be taken even that which he seemeth to have.* The context of this verse is the parable of the sower, the seed, and the soils. Without fully explaining the parable, I will give a brief summary. The four different types of soil, represents four different kinds of hearts. Their receptivity to the word is determined by the condition of their heart. It is interesting that the Word was never made to be received in our mind, but in our hearts. That is why David hid his word in his heart.

With that being said the seed represented the Word of God. The first seed of the Word that is received is the gospel. At that point in time, the Holy Spirit comes to dwell inside of the human heart. He acts as the fertilizer of the soil which gives life to all other seeds of the Word which are planted in the soil. Just as God spoke in the beginning when he created the world, and plants grew out of the soil, so too the Holy Spirit speaks to us, and causes those seeds to sprout. When Jesus says "take heed how ye hear", he is referring to the Holy Spirit meaning that we can hear Him to varying degrees. A prophet may not hear him perfectly, and because of that, it may cause him to get a prophecy wrong, but that does not mean that he needs to die. Nor does it mean that the prophecy, or the prophet for that matter, weren't from God. The Lord was using such a high standard that offence may abound, that everyone including the prophet could rely on his grace!

With that being said, there may be another reason why the word of a prophet will not come to pass. *Isaiah 7:1-9 - And it came to pass in the days of Ahaz the son of Jotham, the son of Uzziah, king of Judah, that Rezin the king of Syria, and Pekah the son of Remaliah, king of Israel, went up toward Jerusalem to war against it, but could not prevail against it. 2 And it was told the house of David, saying, Syria is confederate with Ephraim. And his heart was moved, and the heart of his people, as the trees of the wood are moved with the wind. 3 Then said the Lord unto Isaiah, Go forth now to meet Ahaz, thou, and Shear-jashub thy son, at the end of the conduit of the upper pool in the highway of the fuller's field; 4 and say unto him, Take heed, and be quiet; fear not, neither be fainthearted for the two tails of these smoking firebrands, for the fierce anger of Rezin with Syria, and of the son of Remaliah. 5 Because Syria, Ephraim, and the son of Remaliah, have taken evil counsel against thee, saying, 6 Let us go up against Judah, and vex it, and let us make a breach therein for us, and set a king in the midst of it, even the son of Tabeal: 7 thus saith the Lord God, It shall not stand, neither shall it come to pass. 8 For the head of Syria is Damascus, and the head of Damascus is Rezin; and within threescore and five years shall Ephraim be broken, that it be not a people. 9 And the head of Ephraim is Samaria, and the head of Samaria is Remaliah's son. If ye will not believe, surely ye shall not be established.* In many words, this passage is basically saying that Pekah, the king of Israel, and Rezin, the king of Syria, made an alliance together to fight against Ahaz, the king of Judah, but they did not prevail. He was scared as were the hearts of his people. But, the Lord reassured him that their alliance would come to nought to the point that Israel would be taken away from being a nation. This word was meant to establish Ahaz and his kingdom. If the word came to pass, then he and his kingdom would be established against the attacks of Pekah, and Rezin. But the Lord gave a prerequisite for that to happen. He said, "if ye will not believe, surely ye shall not be established." In other words, what he is saying is that he needed to believe the word that he had just been given, and act in faith on it for it to come to pass. But, if he didn't believe in it, and he didn't act in faith on it, then it wouldn't come to pass. This tells us that sometimes prophetic words do not come to pass because the words are given to those who do not believe them. There is nothing wrong with the word, or for the prophet for that matter, the problem lies with the faith of the person who receives the word. I understand that this principle could be abused by those who are called prophets now a days, but I encourage the prophets to think soberly before using this argument to validate why a specific word did not come to pass. The Bible says in *James 3:1 - My brethren, be not many masters, knowing that we shall receive the greater condemnation.* Teachers will stand before God, and will answer to Him for what they said, and by application prophets will too. This isn't meant to strike fear in the hearts of every prophet, but it is meant to be sobering to them. The truth is that this is true for any Word of God whether it is prophetic or not. The Bible says in *Hebrews 4:2 - For unto us was the gospel preached, as well as unto them: but the word preached did not profit them, not being mixed with faith in them that heard it.* The writer of Hebrews just said that though the word was preached to them, it didn't profit them one bit. Why? Because it was not "mixed with faith". He basically just said that the Bible is worthless without the faith to walk it out, or make it a reality. That is a pretty intense verse but God doesn't just want us to be hearers of the Word, he wants us to be doers of it! Later in this same book, the writer of Hebrews writes in *Hebrews 11:32-33 - And what shall I more say? for the time would fail me to tell of Gedeon, and of Barak, and of Samson, and of Jephthae; of David also, and Samuel, and of the prophets: 33 who through faith subdued kingdoms, wrought righteousness, obtained promises, stopped the mouths of lions.* He just said that the promises of God are obtained through faith. God's job is to fulfill his promises, our job is to believe them. If we do not believe in them, then we are not in a position to receive them, and therefore God can't fulfill them. Whether it is a promise, a prophetic word, or the Word of God, faith is required to see them fulfilled.

Many cessationists oppose the doctrine of the baptism of the Spirit by quoting *John 7:39 - (But this spake he of the Spirit, which they that believe on him should receive: for the Holy Ghost was not yet given; because that Jesus was not yet glorified.)* It is said that the Spirit couldn't be given until Jesus was glorified. Usually they then quote *Acts 2:33 - Therefore being by the right hand of God exalted, and having received of the Father the promise of the Holy Ghost, he hath shed forth this, which ye now see and hear.* It is said that Jesus was "by the right hand of God exalted" before the believers "received of the Father the promise of the Holy Ghost". It is concluded that Jesus wasn't exalted until Jesus ascended to the right hand of the Father, then they could receive the Holy Spirit. These verses are quoted to prove that the disciples did not receive the Spirit in *John 20:21-22*, they were simply promised the Spirit in these verses. It is interesting the Greek word for "being exalted" is an aorist tense participle meaning that it is referring to an undefined action. It is most likely a constative aorist which would simply point to the fact that he had been glorified. It could be a consummative aorist which is pointing to the fact that he had been glorified. In this case, it would indicate the finished action of being glorified. Either way, it is in the aorist tense which refers to an undefined action. This fact in itself does prove that Jesus was glorified before he ascended, but it does allow for it. With that being said I do believe that it supports a timeframe for his glorification before the cross. As we have already seen, the disciples could not receive the Spirit until Jesus had been glorified. Two questions then must be answered. Why couldn't they receive the Spirit until he had been glorified, and when was he actually glorified? Let's start by looking at *Philippians 2:5-11 - Let this mind be in you, which was also in Christ Jesus: 6 who, being in the form of God, thought it not robbery to be equal with God: 7 but made himself of no reputation, and took upon him the form of a servant, and was made in the likeness of men: 8 and being found in fashion as a man, he humbled himself, and became obedient unto death, even the death of the cross. 9 Wherefore God also hath highly exalted him, and given him a name which is above every name: 10 that at the name of Jesus every knee should bow, of things in heaven, and things in earth, and things under the earth; 11 and that every tongue should confess that Jesus Christ is Lord, to the glory of God the Father.* Notice that the Bible says "Wherefore God also hath highly exalted him". This means that Paul just wrote the reason for why God had exalted Jesus. The reason was because Jesus, who was God, became a man, became a servant, humbled himself, and died on the cross for all. As a result, God had "given him a name which is above every name" so "that every tongue should confess that Jesus Christ is Lord". It is interesting that every tongue will confess that Jesus is Lord because he humbled himself, became a man, and died on the cross. It is also interest in context, the Bible says something similar in *Acts 2:32-36 - This Jesus hath God raised up, whereof we all are witnesses. 33 Therefore being by the right hand of God exalted, and having received of the Father the promise of the Holy Ghost, he hath shed forth this, which ye now see and hear. 34 For David is not ascended into the heavens: but he saith himself, The Lord said unto my Lord, Sit thou on my right hand, 35 until I make thy foes thy footstool. 36 Therefore let all the house of Israel know assuredly, that God hath made that same Jesus, whom ye have crucified, both Lord and Christ.* Peter is preaching to the Jews, and he is quoting from the Old Testament to prove that Jesus is the Messiah. He cites the fact that Jesus truly did rise from the dead, and that he ascended into heaven at the right hand of the Father to prove that he was "both Lord and Christ". The question is when did God make Jesus "both Lord and Christ"? The Bible tells us in *Matthew 28:18 - And Jesus came and spake unto them, saying, All power is given unto me in heaven and in earth.* The Greek word for "power" is ἐξουσία exousía, (in the sense of ability); privilege, i.e. (subjectively) force, capacity, competency, freedom, or (objectively) mastery (concretely, magistrate, superhuman, potentate, token of control), delegated influence:—authority, jurisdiction, liberty, power, right, strength. This word means authority many times in the New Testament, and I believe that it does here. Jesus had been given all authority in heaven, and in earth before he ascended to heaven. Why? Because Jesus had already been made "both Lord and Christ." This is why "that at the name of Jesus every knee should bow, of things in heaven, and things in earth, and things under the earth; and that every tongue should confess that Jesus Christ is Lord". But when exactly was he glorified? Jesus said in *John 12:23-24 - And Jesus answered them, saying, The hour is come, that the Son of man should be glorified. 24 Verily, verily, I say unto you, Except a corn of wheat fall into the ground and die, it abideth alone: but if it die, it bringeth forth much fruit. 25 He that loveth his life shall lose it; and he that hateth his life in this world shall keep it unto life eternal. 26 If any man serve me, let him follow me; and where I am, there shall also my servant be: if any man serve me, him will my Father honour.* The hour was come that Jesus would be glorified. What hour? The hour that he died. How do I know? I know because of the very next verse. Unless a grain of wheat falls into the ground and dies, it abides alone, but if it dies, then it brings forth much fruit. He is saying that if he wouldn't die, then no one would be able to come to him in repentance and faith in his finished work. But if he did die, then many would come to him in repentance, and believe on him. He set an example for us to follow. Of course, he was not asking us to die on the cross just as he did, though if it comes to that, then I ask that God gives us all grace. He was saying that we need to die to ourselves on a daily basis. We need to crucify self on a daily basis to bring forth much fruit, and follow him. I believe the hour that he died on the cross was the hour that he was glorified. How do I know? Jesus prayed in *John 17:1 - These words spake Jesus, and lifted up his eyes to heaven, and said, Father, the hour is come; glorify thy Son, that thy Son also may glorify thee:* This was hours before he was to be arrested, tried, beaten, mocked, and ultimately crucified. He asked the Father to glorify him because the hour was come. What hour? The hour that he died on the cross.

We know that Jesus was glorified, when he died on the cross because the Bible says in *Luke 24:25-26 - Then he said unto them, O fools, and slow of heart to believe all that the prophets have spoken: 26 ought not Christ to have suffered these things, and to enter into his glory? 27 And beginning at Moses and all the prophets, he expounded unto them in all the scriptures the things concerning himself.* With the two disciples on the road to Emmaus, Jesus taught them everything concerning himself starting with the law, and the prophets, and all the Scriptures. He specifically taught them that he was to suffer, and afterwards to enter into his glory. I find it interesting that he said that he would "enter into his glory". He did not say that he would "enter into glory". Why was it "his glory"? Because it had been given to him. In other words, after Jesus suffered he was glorified, not after he ascended.

We answered the question of when Jesus was glorified, but why couldn't anyone receive the Spirit until Jesus was glorified? The same passage of Scripture that cessationists use to prove that the disciples couldn't have received the Spirit actually explains why the Spirit couldn't be given until Jesus was glorified. They usually quote *John 16:7 - Nevertheless I tell you the truth; It is expedient for you that I go away: for if I go not away, the Comforter will not come unto you; but if I depart, I will send him unto you.* It is said by cessationists that when Jesus said that he would "go away", he was referring to his ascension. If he was referring to his ascension, the Holy Spirit would not come to them, and the disciples did not receive the Spirit in *John 20:21-22*. I don't believe that he was referring to his ascension. If we just put this verse in context the Bible says in *John 16:7-11 - Nevertheless I tell you the truth; It is expedient for you that I go away: for if I go not away, the Comforter will not come unto you; but if I depart, I will send him unto you. 8 And when he is come, he will reprove the world of sin, and of righteousness, and of judgment: 9 of sin, because they believe not on me; 10 of righteousness, because I go to my Father, and ye see me no more; 11 of judgment, because the prince of this world is judged.* The Holy Spirit would not come, until Jesus went away, but the question is why? The answer to that question is because the Holy Spirit couldn't convict the world of sin, of righteousness, and judgement until Jesus died. He convicts the world of their sin in order that they can repent, believe in Christ, and accept his finished work on the cross. He convicts believers that they have been made righteous by believing in Christ, and accepting his finished work on the cross, and he convicts those who refuse to repent, believe in Christ, and accept his finished work on the cross of judgement because if the prince of this world's system is judged, then those who partake in it will also surely be judged. All three of these things are tied to Christ's death on the cross. In other words, the Holy Spirit couldn't come until Christ died, and fulfill his work so that he could start his work of convicting the world of sin, of righteousness, and of judgement.

Some people might object by saying that Jesus was truly referring to his ascension because he said in *John 16:5 -But now I go my way to him that sent me; and none of you asketh me, Whither goest thou?* He specifically said that he went his "way to him that sent me", therefore he must've been referring to his ascension. He may have been, but I don't believe that he was given the fact that the context speaks of the Holy Spirit coming to convict the world of sin, of righteousness, and of judgement. I believe that Jesus did ascend to heaven during those three days that he departed from this world. Why do I believe that? The Bible says in *Ephesians 4:8-10 - Wherefore he saith, When he ascended up on high, he led captivity captive, and gave gifts unto men. 9 (Now that he ascended, what is it but that he also descended first into the lower parts of the earth? 10 He that descended is the same also that ascended up far above all heavens, that he might fill all things.)* I believe that this passage teaches that during the three days, and three nights that Jesus was dead, he ascended up to heaven taking all the Old Testament saints with Him. The Old Testament saints went to a compartment of hell referred to as Abraham's bosom or paradise before Jesus died on the cross. The Bible says in *Luke 16:19-23 - There was a certain rich man, which was clothed in purple and fine linen, and fared sumptuously every day: 20 and there was a certain beggar named Lazarus, which was laid at his gate, full of sores, 21 and desiring to be fed with the crumbs which fell from the rich man's table: moreover the dogs came and licked his sores. 22 And it came to pass, that the beggar died, and was carried by the angels into Abraham's bosom: the rich man also died, and was buried; 23 and in hell he lift up his eyes, being in torments, and seeth Abraham afar off, and Lazarus in his bosom.* The rich man obviously wasn't saved, but Lazarus was. They both died, and Lazarus went to Abraham's bosom, or paradise, and the rich man went to hell. It is obvious that saints went to Abraham's bosom because when Lazarus died, "he was carried by the angels into Abraham's bosom", the same place where Abraham himself was. We know that Abraham's bosom was in hell because the rich man could see Lazarus, and Abraham when he was in hell. Not to mention that the Bible also says in *Luke 16:26 - And beside all this, between us and you there is a great gulf fixed: so that they which would pass from hence to you cannot; neither can they pass to us, that would come from thence.* This seems to indicate that hell, and Abraham's bosom was in the same place, but there was a gulf between them. When Jesus was on the cross he told the thief that believed in him in *Luke 23:43 - And Jesus said unto him, Verily I say unto thee, To day shalt thou be with me in paradise.* He said that he would be with him in "paradise" after he believed on Christ. This means that Jesus was in paradise for at least one day, but it also means that Abraham's bosom, and paradise are the same place referred to by different names. Paul wrote in *II Corinthians 12:2-4 - knew a man in Christ above fourteen years ago, (whether in the body, I cannot tell; or whether out of the body, I cannot tell: God knoweth;) such an one caught up to the third heaven. 3 And I knew such a man, (whether in the body, or out of the body, I cannot tell: God knoweth;) 4 how that he was caught up into paradise, and heard unspeakable words, which it is not lawful for a man to utter.* Paul was caught up to heaven, and he saw things which it was not lawful for a man to utter. I have no idea what he saw, but I wish I did. Praise God we will see the same things one day. It is interesting that he mentions that he was caught up into paradise. I have no idea what happened, but I know that it was significant. I know that it is no longer in the same place as hell as it was before Christ died, but that it is now in the same place as heaven after he died. Let's look again at what the Bible says in *Ephesians 4:8-10 - Wherefore he saith, When he ascended up on high, he led captivity captive, and gave gifts unto men. 9 (Now that he ascended, what is it but that he also descended first into the lower parts of the earth? 10 He that descended is the same also that ascended up far above all heavens, that he might fill all things.)* This passage tells us that Jesus "led captivity captive" when he "ascended on high". What does this mean? The Greek word for "led captivity" is αἰχμαλωτεύω aichmalōteúō, aheekh-mal-o-tew'-o; to capture :—lead captive. It means exactly what it says. The Greek word for "captive" is αἰχμαλωσία aichmalōsía, aheekh-mal-o-see'-ah; captivity:— captivity. In this verse, I believe that he is saying that he led captivity itself captive. I believe this captivity includes the captivity to sin, and to the devil, and that it refers to spiritual slavery. I believe that Paul is teaching that Jesus lead any and all spiritual slavery captive. This slavery results in plethora of problems including emotional issues. But, this verse is quoted from *Psalm 68:17-18-The chariots of God are twenty thousand, even thousands of angels: the Lord is among them, as in Sinai, in the holy place. 18 Thou hast ascended on high, thou hast led captivity captive: thou hast received gifts for men; yea, for the rebellious also, that the Lord God might dwell among them.* This passage clearly refers to war seeing that it speaks of the "chariots of God". Jesus won the victory on the cross, and he "ascended on high" to receive gifts for men. As he did so he "led captivity captive" The Hebrew word for "thou hast led captivity" is שְׁבִי sh^ebîy, sheb-ee'; exiled; captured; as noun, exile (abstractly or concretely and collectively); by extension, booty:—captive(-ity), prisoners, × take away, that was taken. He led the prisoners, the exiled, and the captured captives. In other words, when he ascended on high, he led those which were exiled from his presence. I believe he is referring to the Old Testament saints who were living in paradise. It seems as though instead of just leading them to heaven, he took all of paradise with Him. I also believe that it was at this time that Jesus went to heaven to place his blood on the mercy seat for the Bible says in *Hebrews 9:12 - neither by the blood of goats and calves, but by his own blood he entered in once into the holy place, having obtained eternal redemption for us.* This would fit well with the context of *John 16:5-11 - But now I go my way to him that sent me; and none of you asketh me, Whither goest thou? 6 But because I have said these things unto you, sorrow hath filled your heart. 7 Nevertheless I tell you the truth; It is expedient for you that I go away: for if I go not away, the Comforter will not come unto you; but if I depart, I will send him unto you. 8 And when he is come, he will reprove the world of sin, and of righteousness, and of judgment: 9 of sin, because they believe not on me; 10 of righteousness, because I go to my Father, and ye see me no more; 11 of judgment, because the prince of this world is judged.* It seems as though Jesus was glorified when he died on the cross, departed from this world to lead the Old Testament saints into the presence of God bringing paradise with him, at which time he sprinkled his blood on the mercy seat in heaven, and rose from the dead to personally send the Holy Spirit to his disciples when he breathed on them the breath of life which enabled the Holy Spirit to convict the world of sin of righteousness, and of judgment.

Many people who have opposed the Charismatic church use different verses as a source of their opposition. One of these verses is *Ephesians 2:19-21 - Now therefore ye are no more strangers and foreigners, but fellowcitizens with the saints, and of the household of God; 20 and are built upon the foundation of the apostles and prophets, Jesus Christ himself being the chief corner stone; 21 in whom all the building fitly framed together groweth unto an holy temple in the Lord:* It is said that the apostles and prophets were the foundation of the church because they received revelation from the Lord to write the Holy Scriptures. Then another passage that is then quoted is *Ephesians 3:1-6 - For this cause I Paul, the prisoner of Jesus Christ for you Gentiles, 2 if ye have heard of the dispensation of the grace of God which is given me to you-ward: 3 how that by revelation he made known unto me the mystery; (as I wrote afore in few words, 4 whereby, when ye read, ye may understand my knowledge in the mystery of Christ) 5 which in other ages was not made known unto the sons of men, as it is now revealed unto his holy apostles and prophets by the Spirit; 6 that the Gentiles should be fellowheirs, and of the same body, and partakers of his promise in Christ by the gospel:* It is pointed out that God revealed his truth to his holy apostles and prophets. The conclusion that is made is that the purpose office of the apostle, or prophet was to receive the Scripture by divine revelation. Then the qualifications of an apostle are usually given by quoting *Acts 1:20-22 - For it is written in the book of Psalms, Let his habitation be desolate, and let no man dwell therein: and his bishoprick let another take. 21 Wherefore of these men which have companied with us all the time that the Lord Jesus went in and out among us, 22 beginning from the baptism of John, unto that same day that he was taken up from us, must one be ordained to be a witness with us of his resurrection.* This passage is in reference to Judas Iscariot. The apostles were looking for a replacement for Judas, and these were the qualities that were listed in this passage for his replacement. Therefore it is said that these were the qualities required to be an apostle. These qualities include being with Jesus from the time that he was baptized until he ascended, and that they were a witness of his resurrection by beholding Christ as a man physically before he ascended. After this passage is quoted, then cessationists usually quote from *II Corinthians 12:12 - Truly the signs of an apostle were wrought among you in all patience, in signs, and wonders, and mighty deeds.* It is said that the signs of an apostle were the signs, wonders, and mighty deeds. Since the apostles were the ones that received the Scriptures by divine revelation, the signs, wonders, and mighty deeds confirmed the word which was written. Since the New Testament is completed, we don't need signs, wonders, and mighty deeds to confirm the word. The sign gifts had a purpose, but fulfilled their purpose with the completion of the New Testament. Furthermore, it is taught that the role of the apostle and prophet was to receive by divine revelation the Holy Scriptures from God, and since the New Testament is completed, the role of the apostle, and prophet has fulfilled their purpose as well, and are therefore no longer needed. *Acts 1:19-22* is then usually pointed to as proof that there are no more apostles living today because there is no one alive today that walked with Jesus during his earthly ministry from the time that he was baptized by John to the time that he ascended, and that no one alive today is a witness of Christ beholding him physically after his resurrection.

  I have already gone through all these arguments earlier in this book, but I bring them up again for the sake of repetition. Peter wrote in *II Peter 1:12 - Wherefore I will not be negligent to put you always in remembrance of these things, though ye know them, and be established in the present truth.* If repetition was good enough for Peter, than it is good enough for me too! First of all them me start with *II Corinthians 12:12 - Truly the signs of an apostle were wrought among you in all patience, in signs, and wonders, and mighty deeds.* The Greek word for "apostle" is ἀπόστολος apóstolos, a delegate; specially, an ambassador of the Gospel; officially a commissioner of Christ ("apostle") (with miraculous powers):—apostle, messenger, he that is sent. An apostle is an ambassador of the gospel. In our language today, we might refer to them as missionaries. Proof that apostles were ambassadors of the gospel is found in *I Corinthians 9:2 - If I be not an apostle unto others, yet doubtless I am to you: for the seal of mine apostleship are ye in the Lord.* The Corinthian believers themselves were the seal, or proof of Paul's apostleship, not the Scriptures that he wrote. Why? Because they believed on Christ as a result of his ministry of preaching the gospel. Barnabas is also mentioned as being an apostle on a missionary journey in *Acts 14:14 - Which when the apostles, Barnabas and Paul, heard of, they rent their clothes, and ran in among the people, crying out.* The Bible tells us in *Romans 1:5 - by whom we have received grace and apostleship, for obedience to the faith among all nations, for his name: 6 among whom are ye also the called of Jesus Christ:* Paul is writing to the believers at Rome, and he said they had received apostleship for the obedience to the faith among all nations. In other words, they had received apostleship to share the gospel, so that the people of all nations would turn to the Lord, and walk in obedience by faith with Him! What is interesting is that the Greek word for "obedience" is most likely an Accusative of purpose meaning Paul is making us completely sure that he is saying that he received his apostleship for this purpose. It is also interesting to note that he includes the Roman believers in this statement. They had received apostleship for the obedience to the faith among all nations as well. I know that Paul was referring to them because there is no reference to any of the other apostles in the context, nor is there any co-authors to this book which means that the Roman believers themselves were the ones to whom Paul was referring to. Not only was Paul an apostle, but apparently all the Roman believers were given apostleship. By application, this statement extents to all believers today. This is not to say that all believers are apostles, but it is the responsibility of all believers to share the gospel. As ambassadors of the gospel they will have signs follow them as they preach the gospel. *Mark 16:15-20 - And he said unto them, Go ye into all the world, and preach the gospel to every creature. 16 He that believeth and is baptized shall be saved; but he that believeth not shall be damned. 17 And these signs shall follow them that believe; In my name shall they cast out devils; they shall speak with new tongues; 18 they shall take up serpents; and if they drink any deadly thing, it shall not hurt them; they shall lay hands on the sick, and they shall recover. 19 So then after the Lord had spoken unto them, he was received up into heaven, and sat on the right hand of God. 20 And they went forth, and preached every where, the Lord working with them, and confirming the word with signs following. Amen.*

Jesus commanded his disciples to preach the gospel. Immediately after he did so, he told them "these signs follow them that believe". The Greek word for "them that believe" is πιστεύσασιν. It is a participle. A participle is a verbal adjective. This particular participle is functioning as a substantival participle meaning that is functioning as a direct object. In other words, as a verbal adjective this word is describing these people as the people that people. What do they believe? In the context, it seems as though it is referring to those who believe the gospel. In other words, anyone who is saved is able to partner with God to perform miracles. I also believe that this means that faith is required to perform such miracles. How do I know? I know because the first miracle on this list is to cast out devils in his name. When Jesus was on the mountain of transfiguration with Peter, James, and John, the rest of his disciples were trying to cast out a devil out of the son of the man who had brought him to them. Jesus comes down, and casts it out. The Bible says in *Matthew 17:19-21 - Then came the disciples to Jesus apart, and said, Why could not we cast him out? 20 And Jesus said unto them, Because of your unbelief: for verily I say unto you, If ye have faith as a grain of mustard seed, ye shall say unto this mountain, Remove hence to yonder place; and it shall remove; and nothing shall be impossible unto you. 21 Howbeit this kind goeth not out but by prayer and fasting.* Jesus flat out tells them that their own unbelief was the cause for which they couldn't cast out this devil. In other words, faith is required to cast out devils, and therefore faith is required to perform all the other miracles mentioned in *Mark 16:17-18*. In this passage, Jesus is not saying that demons only come out by prayer and fasting, he is saying that unbelief only comes out by prayer and fasting. Prayer and fasting purges the unbelief out of us so we can believe in him to perform miracles. As we have seen, faith is required to perform miracles. As ambassadors of the gospel, apostles should preach the gospel, and believe in the Lord to confirm his word through miracles because it is through the miracles that he confirms his word being preached by the apostles. Also notice that in context, the Lord is using these miracles to confirm the gospel. He was not using the miracles to confirm the message of the New Testament until the so-called "transition period" was fulfilled with the completion of the Word of God in its entirety. He was, and still does use miracles to confirm the gospel message to unbelievers, not to the church.

If apostles are ambassadors of the gospel, and sign gifts were used to edify the church, and confirm the gospel to unbelievers, then wouldn't it make sense that we still need apostles to preach the gospel, and signs and wonders to confirm it? Seeing that there are still unreached people groups in the world, the answer should be obvious. We still need both.

Let's look again at *Acts 1:20-22 - For it is written in the book of Psalms, Let his habitation be desolate, and let no man dwell therein: and his bishoprick let another take. 21 Wherefore of these men which have companied with us all the time that the Lord Jesus went in and out among us, 22 beginning from the baptism of John, unto that same day that he was taken up from us, must one be ordained to be a witness with us of his resurrection.* These were not the qualifications of every apostle, they were simply the qualifications that disciples decided on for the replacement of Judas. How do I know? I know because Paul wouldn't fit in these qualifications. He wasn't walking with the Lord from the time that he was baptized by John until the day that he ascended. Barnabas may or may not have fit those qualifications as well, and yet they are both referred to as apostles. *Acts 14:14 - Which when the apostles, Barnabas and Paul, heard of, they rent their clothes, and ran in among the people, crying out.* Why then were they both called apostles? Because they were both ambassadors of the gospel. This verse is written in the context of a missionary journey taken both by Paul and Barnabas. These qualifications were given for the replacement of Judas seeing that the Scripture says "and his bishoprick let another take". The Greek word for "bishoprick" is ἐπισκοπή episkopē,; inspection (for relief); by implication, superintendence; specially, the Christian "episcopate":—the office of a "bishop", bishoprick, visitation. It was Judas' office of a bishop that was being fulfilled by another. For that person to fulfill that specific bishoprick or office, they would've needed those qualification to be effective in carrying out the responsibilities which God intended for Judas. God can and will raise up another to do his will for our lives if we choose not to. The Bible says in *Esther 4:13-14 - Then Mordecai commanded to answer Esther, Think not with thyself that thou shalt escape in the king's house, more than all the Jews. 14 For if thou altogether holdest thy peace at this time, then shall there enlargement and deliverance arise to the Jews from another place; but thou and thy father's house shall be destroyed: and who knoweth whether thou art come to the kingdom for such a time as this?* Haman was planning on trying to kill all the Jews living in the Persian empire. Mordecai, Ester's cousin, told her that if she would remain quiet, then she would be killed, but God would raise another deliverer to fulfill his will to protect his people. This is exactly what is happening in *Acts 1:15-22*. Another was taking Judas' place as an apostle to fulfill the role that God had intended for his life.

Some have questioned the charismatic movement by asking whether or not we believe that there are men who live up to the caliber of the apostle Peter, or the apostle Paul. First of all, the reason why the apostles were such amazing men of God wasn't because of their office. There are many today that are ambassadors of the gospel. They were such amazing men of God because of their walk with Him. They were willing to suffer so much for their great King. Second, I do not think it to be wise to compare ourselves among ourselves, but there have been some great men of faith even in our generation who have suffered just as much for their King as the apostle Peter, and the apostle Paul, yet were still amazing witnesses for Him. I think of names such as Richard Wormbrand, Brother Yun, or the Dietrick Bonhoffer, among thousands of unnamed pastors who suffered at the hands of men, yet remained true to the Lord.

With that being said, let's look again at *Ephesians 2:19-21 - Now therefore ye are no more strangers and foreigners, but fellowcitizens with the saints, and of the household of God; 20 and are built upon the foundation of the apostles and prophets, Jesus Christ himself being the chief corner stone; 21 in whom all the building fitly framed together groweth unto an holy temple in the Lord:* The apostles and prophets aren't the foundation of the church. They didn't even lay the foundation of the Church by leaving us the Word of God. How do I know? The Bible says in *I Corinthians 3:9-11 - For we are labourers together with God: ye are God's husbandry, ye are God's building. 10 According to the grace of God which is given unto me, as a wise masterbuilder, I have laid the foundation, and another buildeth thereon. But let every man take heed how he buildeth thereupon. 11 For other foundation can no man lay than that is laid, which is Jesus Christ.* This is obviously a parallel passage. It speaks of the church as a building. It speaks of laying a foundation to this building, and it speaks of Jesus being that foundation. All of these truths are found in *Ephesians 2:19-21*. But, this passage clarifies *Ephesians 2:19-21*. This passage tells us that the foundation of the apostles and prophets is Jesus Christ, and they simply laid the foundation. How do I know? Because "other foundation can no man lay than that which is laid, which is Jesus Christ." There is no other foundation. It's Him! The glorious Son of God is the only foundation of the church corporately, and of the individuals which make up the church. So how did Paul lay the foundation? Before a building exists a foundation must be laid. The only way a church can exist is by sharing the gospel with individual people. Once they receive the gospel, then the foundation of their Christian life is established in their relationship with Him. This makes sense seeing that the apostles are ambassadors of the gospel. Paul even wrote in *Romans 15:20 - Yea, so have I strived to preach the gospel, not where Christ was named, lest I should build upon another man's foundation:* he didnt want to lay a foundation on another man's work by sharing the gospel. In other words, he is saying that he laid the foundation of the churches that he planted by sharing the gospel, not by writing the Scriptures. If the apostles laid the foundation of the church by sharing the gospel with individuals so they could establish their own relationship with Jesus, then how did the prophets contributed to the foundation? The prophets contributed to the foundation by strengthen the church's relationship with Jesus, who is it's foundation by speaking words of edification, exhortation, and comfort directly from him to them.

There are other reasons why I know that Paul was not referring to the Scriptures as the foundation which the apostles, and prophets left behind. First of all, it was not inherent to the office of an apostle to write the Scriptures. If it was, then all the apostles would've wrote books of the Bible, but Andrew didn't, Philip didn't, and neither did Thomas just to name a few. The apostles were simply ambassadors of the gospel, which is why Barnabas is referred to as an apostle. Their office would be similar to a missionary today, and I would even go as far to say that it is the Bible term for a missionary. Second it wasn't inherent to the role of a prophet either because Agabus would've written a book as well, but he didn't. Prophets simply spoke words of edification, exhortation, and comfort directly, and supernaturally from God to his people concerning the secrets of their hearts to touch them in a very deep way. If that is the case, then why did some of the apostles write the Scriptures? The answer is simple. The answer is that it was the will of God for them to write certain books of the Bible. Some of the apostles wrote books of the Bible, and some didn't, but they were all ambassadors of the gospel. Similarly today, some pastors write books because it is the will of God for them to write books, and some pastors don't because it is not the will of God for them to write books, but all pastors should care for their flocks.

It has been taught by cessationists that the gifts were used to confirm the Word which was being written by the apostles and prophets during the time of the "transition period" when God was transitioning from using the nation of Israel as a whole to using the Gentiles. This transition period was the time when the church began to the time when the New Testament was finished. Paul writes in *I Corinthians 1:22 - For the Jews require a sign, and the Greeks seek after wisdom.* The reason why the Jews required a sign was because God worked signs and wonders throughout the Jews history in his dealings with them. If God was going to start working through a new entity known as the church, then he would have to confirm it to the Jews for them to believe in the words being spoken and written by the members of this new entity. This is exactly what the writer of Hebrews writes in *Hebrews 2:3-4 - how shall we escape, if we neglect so great salvation; which at the first began to be spoken by the Lord, and was confirmed unto us by them that heard him; 4 God also bearing them witness, both with signs and wonders, and with divers miracles, and gifts of the Holy Ghost, according to his own will?* God did in fact confirm the word which was spoken by the apostles to the Jews with these signs and wonders, diverse miracles, and gifts of the Holy Ghost. Once the New Testament was completed, then the sign gifts had fulfilled their purpose in confirming the Word to the Jews, and passed off the scene when the church was well established. We know this because the Greek word for "confirmed" is probably a consummative aorist pointing to the completed action of it. First of all, as I have already mentioned several times before, there was no transition period. How do I know? Because Jesus Christ acts according to his Word "yesterday, and to day, and for ever" meaning that he was acting according to his word by working through the sign gifts in the early church, and he continues to do so today as well. Second in this passage it specifically mentions a "so great salvation" indicating that the word which the Lord confirmed to the Jews was the gospel. To be doubly sure of this, the Greek word for "confirmed" in this verse is the same Greek word for "confirming" in *Mark 16:20 - And they went forth, and preached every where, the Lord working with them, and confirming the word with signs following. Amen.* In this verse the Greek word for "confirming" is βεβαιόω bebaióō; to stabilitate (figuratively):—confirm, (e-)stablish. It is a present tense participle. More specifically, it is probably either a durative present meaning that he continually confirmed the word in the past which continues in the present time, or it is a customary present tense participle meaning that it the custom of God to confirm the word by signs and wonders to unbelievers on the behalf of those who have faith to step out and believe that he will confirm their word. It is also interesting that the

Greek word for "also bearing them witness" from *Hebrews 2:4*, is also a present tense participle. This could also be a durative present, though it is probably closer to a customary present meaning that it is God's custom to bear witness to the words of those who have the faith witness to unbelievers, and who step out and believers that he will with signs and wonders. As we have already seen that the context speaks of the gospel, not the New Testament. *Mark 16:15 - And he said unto them, Go ye into all the world, and preach the gospel to every creature.* All this still proves that God confirmed the gospel to the Jews, but if he only confirmed the gospel to the Jews, then why did Paul incorporate miracles, signs, and wonders in his gospel-preaching ministry to the Gentiles? *Romans 15:18-19 - For I will not dare to speak of any of those things which Christ hath not wrought by me, to make the Gentiles obedient, by word and deed, 19 through mighty signs and wonders, by the power of the Spirit of God; so that from Jerusalem, and round about unto Illyricum, I have fully preached the gospel of Christ.* This is further proof that there was no transition period because miracles signs and wonders were not just used to preach the gospel to the Jews during the days of the early church. He didn't just use them to help the Jews transition to a new entity known as the church, he used them to confirm the word to the Gentiles. There was no transition for the Gentiles. God had never worked with the Gentiles. His chosen people were the Jews. In fact, it was probably less of a transition for the Gentiles to become part of the church, than it was for them to become part of the nation of Israel. I understand that there may have been a transition in the fact that salvation was found in Christ alone, not through Judaism, but even that isn't near the same transition that the Jews had to go through, yet Paul still used signs and wonders to preach the gospel to them. Why? Not because he was trying to aid the Jews to believe in him during a so called "transition" period, but because as Nicodemus said in *John 3:2 - the same came to Jesus by night, and said unto him, Rabbi, we know that thou art a teacher come from God: for no man can do these miracles that thou doest, except God be with him.* God confirmed his word to them so that they understood that he was speaking directly to them because no man can perform these miracles unless God is with them.

When talking about the spiritual gifts, some people have gone so far to say that the reason why there are miracles that happen in the Charismatic church is because they are done through the power of the devil. Can you imagine the audacity of saying such a claim? Do you understand the implications of that? That statement says that a born again child of God is working in connection with the devil. In fact, it means that an entire community of born again Christians have been working in connection with the devil for the last hundred years. Granted, we have seen that there are charismatic churches that don't operate in accordance with Scripture. Sometimes, they operate against the commands of Scripture. Honestly, there may be some demonic activity happening under the guise of Charismatic Christianity. With all that being said, just because some do, that doesn't mean that every charismatic church does. It does not mean that every charismatic church doesn't operate in accordance with Scripture. It doesn't mean that every charismatic church is operating against the commands of Scripture, and it doesn't mean that demonic activity is occurring under the guise of Christianity in every Charismatic church. But if truth be told, other non-charismatic churches do the same thing, it just manifests in a different way. I encourage all Christians to minister in accordance with the Word of God. One thing I find interesting is the Pharisees said the same thing about Jesus! And they did it more than once! *Matthew 12:24-28 - But when the Pharisees heard it, they said, This fellow doth not cast out devils, but by Beelzebub the prince of the devils. 25 And Jesus knew their thoughts, and said unto them, Every kingdom divided against itself is brought to desolation; and every city or house divided against itself shall not stand: 26 and if Satan cast out Satan, he is divided against himself; how shall then his kingdom stand? 27 And if I by Beelzebub cast out devils, by whom do your children cast them out? therefore they shall be your judges. 28 But if I cast out devils by the Spirit of God, then the kingdom of God is come unto you.* I am not calling anyone a a Pharisee, but I am, however, pointing out a trap that can be easy to fall into. They said that the only way that Jesus casted out devils was through the power of Satan himself. Jesus tells them that a kingdom divided against itself will be destroyed. He is specifically referring to the devil's kingdom, but the same principle applies to the kingdom of God. A kingdom divided against itself cannot stand. It just won't operate the way it should. There won't be unity, there will be strife. We should not be divided against each other as Christians. We need to be unified in our attempt to reach the lost for Christ. If we are divided against ourselves, then the kingdom of God will not stand the way it should. He said that if a house is divided against itself, then cannot stand. If Satan could cast out Satan, then it would be counterproductive for his kingdom. Jesus said that it couldn't stand, and that it would be brought to destruction. So it is today. The miracles done in the charismatic church are not done by the power of Satan, but by the power of God. Apparently, their children were casting out devils seeing that Jesus mentions it. As a result, Jesus also told them that their children will be their judges. Why? Because He said in *Mark 16:17 - And these signs shall follow them that believe; In my name shall they cast out devils; they shall speak with new tongues;* They believed and therefore they were able to cast out devils. In verse 28, Jesus said that the kingdom of God was come to them. He also said that the casted out devils by the Spirit of God. What did he mean by his kingdom? He meant that his Lordship was being manifested to them before their eyes. Jesus is the King of kings, and the Lord of lords. There is no devil that can stand in His way. That is my Savior, glory to God, Amen. It was by the work of the Holy Spirit that these devils were cast out. The Pharisees that clung so tightly to their beliefs in God, were the same ones that were calling the work of His Spirit, the work of the devil. We have to be careful not to do the same thing. The Bible tell us in *John 3:1-2 - There was a man of the Pharisees, named Nicodemus, a ruler of the Jews: 2 the same came to Jesus by night, and said unto him, Rabbi, we know that thou art a teacher come from God: for no man can do these miracles that thou doest, except God be with him.* This chapter records the conversation between Jesus and Nicodemus. Nicodemus was a ruler of the Jews. Later on in this passage Jesus refers to him as a master, or a teacher of Israel. Nicodemus didn't have everything right, but he did come to Jesus with the right heart, and he did have quite a bit of Biblical knowledge. He said that no one could do the miracles that Jesus did, except God was with Him. Can we do the miracles of Jesus? We can if God is with us. In fact Jesus said in *John 14:12 - Verily, verily, I say unto you, He that believeth on me, the works that I do shall he do also; and greater works than these shall he do; because I go unto my Father.* Jesus, our Lord and Savior said that we could the same works the he did if we would just believe. He even extended it farther by saying that we could do greater works then He did if we would just believe. That is amazing! I am not willing to lower the bar of Scripture to my own understanding, I would rather keep the bar where the Scriptures set it, and reach as high as I can to meet it. Another passage that deals with this same subject is *Mark 9:38-39 - And John answered him, saying, Master, we saw one casting out devils in thy name, and he followeth not us: and we forbad him, because he followeth not us. 39 But Jesus said, Forbid him not: for there is no man which shall do a miracle in my name, that can lightly speak evil of me.* The disciples saw someone casting out devils in the name of the Lord, and they forbid him from doing so. As a side note it is easy for us as Christians to forbid others that are doing the work of the Lord in His name because they "followeth not us", or because they are not part of our circles. This ought not be. We should be like Paul who rejoice that the gospel was being preached. *Philippians 1:18 - What then? notwithstanding, every way, whether in pretence, or in truth, Christ is preached; and I therein do rejoice, yea, and will rejoice.* Paul rejoiced that the gospel was being preached whether it was being preached in pretence or in truth. We should as well. In the context of *Mark 9:38-39*, we are dealing with casting out devils. Jesus said that no man that does a miracle in His name, whether it be casting out a devil or any other miracle, could lightly speak evil of him. That sounds a little bit different than casting out devils, or doing miracles through the power of the devil. *I Corinthians 12:3 - Wherefore I give you to understand, that no man speaking by the Spirit of God calleth Jesus accursed: and that no man can say that Jesus is the Lord, but by the Holy Ghost.* The person that does a miracle in the name of Jesus is probably not going to speak evil about Him. In fact, he is more likely to say that Jesus is Lord than to curse Him.

It has only been recently that the charismatic movement formed. The charismatic movement officially formed out of what is referred to as the Azusa Street Revival in 1906. Those that oppose the charismatic movement often cite the fact that before this the church has not believed in them since the days of the apostles. If this is truly is of God, then why hasn't the church believed in miracles since the days of the apostles? If God's people who have the Holy Spirit dwelling inthem who guides them into truth, then why haven't God's people been guided into truth before 1906? Those are valid questions. I would also like to point something out. The pre-tribulation rapture wasn't accepted by the church until John Darby formulated his view of the rapture in 1827. This view of the rapture is widely known and accepted among Christians, and yet, it only appeared roughly 80 years before the charismatic revival. The truth is that not even all the early church believed in it, just as not all Christians in our day believe in it. At least Christians could see the sign gifts in use, and are recorded in the Scriptures. Dwight Pentecost quotes James Orr's book *The Progress of Dogma*, in his own book *Things to Come* by writing,

It should be observed that each era of church history has been occupied with a particular doctrinal controversy, which has become the object of discussion, revision, and formulation, until there was a general acceptance of what the Scripture taught. The entire field of theology was thus formulated through the age. It was not until the last century that the field of Eschatology became a matter to which the mind of the church was turned. This has well been developed by Orr, who writes:

> Has it ever struck you…what a singular *parallel* there is between the historical course of dogma, in the one hand, and the scientific order of the text-books on systematic theology on the other? The history of dogma, as you speedily discover is simply the system of theology spread out through the centuries…and this not only regards its general subject-matter, but even as respects the definite succession of its parts…One thing, I think it shows unmistakably, viz., that neither arrangement is arbitrary – that there is law and reason underlying it; and another thing which forces itself upon us is, that the law of these two developments – the logical and historical-is the same.
>
> … the second century in the history of the Church – what was that? The age of *Apologetics* and the vindication of *the fundamental ideas of all religion* – of the *Christian* especially – in conflict with Paganism and with Gnostics.
>
> We pass to the next stage of the development, and what do we find there? Just what comes next in the theological system – *Theology Proper* – The Christian doctrine of God, and specially the doctrine of the Trinity. This period is covered by the *Monarchian, Arian,* and *Macedonian* controversies in the third and fourth centuries.
>
> …What comes next? As in the logical system theology is succeeded by *Anthropology*, so in the history of dogma the controversies I have named are followed in the beginning of the fifth century by the *Augustinian* and *Pelagian* controversies, in which …the center of interest shifts from God to man.

...From the time of Augustine's death we see the Church entering on that long and distracting series of controversies known as Christological – *Nestorian, Eutychian, Monophysite, Monothelite* – which kept in continual ferment, and rent it with the most unchristlike passions during the fifth and sixth, on even till near the end of the seventh, centuries.

...Theology, Anthropology, Christology have each had its day – in the order of the theological system, which the history still carefully follows, [but] it was not the turn of *Soteriology*... [until] the next step, that taken by the Reformers in the development of the *Application of Redemption*. This...is the next great division of the theological system.

What now shall I say of the remaining branch of the theological system, the Eschatological? An Eschatology, indeed, there was in the early church, but it was not theologically conceived; and a Mythical Eschatology there was in the Mediaeval Church – an Eschatology of Heaven, Hell, and Purgatory...but the Reformation swept this away, and with its sharply contrasted states of bliss and woe, can hardly be said to have put anything in its place, or even to have faced very distinctly the difficulties of the problem...Probably I am not mistaken in thinking that, besides the necessary revision of the theological system as a whole, which could not properly be undertaken till the historical development I have sketched had run its course, the modern mind has given itself with special earnestness to eschatological questions, moved thereto, perhaps, by the solemn impression that on it the ends of the world have come, and that some great crisis in the history of human affairs is approaching.

This whole argument of the progress of dogma would be our strongest argument against the post-tribulation rapturist who argues that doctrine must be rejected because it was not clearly taught in the early church. [43]

In every age of the church, there has been some controversy and debate over theological issues. These theological debates have forced the church to make a decision as to what she will believe. There are certainly exceptions to this, but these areas of theology recovered by these debates are considered to be orthodox teaching by all Christians. By quoting Orr, Pentecost argues that there have been debates throughout church history until orthodox doctrine has generally been agreed upon. This is true with the doctrine of the pre-tribulation rapture. Many, though not all, Christians believe that the rapture will occur before the tribulation. It is generally accepted as orthodox teaching, but it was not accepted as such until J.N. Darby proposed his view of the rapture in 1827. Orr writes that the church was been thinking of eschatological questions because it may have been possible that the Holy Spirit was putting an impression on it to do so in light of the ever-encroaching coming judgement in the tribulation period. I find it interesting that about the time that Orr was penning these words, the Azusa Street Revival was also taking place which many have pointed to as the origin of Charismatic Christianity. It may be possible that God was reminding people of the end times to motivate them to witness to the lost to warn them of the coming judgement, and to exhort them to receive Jesus Christ as their Savior to avoid that judgement in the rapture, then He proceeded to create a controversy concerning the Holy Spirit who empowers the church to carry out its mission to preach the gospel to every creature so that he could establish doctrine that taught more explicitly about the Holy Spirit's ministry through believers. Yes, doctrine concerning Charismatic Christianity has been ignored for very good reasons since the apostles. Other areas of doctrines needed more attention due to the controversies in different time periods of the church. Just as the doctrine of the pre-tribulation rapture was not believed for the majority of the history of the church until 1827, the doctrine concerning Charismatic Christianity was not believed or has been given attention, but that doesn't make either of those areas of doctrine wrong. Now that this controversy is active today, is it possible that God is using that to establish orthodox teaching concerning the Holy Spirit according to the Scriptures in our day? That is a question that we must ask ourselves, and seek the Lord and the Scriptures for the answers.

Chapter 8

The Baptism of the Spirit

The baptism of the Spirit is necessary in our churches, but its existence has been debated for years. Many people have preconceptions about it, but if we just look at the Scriptures objectively, then it will lead us to the right conclusions.

Acts 1:8 - But ye shall receive power, after that the Holy Ghost is come upon you: and ye shall be witnesses unto me both in Jerusalem, and in all Judæa, and in Samaria, and unto the uttermost part of the earth. I think this verse adequately describes the Baptism of the Spirit. It is an event in the believer's life when the Holy Ghost comes "upon" them. The reason that He does so is to empower them for some type of service that they couldn't do adequately themselves. In this particular instance, he's referring to the disciples becoming his witnesses. This is a problem for some people because they believe that this is the event when the Holy Ghost was sent from God to baptize those believers into the body of Christ, and the church had begun as a result. There are a couple problems with this. First of all, let's look at the word church in the Greek. ἐκκλησία ekklēsía, ek-klay-see'-ah; a calling out, i.e. (concretely) a popular meeting, especially a religious congregation (Jewish synagogue, or Christian community of members on earth or saints in heaven or both):—assembly, church. That is the Strong's definition for "church" in *Acts 2:47 - praising God, and having favour with all the people. And the Lord added to the church daily such as should be saved.* Many people call it a called out assembly of believers. I understand that this verse is the last verse in *Acts 2*, and this was after the events on the day of Pentecost. My question is this. Wasn't there a called out assembly of believers before *Acts 2*? There were 120 believers all in the upper room waiting to be endued with power from on high, and praying together. That sounds like a called out assembly of believers to me. It fits with Strong's definition. Some people may say that was before the Spirit came. Was it? *John 20:19-22 - Then the same day at evening, being the first day of the week, when the doors were shut where the disciples were assembled for fear of the Jews, came Jesus and stood in the midst, and saith unto them, Peace be unto you. 20 And when he had so said, he shewed unto them his hands and his side. Then were the disciples glad, when they saw the Lord. 21 Then said Jesus to them again, Peace be unto you: as my Father hath sent me, even so send I you. 22 And when he had said this, he breathed on them, and saith unto them, Receive ye the Holy Ghost.* Cate writes,

> Some think the disciples received the Holy Spirit before Pentecost according to *John 20:19-23*. This was spoken in view of the coming of the Holy Spirit at Pentecost. The disciples were behind closed doors, afraid to face the Jews with the resurrection story. (v. 19). Then came Jesus and stood in the midst, and saith unto them, "Peace be unto you." Then to dispel their FEARS, He assured them that He was alive (vs. 20) "Then said Jesus unto them AGAIN, Peace be unto you:" He said this to them the second time, because He was about to tell them that He was going to send them out to a crowd of Jews (at Pentecost) of which they were then afraid. So he continued by saying, "As my Father hath sent me, even so send I you" (v. 21). This was spoken in view of Pentecost because we know they did not go out until Pentecost. To assure them that they were not going out AFRAID and LIFELESS as they were then, "He BREATHED [a symbol of LIFE and POWER which they received at Pentecost] on them, and saith unto them, Receive ye the Holy Ghost" (v. 22). After thus assuring them that this power would come FROM HIM (Acts 2:33), He spake again in verse 23 of their going out at Pentecost. It is clear from this passage that the Holy Spirit was to equip the disciples to face the world, without "FEAR" with the gospel message. This they did not do until Pentecost. The statement, "Receive ye the Holy Ghost:" is in connection with the statement, "Even so send I you." This commission and the power to perform it must be viewed together. If they received the Holy Spirit at that time, they should have started performing their commission at that time. But he fact that they did not go out at that time shows that they were waiting for the Holy Spirit at Pentecost to empower them without "FEAR."[44]

Let's look at this passage again. *John 20:18-22 - Mary Magdalene came and told the disciples that she had seen the Lord, and that he had spoken these things unto her. 18 Then the same day at evening, being the first day of the week, when the doors were shut where the disciples were assembled for fear of the Jews, came Jesus and stood in the midst, and saith unto them, Peace be unto you. 20 And when he had so said, he shewed unto them his hands and his side. Then were the disciples glad, when they saw the Lord. 21 Then said Jesus to them again, Peace be unto you: as my Father hath sent me, even so send I you. 22 And when he had said this, he breathed on them, and saith unto them, Receive ye the Holy Ghost.* Cate is right. They were in this room for fear. I don't know if I ever have been so afraid that I have locked myself in some place. It doesn't seem as though they believed the message of Mary seeing that they were still locked in this same room. It also seems as though the disciples were still in unbelief, and it probably didn't help that Jesus instantly appeared in the midst of them. He said that peace was available to them, and that he wanted to give it to them. Jesus is amazing. After they had walked with him for three and half years, they deserted him at the time that he needed them the most, and the first thing he said to them was, "Peace be unto you." Jesus is so patient, and so gracious. I am so thankful for that! Then he showed them his hands and his feet. They saw the scars that were in his hands and feet, and the disciples were glad after they saw his scars. They weren't glad that he had been crucified, but because he had been resurrected. Then Jesus tells them something very interesting. *John 20:21 - Then said Jesus to them again, Peace be unto you: as my Father hath sent me, even so send I you.* Jesus said peace was available to them. Then he said "as my Father hath sent me, even so send I you." John the Baptist spoke of Jesus in *John 3:34 - For he whom God hath sent speaketh the words of God: for God giveth not the Spirit by measure unto him.* The Greek word for "measure" in this verse is μέτρον métron; a measure ("metre"), literally or figuratively; by implication, a limited portion (degree):—measure. Apparently there are varying degrees, or portions of the Spirit of God. Paul said in *Philippians 1:19 - For I know that this shall turn to my salvation through your prayer, and the supply of the Spirit of Jesus Christ.* The one that God sends speaks his word. Again, John was speaking of Jesus. Jesus certainly spoke the words of God. God doesn't give the Spirit by measure to the one that he sends. This means that God doesn't give a limited amount of the Spirit of God to those that he sends. When did he give the Spirit to Jesus? *Matthew*

3:16-17 - And Jesus, when he was baptized, went up straightway out of the water: and, lo, the heavens were opened unto him, and he saw the Spirit of God descending like a dove, and lighting upon him: 17 and lo a voice from heaven, saying, This is my beloved Son, in whom I am well pleased. This is when Jesus was baptized by John the Baptist. Right after he was baptized the Spirit of God descended upon him like a dove. Then God spoke from heaven saying, "This is my beloved Son, in whom I am well pleased." It is interesting even the holy Son of God was given the Spirit by the Father. Notice that the Spirit lighted "upon" him, not in him. Which means that Jesus was empowered by the Spirit to fulfill the Father's will. How do I know? The Bible says in *Acts 1:1-2 - The former treatise have I made, O Theophilus, of all that Jesus began both to do and teach, 2 until the day in which he was taken up, after that he through the Holy Ghost had given commandments unto the apostles whom he had chosen:* The Greek words for "Holy Ghost" is πνεύματος ἁγίου. The word specifically for "Ghost" is πνεύματος, and it is an ablative of agency meaning that the Holy Ghost was the agent through which Jesus operated. He relied on the power of the Holy Ghost to give us an example to follow. For he said himself in *Luke 6:40 - The disciple is not above his master: but every one that is perfect shall be as his master.* John said that the one whom God sends, speaks the words of God, and is not given the Spirit by measure. Jesus told his disciples, "As my Father hath sent me, even so send I you." Jesus sent his disciples the same way that God sent him. God did not send him with a limited amount of the Spirit. This means that Jesus wasn't going to send his disciples with a limited amount of the Spirit. Is it that hard to believe that God sent his Spirit to them twice? Cate writes, "So he continued by saying, "As my Father hath sent me, even so send I you" (v. 21). This was spoken in view of Pentecost because we know they did not go out until Pentecost." [45] As we have already seen that God doesn't give a limited degree, measure, or portion of the Holy Spirit to whom he sends. This is why they were not sent forth to preach right away. They only had received a limited amount of the Spirit of God in *John 20:22*, so they were waiting until the Spirit came upon them so they could receive power. *Acts 1:8 - But ye shall receive power, after that the Holy Ghost is come upon you: and ye shall be witnesses unto me both in Jerusalem, and in all Judæa, and in Samaria, and unto the uttermost part of the earth.* They would receive "power after the Holy Ghost was come upon them." They would receive the power they needed to fulfill the command of Jesus to go and preach the gospel to every creature, but it was only after the Holy Ghost "was come upon" them. They would not receive power before the Holy Spirit "was come upon" them. It was only after this event that they would receive this power. Cate writes, "To assure them that they were not going out AFRAID and LIFELESS as they were then, "He BREATHED [a symbol of LIFE and POWER which they received at Pentecost] on them, and saith unto them, Receive ye the Holy Ghost" (v. 22)."[46] This was not a symbol of life and power. This was actually a source of life and power. How do I know? The Greek word for "he breathed on" is ἐμφυσάω emphysáō, em-foo-sah'-o and φυσάω physáō (to puff) to blow at or on:—breathe on. The Septuagint is the Greek translation of the Hebrew Old Testament. This is the same Greek word that is found in the Septuagint in an interesting verse. *Genesis 2:7 - And the Lord God formed man of the dust of the ground, and breathed into his nostrils the breath of life; and man became a living soul.* The Hebrew word for "and breathed" is נָפַח nâphach, naw-fakh'; a primitive root; to puff, in various applications (literally, to inflate, blow hard, scatter, kindle, expire; figuratively, to disesteem):—blow, breath, give up, cause to lose (life), seething, snuff. Guess what Greek word was used to translate this Hebrew word into the Septuagint. That's right it is ἐμφυσάω. Let's take another look at *Genesis 2:7 - And the Lord God formed man of the dust of the ground, and breathed into his nostrils the breath of life; and man became a living soul.* Again the Hebrew word for "and breathed" is נָפַח nâphach. This is the same Hebrew word for "and breathe" used in *Ezekiel 37:9 - Then said he unto me, Prophesy unto the wind, prophesy, son of man, and say to the wind, Thus saith the Lord God; Come from the four winds, O breath, and breathe upon these slain, that they may live.* Ezekiel was to prophesy to the wind. This Hebrew word for "wind" is רוּחַ rûwach, roo'-akh; from H7306; wind; by resemblance breath, i.e. a sensible (or even violent) exhalation; figuratively, life, anger, unsubstantiality; by extension, a region of the sky; by resemblance spirit, but only of a rational being (including its expression and functions):—air, anger, blast, breath, × cool, courage, mind, × quarter, × side, spirit(-ual), tempest, × vain, (whirl-)wind(-y). It is the same word translated as "and the Spirit" in *Genesis 1:2 - And the earth was without form, and void; and darkness was upon the face of the deep. And the Spirit of God moved upon the face of the waters.* In other words, Ezekiel was to prophesy to the Spirit to breathe on these slain soldiers that they would "live". The Hebrew word for "the breath" in *Genesis 2:7 - And the Lord God formed man of the dust of the ground, and breathed into his nostrils the breath of life; and man became a living soul* is נְשָׁמָה nᵉshâmâh, nesh-aw-maw'; a puff, i.e. wind, angry or vital breath, divine inspiration, intellect. or (concretely) an animal:—blast, (that) breath(-eth), inspiration, soul, spirit. It is the same Hebrew word used for "and the breath" in *Job 33:4 - The Spirit of God hath made me, and the breath of the Almighty hath given me life.* This means that when the Spirit of God breathes upon someone dead, they come to life, and that His breathe gives life. What does all of this mean? Because the Hebrew word for "and breathed" was translated as ἐμφυσάω, it means that it refers to the same kind of action that happened in *Genesis 2:7*. When Jesus breathed on his disciples, it was the same kind of action that happened when God breathed into Adam's nostrils the breath of life. It is the same kind of action that happened when the Spirit breathed on the dry bones to become an army, with the breathe that gives life. What's going on in this passage? Jesus is breathing on his disciples the breath of life, they are receiving the Spirit, and they are becoming brand new creations. *II Corinthians 5:17 - Therefore if any man be in Christ, he is a new creature: old things are passed away; behold, all things are become new.* The Greek word for "creature" is κτίσις ktísis, ktis'-is; original formation (properly, the act; by implication, the thing, literally or figuratively):—building, creation, creature, ordinance. If any man is in Christ, then he is a new creation. When do we become a new creation? The prerequisite to being a new creation is that we are in Christ. Anyone outside of Christ is not a new creation. Only those in Christ are new creations. How and when do we get placed "in Christ"? *I Corinthians 12:12-13 - For as the body is one, and hath many members, and all the members of that one body, being many, are one body: so also is Christ. 13 For by one Spirit are we all baptized into one body, whether we be Jews or Gentiles, whether we be bond or free; and have been all made to drink into one Spirit.* It is by one Holy Spirit that we are baptized into the body of Christ. This is how we end up "in Christ". When this happens we are "made to drink into one Spirit". In other words, we receive the Spirit when we are baptized into Christ. This means that when Jesus breathed on the disciples they became new creatures in Christ. At that point they were baptized into the body of Christ, and received the Spirit in the process. This means two things. It means that this is truly when the church began. Some might argue saying that only ten of the disciples were in this room. All of Christ's followers were not present. Neither were they in *Acts 2*. The Bible says in *Acts 1:15 - And in those days Peter stood up in the midst of the disciples, and said, (the number of names together were about an hundred and twenty,)* There were 120 disciples of the Lord in the upper room. Paul writes in *I Corinthians 15:6 - after that, he was seen of above five hundred brethren at once; of whom the greater part remain unto this present, but some are fallen asleep.* The context tells us of the witnesses who saw Jesus after his resurrection. We know this to be before Pentecost because they witnessed him after his resurrection. The only time that they could've done that was before his ascension. None of these witnesses could've witnessed Him after Paul who witnessed him on the road to Damascus. There were over five hundred "brethren" that saw Jesus after his resurrection. All of Christ's followers were not in the upper room. They were acting like a church. They were acting as a unit in one body. They made decisions. They prayed. They shared some Scriptures, they were acting like the way that the church should act. This also means that when Jesus breathed on his disciples they truly did receive the Spirit. He wanted to give his disciples peace. They were full of fear sitting behind closed doors, but when Jesus appeared to them, he said, "peace be unto you". *Galatians 5:22-23 - But the fruit of the Spirit is love, joy, peace, longsuffering, gentleness, goodness, faith, 23 meekness, temperance: against such there is no law.* The fruit of the Spirit is love, joy, "peace". When they received the Spirit, they also received real peace. Jesus did more for them, than just comfort them. He gave them real peace. Peace only comes from God through agency of the Holy Spirit.

Many people deny that the disciples actually received the Spirit in *John 20:22* by citing *John 7:37-39 - In the last day, that great day of the feast, Jesus stood and cried, saying, If any man thirst, let him come unto me, and drink. 38 He that believeth on me, as the scripture hath said, out of his belly shall flow rivers of living water. 39 (But this spake he of the Spirit, which they that believe on him should receive: for the Holy Ghost was not yet given; because that Jesus was not yet glorified.)* It is particularly quoted that "the Holy Ghost was not yet given; because that Jesus was not yet glorified." It is said that Jesus was not glorified until he ascended to heaven, after the resurrection, and after he breathed on his disciples in *John 20:21-21.* At which time they usually quote *Acts 2:33 - Therefore being by the right hand of God exalted, and having received of the Father the promise of the Holy Ghost, he hath shed forth this, which ye now see and hear.* First of all, when the Bible says "the Holy Ghost was not yet given; because that Jesus was not yet glorified" it shows us that there is a connection between the glorification of Jesus, and the Spirit being given. Many have said that this connection is the fact the Jesus needed to be glorified before the Spirit could be given. I agree. But, why? The truth is that the glorification of Jesus is not tied to his ascension, it is tied to his suffering. This is why the Bible says in *Philippians 2:5-11 - Let this mind be in you, which was also in Christ Jesus: 6 who, being in the form of God, thought it not robbery to be equal with God: 7 but made himself of no reputation, and took upon him the form of a servant, and was made in the likeness of men: 8 and being found in fashion as a man, he humbled himself, and became obedient unto death, even the death of the cross. 9 Wherefore God also hath highly exalted him, and given him a name which is above every name: 10 that at the name of Jesus every knee should bow, of things in heaven, and things in earth, and things under the earth; 11 and that every tongue should confess that Jesus Christ is Lord, to the glory of God the Father.* In other words, God is the one who highly exalted Jesus, and he did so because of his death. In fact, it says that he gave him a name above every name, that every tongue should confess that he is Lord. Let's look at the context of *Acts 2:33-36 - Therefore being by the right hand of God exalted, and having received of the Father the promise of the Holy Ghost, he hath shed forth this, which ye now see and hear. 34 For David is not ascended into the heavens: but he saith himself, The Lord said unto my Lord, Sit thou on my right hand, 35 until I make thy foes thy footstool. 36 Therefore let all the house of Israel know assuredly, that God hath made that same Jesus, whom ye have crucified, both Lord and Christ.* Literally three verses later, the Bible specifically says that God made Jesus "both Lord and Christ". This is the reason why Jesus told his disciples in *Matthew 28:18 - And Jesus came and spake unto them, saying, All power is given unto me in heaven and in earth.* All authority had been given him because God made him both Lord and Christ. This is why "every knee should bow, of things in heaven, and things in earth, and things under the earth; 11 and that every tongue should confess that Jesus Christ is Lord". Further proof that the glorification of Christ is tied to his death can be found in *John 12:23-24 - And Jesus answered them, saying, The hour is come, that the Son of man should be glorified. 24 Verily, verily, I say unto you, Except a corn of wheat fall into the ground and die, it abideth alone: but if it die, it bringeth forth much fruit.* Right after Jesus speaks of the hour coming that he should be glorified, he said that unless a grain of wheat falls into the ground, and "die", it remains alone. He is tying the hour of his glorification to the time of his death. This is why Jesus prayed in *John 17:1 - These words spake Jesus, and lifted up his eyes to heaven, and said, Father, the hour is come; glorify thy Son, that thy Son also may glorify thee:* Right before he was arrested, tried, beaten, mocked, and crucified, he prayed that the Father would glorify him because his hour was come. This is all confirmed by *Luke 24:25-27 - Then he said unto them, O fools, and slow of heart to believe all that the prophets have spoken: 26 ought not Christ to have suffered these things, and to enter into his glory? 27 And beginning at Moses and all the prophets, he expounded unto them in all the scriptures the things concerning himself.* On the road to Emmaus, he explained to these two disciples all things concerning himself out of the law, the prophets, and all the Scriptures that he should suffer, and "enter into his glory", not after he ascended, but after he suffered. The Holy Spirit couldn't be given until Jesus was glorified until Jesus suffered, bled, and died. The reason why He couldn't be given until Jesus suffered and died is actually found in a verse that cessationists use to oppose the baptism of the Spirit. The Bible says in *John 16:7 - Nevertheless I tell you the truth; It is expedient for you that I go away: for if I go not away, the Comforter will not come unto you; but if I depart, I will send him unto you.* It is said that Jesus was referring to his ascension when he said that he would "go away" which was after he breathed on them in *John 20:22*. Therefore, the disciples did not receive the Spirit then, but only simply received a promise that they would receive the Spirit. I would argue with that reasoning by stating that Jesus did truly "go away" before then. Look at the context, this is right before he died. In a matter of hours, Jesus would be arrested, tried, and unlawfully hung on the cross. He died on the cross, and was buried in the tomb of Joseph of Aramethea, and went to paradise. He truly did go away, and came back to personally send the Spirit to them by breathing on them so they became new creations in Christ. How do I know this to be the correct interpretation? I know because of the context. Right after he said this, Jesus explains in *John 16:8-11 - And when he is come, he will reprove the world of sin, and of righteousness, and of judgment: 9 of sin, because they believe not on me; 10 of righteousness, because I go to my Father, and ye see me no more; 11 of judgment, because the prince of this world is judged.* The Holy Spirit convicts the world of sin of righteousness, and of judgement. He convicts the world of their sin so that they repent from it, turn to God, and believe in Christ's death on the cross. He convicts those who do that they have been made righteous by believing in Christ's death on the cross, and he convicts those of judgement who remain in the world, refuse to come Him, and believe in his death on the cross because if the prince of this world is judged, then they will face judgement as well. All three of these things are connected to his death on the cross. The Holy Spirit couldn't come, and convict the world of these three things because Jesus had to die on the cross for him to fulfill his work before the Holy Spirit could begin his work of convicting the world of sin, righteousness, and judgement.

Some might argue by saying that Jesus also said in *John 16:5 - But now I go my way to him that sent me; and none of you asketh me, Whither goest thou?* The Bible does say that Jesus said that he would go his "way to him that sent" him, therefore Christ could've been referring to his ascension. He could've, but that does not necessarily mean that he did. I personally believe that He ascended to heaven during the three days after he died. Why? The Bible says in *Ephesians 4:8-10 - Wherefore he saith, When he ascended up on high, he led captivity captive, and gave gifts unto men. 9 (Now that he ascended, what is it but that he also descended first into the lower parts of the earth? 10 He that descended is the same also that ascended up far above all heavens, that he might fill all things.)* Before we understand this passage, it would be helpful to look at *Luke 16:19-23 - There was a certain rich man, which was clothed in purple and fine linen, and fared sumptuously every day: 20 and there was a certain beggar named Lazarus, which was laid at his gate, full of sores, 21 and desiring to be fed with the crumbs which fell from the rich man's table: moreover the dogs came and licked his sores. 22 And it came to pass, that the beggar died, and was carried by the angels into Abraham's bosom: the rich man also died, and was buried; 23 and in hell he lift up his eyes, being in torments, and seeth Abraham afar off, and Lazarus in his bosom.* The rich man was not saved, and Lazarus obviously was because he was "carried by angels into Abraham's bosom". We know that this was the place where the Old Testament saints resided because Abraham himself was there. It seems as though Abraham's bosom was in a place that also contained hell. The rich man could see Abraham's bosom, and could see Abraham in it. Not to mention that Abraham said himself in *Luke 16:26 - And beside all this, between us and you there is a great gulf fixed: so that they which would pass from hence to you cannot; neither can they pass to us, that would come from thence.* There was a gulf fixed between Abraham, and the rich man that no one could pass over. Abraham's bosom is also referred to as paradise in the Scriptures. How do we know? The Bible tells us in *Luke 23:43 - And Jesus said unto him, Verily I say unto thee, To day shalt thou be with me in paradise.* Jesus referred to the place that the Old Testament saints departed to as paradise, which means that paradise is the same place as Abraham's bosom. Paul wrote in *II Corinthians 12:2-3 - I knew a man in Christ above fourteen years ago, (whether in the body, I cannot tell; or whether out of the body, I cannot tell: God knoweth;) such an one caught up to the third heaven. 3 And I knew such a man, (whether in the body, or out of the body, I cannot tell: God knoweth;) 4 how that he was caught up into paradise, and heard unspeakable words, which it is not lawful for a man to utter.* Paul was caught up to heaven, and he heard unspeakable words which were not lawful for him to utter. He also said that he was caught up into paradise. I don't know what happened, but before Christ died, paradise was in the same place as hell, but after his death it seems as though it was in the same place as heaven. Let's look again at *Ephesians 4:8-10 - Wherefore he saith, When he ascended up on high, he led captivity captive, and gave gifts unto men. 9 (Now that he ascended, what is it but that he also descended first into the lower parts of the earth? 10 He that descended is the same also that ascended up far above all heavens, that he might fill all things.)* The Greek word translated as "led captivity" is αἰχμαλωτεύω aichmalōteúō, aheekh-mal-o-tew'-o; to capture :—lead captive. Whereas the Greek word for "captive" is αἰχμαλωσία aichmalōsía, aheekh-mal-o-see'-ah; captivity:—captivity. I believe that Paul is saying that Jesus led captivity itself captive. I believe this captivity is a spiritual slavery, which includes slavery to sin, and to the devil. Though spiritual slavery doesn't always cause emotional issues such as anxiety, depression, and insecurities, many times it does. Praise God that he took it captive, and that we can find freedom from those things through him! This passage is actually quoted from *Psalm 68:17-18 - The chariots of God are twenty thousand, even thousands of angels: the Lord is among them, as in Sinai, in the holy place. 18 Thou hast ascended on high, thou hast led captivity captive: thou hast received gifts for men; yea, for the rebellious also, that the Lord God might dwell among them.* This passage obvious refers to battle seeing that it mentions "the chariots of God". Jesus conquered the devil with his death on the cross. After which time he ascended on high, and led captivity captive. The Hebrew word for "thou has led captivity" is שְׁבִי sh^{e}bîy, sheb-ee'; exiled; captured; as noun, exile (abstractly or concretely and collectively); by extension, booty:—captive(-ity), prisoners, × take away, that was taken. This means that he lead the exiled, the captured, the prisoners captive. He led those who were exiled from the presence of God into his very presence when he ascended on high. We know this ascension is a different ascension than his ascension after his resurrection because he did not lead captivity captive at his ascension after his resurrection. These exiles seem to be the Old Testament saints. Instead of simply leading them to heaven, it seems as though he took all of paradise to heaven with them. I personally believe that it was at this time that Jesus entered into heaven and sprinkled his blood on the mercy seat for the Bible says in *Hebrews 9:12 - neither by the blood of goats and calves, but by his own blood he entered in once into the holy place, having obtained eternal redemption for us.* It seems as though this explanation fits well with the context of *John 16:5-11 - But now I go my way to him that sent me; and none of you asketh me, Whither goest thou? 6 But because I have said these things unto you, sorrow hath filled your heart. 7 Nevertheless I tell you the truth; It is expedient for you that I go away: for if I go not away, the Comforter will not come unto you; but if I depart, I will send him unto you. 8 And when he is come, he will reprove the world of sin, and of righteousness, and of judgment: 9 of sin, because they believe not on me; 10 of righteousness, because I go to my Father, and ye see me no more; 11 of judgment, because the prince of this world is judged.* Jesus said that he would go away to "him who sent" him to lead the Old Testament saints into the very presence of God, and to sprinkle his blood on the mercy seat in heaven, then he would return to the earth to personally send the Holy Spirit to them when he breathed on them the breath of life, and they became new creations in Christ. At which time the Holy Spirit would be able to convict the world of sin, of righteousness, and of judgement, after God had glorified Jesus on the cross.

In other words, *Acts 2:33* does not prove that Jesus wasn't glorified until he ascended to heaven. It just proves that he had been glorified already when he died on the cross, and he simply entered his glory after his sufferings when he rose from the dead. *John 16:5* does not necessarily prove that Jesus was referring to his ascension. Neither does *John 16:7*, nor *John 7:39*, prove that the disciples couldn't have received the Spirit in *John 20:21-22*. In fact, these passages point to the fact that they did receive the Spirit, when Jesus breathed on them the breath of life so that they could be used by him to convict the world of sin, of righteousness, and of judgement through the words which they spoke.

Cate writes,

> After thus assuring them that this power would come FROM HIM (Acts 2:33), He spake again in verse 23 of their going out at Pentecost. It is clear from this passage that the Holy Spirit was to equip the disciples to face the world, without "FEAR" with the gospel message. This they did not do until Pentecost. The statement, "Receive ye the Holy Ghost:" is in connection with the statement, "Even so send I you." This commission and the power to perform it must be viewed together. If they received the Holy Spirit at that time, they should have started performing their commission at that time. But the fact that they did not go out at that time shows that they were waiting for the Holy Spirit at Pentecost to empower them without "FEAR."[47]

As we have already seen this. The power would come from Him after they received the Holy Ghost "upon" them, not in them. *Acts 1:8 - But ye shall receive power, after that the Holy Ghost is come upon you: and ye shall be witnesses unto me both in Jerusalem, and in all Judæa, and in Samaria, and unto the uttermost part of the earth.* We have already seen the connection between the statements, "Receive ye the Holy Ghost" with the statement, "Even so send I you". The connection is that God doesn't give his Spirit by measure to those he sends. He doesn't give them a limited amount. The reason why they were waiting is exactly what Jesus told them in *Luke 24:49 - And, behold, I send the promise of my Father upon you: but tarry ye in the city of Jerusalem, until ye be endued with power from on high.* They were waiting in Jerusalem until they were endued with "power" from on high. They would receive this "power" after that the Holy Ghost would come "upon" them. The Bible tells us in *Luke 4:17-19 - And there was delivered unto him the book of the prophet Esaias. And when he had opened the book, he found the place where it was written, 18 The Spirit of the Lord is upon me, because he hath anointed me to preach the gospel to the poor; he hath sent me to heal the brokenhearted, to preach deliverance to the captives, and recovering of sight to the blind, to set at liberty them that are bruised, 19 to preach the acceptable year of the Lord. 20 And he closed the book, and he gave it again to the minister, and sat down. And the eyes of all them that were in the synagogue were fastened on him.* The Greek word for "he hath sent" is ἀποστέλλω apostéllō, ap-os-tel'-lo; set apart, i.e. (by implication) to send out (properly, on a mission) literally or figuratively:—put in, send (away, forth, out), set (at liberty). It is the same word for "hath sent" in *John 20:21 - Then said Jesus to them again, Peace be unto you: as my Father hath sent me, even so send I you.* It is also the same Greek for "sent" in *John 3:17 - For God sent not his Son into the world to condemn the world; but that the world through him might be saved.* The question is when did the Father send Jesus? He sent him, when he came into this world. He lived for about thirty years as a man before his Father had actually commissioned him. It wasn't until the Spirit of God rested upon him that he was commissioned. After he rose from the dead he told his disciples as my Father hath sent me so I send you. If Jesus was sent by the Father into the world, but had to wait for about thirty years until the Spirit of God rested "upon" him before he was actually commissioned by Him, then it is safe to say that the disciples could wait a few days for the Holy Ghost to come "upon" them to empower them for ministry.

When the Holy Ghost did come "upon" them, they were partaking of the prophecy of Joel. He did not say that the prophecy was fulfilled, but the disciples did partake of it. *Acts 2:16-21- But this is that which was spoken by the prophet Joel; 17 And it shall come to pass in the last days, saith God, I will pour out of my Spirit upon all flesh: and your sons and your daughters shall prophesy, and your young men shall see visions, and your old men shall dream dreams: 18 and on my servants and on my handmaidens I will pour out in those days of my Spirit; and they shall prophesy: 19 and I will shew wonders in heaven above, and signs in the earth beneath; blood, and fire, and vapour of smoke: 20 the sun shall be turned into darkness, and the moon into blood, before that great and notable day of the Lord come: 21 and it shall come to pass, that whosoever shall call on the name of the Lord shall be saved.* Some people say that this was written to the Jews, and that it was for the Jews. I would say that is true. It is written to the Jews and for the Jews. There is a very easy answer to this objection. It is found in *Romans 11:17 - And if some of the branches be broken off, and thou, being a wild olive tree, wert graffed in among them, and with them partakest of the root and fatness of the olive tree.* This is because Israel was the branch that was broken off from the olive tree, and the church has been graft into their place enjoying the blessings and service of God that Israel would have received. There is still a future fulfillment when Jesus sets up his kingdom, and establishes His New Covenant with Israel. Yet, even that future fulfillment of this prophecy still does speak of the baptism of the Holy Spirit. The Spirit is being poured out "upon" all flesh. Notice the results of the pouring out of the Spirit. God's people would dream dreams, they would see visions, and they would prophesy. These are all to be used in service for God emphasizing the fact that the Spirit is poured out upon His people to empower them to serve Him. In fact, the Bible specifically says that He would pour out his Spirit upon His "servants, and His handmaidens." This proves that we receive the Spirit again after we are born again to empower us for service. Something else that should be noted is that all of these things were supposed to happen "before that great and notable day of the Lord come". The church is privileged to be able to partake of the pouring out of the Spirit upon them. The church still can partake of the baptism of the Spirit mentioned in this prophecy because it is still "before the great and notable day of the Lord". Seeing that this prophecy was referring to the same event that Jesus describes as the "baptism of the Spirit" in *Acts 1:5 - For John truly baptized with water; but ye shall be baptized with the Holy Ghost not many days hence*, the Jews will also be baptized in the Spirit when he comes back for them. This is evidenced by the fact that he said that he will "pour out" "of my Spirit" "on my servants and on my handmaidens". He will pour out his spirit upon them when they repent and turn to him at the end of the tribulation. At that time they will be baptized in the Holy Ghost, and fire to purge them of the things which they couldn't repent of such as strongholds as John said that they would be in *Matthew 3:11-12 - I indeed baptize you with water unto repentance: but he that cometh after me is mightier than I, whose shoes I am not worthy to bear: he shall baptize you with the Holy Ghost, and with fire: 12 whose fan is in his hand, and he will throughly purge his floor, and gather his wheat into the garner; but he will burn up the chaff with unquenchable fire.* We know that the Jews will be baptized in both the Spirit and fire to purge them because the church was baptized in the Spirit and fire on the day of Pentecost, and the church was partaking of their baptism. Meaning that this is further proof that the baptism of the Spirit and of fire is the same baptism that the Jews will receive to purge them in order that they can be his servants. He will use the wheat, or the fruit of their lives to make bread. Jesus said in *Matthew 4:4 - But he answered and said, It is written, Man shall not live by bread alone, but by every word that proceedeth out of the mouth of God.* In this verse, bread is being compared to the words of God. Just as we need physical bread to live, we also need the spiritual bread of his words to live. The Greek word for "word" is ῥῆμα rhēma, hray'-mah; an utterance (individually, collectively or specially),; by implication, a matter or topic (especially of narration, command or dispute); with a negative naught whatever:—+ evil, + nothing, saying, word. It is an utterance, which refers to his spoken words which heard when he speaks. This is evidenced by the fact that they are "proceeding out of the mouth of God". In other words, when we are, or when the Jews will be baptized in fire, he is burning up the unusable parts of our lives to purge us from them. At that point, God can use the fruit of our lives, or the "wheat" to produce bread in order to speak to someone else which may very well come in the form of prophecy as he says will happen.

There are many other times in Scripture that the Bible speaks to us about people that had the empowering of the Holy Spirit when He came "upon" them. *Judges 3:8-11 - Therefore the anger of the Lord was hot against Israel, and he sold them into the hand of Chushan-rishathaim king of Mesopotamia: and the children of Israel served Chushan-rishathaim eight years. 9 And when the children of Israel cried unto the Lord, the Lord raised up a deliverer to the children of Israel, who delivered them, even Othniel the son of Kenaz, Caleb's younger brother. 10 And the Spirit of the Lord came upon him, and he judged Israel, and went out to war: and the Lord delivered Chushan-rishathaim king of Mesopotamia into his hand; and his hand prevailed against Chushan-rishathaim. 11 And the land had rest forty years. And Othniel the son of Kenaz died.* I quoted all these verses to put it in context. Othniel was one of the judges that God raised up to deliver the children of Israel from the Mesopotamians. The Spirit of the Lord came upon him to do it. Another example is Gideon. *Judges 6:34 - But the Spirit of the Lord came upon Gideon, and he blew a trumpet; and Abi-ezer was gathered after him.* Gideon was the man that God raised up to be a judge and deliver the children of Israel from the Midianites. *Judges 11:29 - Then the Spirit of the Lord came upon Jephthah, and he passed over Gilead, and Manasseh, and passed over Mizpeh of Gilead, and from Mizpeh of Gilead he passed over unto the children of Ammon.* Jephthah was another judge that the Spirit of the Lord came upon to empower him to deliver the children of Israel from the Ammonites. There are multiple times in the Scriptures that tell us that the Spirit of the Lord came upon Samson. He was definitely empowered by the Lord in a mighty way. Here's just a list of the times that this happened.

Judges 14:6 - And the Spirit of the Lord came mightily upon him, and he rent him as he would have rent a kid, and he had nothing in his hand: but he told not his father or his mother what he had done.

Judges 14:19 - And the Spirit of the Lord came upon him, and he went down to Ashkelon, and slew thirty men of them, and took their spoil, and gave change of garments unto them which expounded the riddle. And his anger was kindled, and he went up to his father's house.

Judges 15:14 - And when he came unto Lehi, the Philistines shouted against him: and the Spirit of the Lord came mightily upon him, and the cords that were upon his arms became as flax that was burnt with fire, and his bands loosed from off his hands. Why multiple times though? Well I suggest that the Spirit left multiple times and came back when he needed Him to. By the time that he was with Delilah the Bible tells us in *Judges 16:20 - And she said, The Philistines be upon thee, Samson. And he awoke out of his sleep, and said, I will go out as at other times before, and shake myself. And he wist not that the Lord was departed from him.* The Bible specifically tells us that Lord had departed from him. I believe the Lord did so because he was caught up in sin. He got so comfortable with the Lord's presence and with his sin that he didn't even know when the Lord left him. That is a very sad statement. Let that never be said about us. Another example is Saul. *I Samuel 11:6 - And the Spirit of God came upon Saul when he heard those tidings, and his anger was kindled greatly.* The Spirit came upon Saul when he first became king. He had heard of threats from Nahash the Ammonite, and He stirred up the people of Israel and won a great battle. Eventually though the Bible says that the Spirit of the Lord left Saul. I believe that this is one of the reasons why Saul committed the great sins that He did. But at one point the Spirit of God did come upon Saul empowering him. *I Samuel 16:13 - Then Samuel took the horn of oil, and anointed him in the midst of his brethren: and the Spirit of the Lord came upon David from that day forward. So Samuel rose up, and went to Ramah.* After David was anointed king, the Spirit of the Lord came upon him and empowered him and he became the best king in Israel's history. *I Samuel 19:23 - And Saul sent messengers to take David: and when they saw the company of the prophets prophesying, and Samuel standing as appointed over them, the Spirit of God was upon the messengers of Saul, and they also prophesied.* There were messengers sent from Saul to David to try to kill him. The Lord stops them by sending the Holy Spirit upon them and instead of doing the will of the enemy they did the will of God and prophesied. The Lord is so gracious. *I Chronicles 12:18 - Then the spirit came upon Amasai, who was chief of the captains, and he said, Thine are we, David, and on thy side, thou son of Jesse: peace, peace be unto thee, and peace be to thine helpers; for thy God helpeth thee. Then David received them, and made them captains of the band.* David was trying to figure out whether these men were Saul's men or if they would be loyal to him. When he asked about their loyalty, the Spirit of the Lord came upon Amasai to empower him to be David's servant. *II Chronicles 15:1 - And the Spirit of God came upon Azariah the son of Oded.* The Spirit of God came upon Azariah to empower him to speak to the king. King Asa has just won an incredible victory and was probably feeling pretty good about himself. That's when Azariah encourages Asa to continue seeking the Lord even when the victory has been won and the hardship was over. *II Chronicles 24:20 - And the Spirit of God came upon Zechariah the son of Jehoiada the priest, which stood above the people, and said unto them, Thus saith God, Why transgress ye the commandments of the Lord, that ye cannot prosper? because ye have forsaken the Lord, he hath also forsaken you.* Zechariah cried out among the people to repent and seek the Lord. Anyone that is crying that to a people caught up in sin needs the empowering of the Lord. *Isaiah 61:1 - The Spirit of the Lord God is upon me; because the Lord hath anointed me to preach good tidings unto the meek; he hath sent me to bind up the brokenhearted, to proclaim liberty to the captives, and the opening of the prison to them that are bound; to proclaim the acceptable year of the Lord, and the day of vengeance of our God; to comfort all that mourn; 3 to appoint unto them that mourn in Zion, to give unto them beauty for ashes, the oil of joy for mourning, the garment of praise for the spirit of heaviness; that they might be called trees of righteousness, the planting of the Lord, that he might be glorified.* This is the mission statement of the Lord Jesus Christ. Jesus quotes all of verse 1, and part of verse 2 when he is first starting his ministry in *Luke 4:18-19 - And Jesus returned in the power of the Spirit into Galilee: and there went out a fame of him through all the region round about. 15 And he taught in their synagogues, being glorified of all. 16 And he came to Nazareth, where he had been brought up: and, as his custom was, he went into the synagogue on the sabbath day, and stood up for to read. 17 And there was delivered unto him the book of the prophet Esaias. And when he had opened the book, he found the place where it was written, 18 The Spirit of the Lord is upon me, because he hath anointed me to preach the gospel to the poor; he hath sent me to heal the brokenhearted, to preach deliverance to the captives, and recovering of sight to the blind, to set at liberty them that are bruised, 19 to preach the acceptable year of the Lord.* I quoted verses 14-17 to put it in context.

Ezekiel 11:5 - And the Spirit of the Lord fell upon me, and said unto me, Speak; Thus saith the Lord; Thus have ye said, O house of Israel: for I know the things that come into your mind, every one of them. This is Ezekiel the prophet. The Spirit of the Lord "fell" from heaven upon him so that he would be empowered to speak the word of the Lord. *Matthew 3:16 - And Jesus, when he was baptized, went up straightway out of the water: and, lo, the heavens were opened unto him, and he saw the Spirit of God descending like a dove, and lighting upon him.* This is the Lord Jesus Christ. Even the Lord Jesus was baptized in the Spirit when at his baptism. Shortly after this he started his public ministry. If he was baptized in the Spirit, how much more should we?

This is not an exhaustive list of all the times that the Holy Spirit came upon individuals. But I just quoted the references from the Old Testament all the way through to the New Testament of how the Spirit of the Lord came upon an individual and empowered them for ministry, i.e. the baptism of the Holy Ghost. Why would it be any different in *Acts 1:8 - But ye shall receive power, after that the Holy Ghost is come upon you: and ye shall be witnesses unto me both in Jerusalem, and in all Judæa, and in Samaria, and unto the uttermost part of the earth?*

There is a teaching among some of the opponents of the Charismatic movement that the Old Testament saints had the Spirit upon them in the Old Testament, but we have the Spirit in us in the New Testament. If that is true, then why was Bezaleel filled with the Spirit? *Exodus 35:30-31 - And Moses said unto the children of Israel, See, the Lord hath called by name Bezaleel the son of Uri, the son of Hur, of the tribe of Judah; 31 and he hath filled him with the spirit of God, in wisdom, in understanding, and in knowledge, and in all manner of workmanship.* If the Old Testament saints only had the Spirit upon them, and not in them, then why does the Bible tell us this in *1 Peter 1:9-11 - receiving the end of your faith, even the salvation of your souls. 10 Of which salvation the prophets have enquired and searched diligently, who prophesied of the grace that should come unto you: 11 searching what, or what manner of time the Spirit of Christ which was in them did signify, when it testified beforehand the sufferings of Christ, and the glory that should follow.* The Old Testament prophets prophesied of the grace that should come to us through salvation, and so they diligently enquired of the Lord about it. Why? Because the

Spirit of Christ was inside of them testifying to them about it. To say that the Old Testament saints didn't have the Holy Spirit inside of them is at best, ignorance of what the Scripture teaches, and at worst willful unbelief in what they teach. In the same light, the Bible says in *Acts 1:8 - But ye shall receive power, after that the Holy Ghost is come upon you: and ye shall be witnesses unto me both in Jerusalem, and in all Judæa, and in Samaria, and unto the uttermost part of the earth.* Jesus said that the Holy Spirit would come "upon" them so that they would receive power to be his witnesses. This is just like what happened in the Old Testament. To say that believers today should only have the Holy Spirit dwelling within them is tantamount to saying that believers in the Old Testament only had the Holy Spirit resting upon them. Both of these teachings are errors that should be addressed.

Similarly, I have heard that we receive all of the Holy Spirit that we ever will receive when we are born again. Soon after that comment is made, another is said. It is said that we don't need more of the Holy Spirit, the Holy Spirit needs more of us. I understand that the Holy Spirit needs more of us, but that doesn't need that we don't need more of Him. To say that we receive all of the Holy Spirit that we ever will when we are born again is also in contradiction to the Scriptures. As we have already seen, the Bible says in *John 3:34 - For he whom God hath sent speaketh the words of God: for God giveth not the Spirit by measure unto him.* The Greek word for "measure" in this verse is μέτρον métron; a measure ("metre"), literally or figuratively; by implication, a limited portion (degree):—measure. Apparently there are varying degrees, or portions of the Spirit of God. Paul said in *Philippians 1:19 - For I know that this shall turn to my salvation through your prayer, and the supply of the Spirit of Jesus Christ.* He doesn't give the Spirit as a limited portion or degree to the ones who God sends. We would all agree that God has chosen us as his church to be his witnesses in this dark world. We would all agree that the Great Commission applies to all of us, and that we need to speak the words of God in order to accomplish it. Therefore, this verse applies to all of the church today. He doesn't want to give his church a limited portion of his Spirit which means that we should not receive all of the Spirit that we will ever get when we are born again, and though we should allow the Spirit to have more of us, we also do need more of the Spirit.

John the Baptist taught about the baptism of the Spirit as well in *Matthew 3:11, Mark 1:8, Luke 3:16,* and in *John 1:33.* These are all cross-references of one another. *Mark 1:8 - I indeed have baptized you with water: but he shall baptize you with the Holy Ghost.* I think this is the one that states it the clearest. He said Jesus would baptize them with the Holy Ghost. I find it interesting that Christ references John and what he said in *Acts 1:5 - For John truly baptized with water; but ye shall be baptized with the Holy Ghost not many days hence.* It is exactly what John said, and it is exactly what happened. The phrase "with the Holy Ghost" is translated from the Greek words in all of these passages. These Greek words are ἐν πνεύματι ἁγίῳ. In particular it is said that πνεύματι is an instrumental of agency meaning which is used to say that God is using the Holy Spirit to baptize us into the body of Christ as in *I Corinthians 12:12-13 - For as the body is one, and hath many members, and all the members of that one body, being many, are one body: so also is Christ. For by one Spirit are we all baptized into one body, whether we be Jews or Gentiles, whether we be bond or free; and have been all made to drink into one Spirit.* Well it is true that the Spirit baptizes us into one body, the body of Christ. It is also true that the Greek word πνεύματι could be an instrumental of agency, but it is also that it could very well be a locative of sphere which would mean that it would be translated as "in the Holy Ghost". I believe that this is a better translation because Jesus said that they would be baptized into the Spirit in *Acts 1:5 - For John truly baptized with water; but ye shall be baptized with the Holy Ghost not many days hence.* This was already after they received the Holy Spirit in *John 20:21-22 - Then said Jesus to them again, Peace be unto you: as my Father hath sent me, even so send I you. 22 And when he had said this, he breathed on them, and saith unto them, Receive ye the Holy Ghost:* This means that John was referring to a different baptism than the baptism that Paul wrote of in *I Corinthians 12:12-13 - For as the body is one, and hath many members, and all the members of that one body, being many, are one body: so also is Christ. 13 For by one Spirit are we all baptized into one body, whether we be Jews or Gentiles, whether we be bond or free; and have been all made to drink into one Spirit.* It also means that these two different baptisms happen at two different times, not at the same time as some suggest. The Holy Spirit baptizes us into the body of Christ at the moment of salvation, but Jesus baptizes us into the Spirit to empower us to serve Him. This doesn't mean that they can't happen at the same time as in *Acts 10* with Cornelius, but when it does it is still two different baptisms happening at the same time which serve two different purposes.

Jesus taught about the baptism of the Spirit in *Luke 11:5-13 - And he said unto them, Which of you shall have a friend, and shall go unto him at midnight, and say unto him, Friend, lend me three loaves; 6 for a friend of mine in his journey is come to me, and I have nothing to set before him? 7 and he from within shall answer and say, Trouble me not: the door is now shut, and my children are with me in bed; I cannot rise and give thee. 8 I say unto you, Though he will not rise and give him, because he is his friend, yet because of his importunity he will rise and give him as many as he needeth. 9 And I say unto you, Ask, and it shall be given you; seek, and ye shall find; knock, and it shall be opened unto you. 10 For every one that asketh receiveth; and he that seeketh findeth; and to him that knocketh it shall be opened. 11 If a son shall ask bread of any of you that is a father, will he give him a stone? or if he ask a fish, will he for a fish give him a serpent? 12 Or if he shall ask an egg, will he offer him a scorpion? 13 If ye then, being evil, know how to give good gifts unto your children: how much more shall your heavenly Father give the Holy Spirit to them that ask him?* Concerning this passage Cate writes,

> In Luke 11:13 we read, "If ye then, being evil, know how to give good gifts unto your children: how much more shall your heavenly Father give the Holy Spirit to them that ask Him?" Because of this verse many think we, in this dispensation, should ask for the Holy Spirit. The disciples could have received the Holy Spirit before the day of Pentecost if they had asked for Him. But we know that they did not ask, because Christ said later, "I will pray the FATHER, and he shall give you another Comforter..." (John 14:16). From this we learn that the Holy Spirit was given in answer to the prayer of Christ, not in answer to the prayer of the disciples. Therefore, when the Holy Spirit came on the day of Pentecost, we read these words "This same Jesus hath God raised up, whereof we all are witnesses. Therefore being at the right hand of God exalted, and HAVING RECEIVED of the FATHER the PROMISE OF THE HOLY GHOST, he hath shed forth this, which ye now see and hear" (Acts 2:32, 33)[48]

As we have already seen the disciples received the Spirit in *John 20:21-22*, then He tells them to wait to receive the Spirit again in *Luke 24:49 - And, behold, I send the promise of my Father upon you: but tarry ye in the city of Jerusalem, until ye be endued with power from on high.* The "promise of my Father" refers to the Holy Spirit. The Holy Spirit would come "upon" them, and that's when they would be "endued with power from on high". That's why Jesus said in *Acts 1:8 - But ye shall receive power, after that the Holy Ghost is come upon you: and ye shall be witnesses unto me both in Jerusalem, and in all Judæa, and in Samaria, and unto the uttermost part of the earth.* They would "receive power" "after" the Holy Ghost came "upon" them. As we have seen so far, it is pretty clear that there is two different occasions when the Holy Ghost was sent. Why would be difficult to believe that we can pray to receive the Holy Spirit again? Especially when the Bible tells us in *Ephesians 1:13 - in whom ye also trusted, after that ye heard the word of truth, the gospel of your salvation: in whom also after that ye believed, ye were sealed with that holy Spirit of promise,* We were "sealed" with the Holy Spirit of promise "after" we "believed". If we are "sealed" with the Holy Spirit of promise "after" we "believed", then why would we ask to receive the Holy Spirit again? The only conclusion I have is that we received the Holy Spirit a second time when He comes "upon" believers. Cate writes,

> In Luke 11:13 we read, "If ye then, being evil, know how to give good gifts unto your children: how much more shall your heavenly Father give the Holy Spirit to them that ask Him?" Because of this verse many think we, in this dispensation, should ask for the Holy Spirit.[49]

Isn't that exactly what Jesus told us to do? I am not trying to condemn Cate, but he is literally arguing with the Scriptures. With that being said, this does not mean that we will not receive the baptism of the Spirit any other way. It does not mean that laying on of hands to receive the Spirit contradicts this verse. Laying on of hands is one way to receive the baptism of the Spirit, and prayer is another way to receive the baptism of the Spirit. This just means that we will receive the baptism of the Spirit if we pray. He continues to write,

> The disciples could have received the Holy Spirit before the day of Pentecost if they had asked for Him. But we know that they did not ask, because Christ said later, "I will pray the FATHER, and he shall give you another Comforter..." (John 14:16). From this we learn that the

Holy Spirit was given in answer to the pray of Christ, not in answer to the prayer of the disciples.[50]

First of all, they did receive the Comforter before Pentecost. The Bible says in *John 20:22 - And when he had said this, he breathed on them, and saith unto them, Receive ye the Holy Ghost.* Second, that occasion may very well have been the answer to Christ' prayer. Third, just because the disciples would pray for the Holy Spirit, doesn't mean they would receive Him before God's chosen time to send Him. We have to wait for our prayer requests to be answered. In fact the Bible says in *Ecclesiastes 3:1-11 - To every thing there is a season, and a time to every purpose under the heaven: 2 a time to be born, and a time to die; a time to plant, and a time to pluck up that which is planted; 3 a time to kill, and a time to heal; a time to break down, and a time to build up; 4 a time to weep, and a time to laugh; a time to mourn, and a time to dance 5 a time to cast stones, and a time to gather stones together; a time to embrace, and a time to refrain from embracing; 6 a time to get, and a time to lose; a time to keep, and a time to cast away; 7 a time to rend, and a time to sew; a time to keep silence, and a time to speak; 8 a time to love, and a time to hate; a time of war, and a time of peace. 9 What profit hath he that worketh in that wherein he laboureth? 10 I have seen the travail, which God hath given to the sons of men to be exercised in it. 11 He hath made every thing beautiful in his time: also he hath set the world in their heart, so that no man can find out the work that God maketh from the beginning to the end.* Solomon is writing here. He is basically saying that there is a time for everything. Then he gets to verse 11 and he writes, "He hath made every thing beautiful in His time." When it comes to the will of God, He has a time for everything. Solomon writes in verse 1, "To every thing there is a season." God has a time for everything, and He will make it beautiful in "His" time. He has a time that he sets for those things which are His will. The time that he set for the disciples to be baptized with the Holy Spirit was at Pentecost. Why did he tell them to ask for the Spirit? Let's look at the passage again. *Luke 11:9-13 - And I say unto you, Ask, and it shall be given you; seek, and ye shall find; knock, and it shall be opened unto you. 10 For every one that asketh receiveth; and he that seeketh findeth; and to him that knocketh it shall be opened. 11 If a son shall ask bread of any of you that is a father, will he give him a stone? or if he ask a fish, will he for a fish give him a serpent? 12 Or if he shall ask an egg, will he offer him a scorpion? If ye then, being evil, know how to give good gifts unto your children: how much more shall your heavenly Father give the Holy Spirit to them that ask him?* In context the disciples just asked Jesus how to pray. And basically he is saying here in a nutshell that we should persevere in prayer until we receive our prayer requests. He says that if a son asks his father for bread will he give him a stone? If he asks for a fish will he give him a serpent? If he asks for an egg will he give him a scorpion? Obviously the answer is no. If we are asking for good things the Father will give them to us. Too many times though we are asking for the stone, serpent, or scorpion, and we don't receive our prayer requests. Why? Because the Father knows what's best for us, and He loves us, and He is not going to give us something that is harmful to us. The reason why He tells us to pray for the Spirit is so that we start desiring the right things. We desire things that "stones", "serpents", and "scorpions", and we don't even know it. God withholds those things from us, and tells us to pray for the Spirit instead. He refers to the Spirit as a good gift rather than a bad gift. Bad gifts are the "stones", "serpents", and "scorpions". So he gives an example of a good gift. He gives us something to ask for, the Holy Ghost. When we ask for the Holy Ghost, it realigns our desires with His, and we are ready to receive the Spirit once again. When we are ready He will give us the Spirit in "His time". Granted, Jesus did pray to the Father that He would send the Spirit. God did grant his prayer request as seen in *John 20:22* and in *Acts 2:2-4*. If we ask for the Holy Ghost, then he will give him to us because we realign our desires to match up with His desires, and we are then in a position to receive that prayer request. The interesting thing about *Luke 11:13* is that he is not speaking of unbelievers. Unbelievers don't ask for the Spirit. Unbelievers may ask many things from God, but before He answers those requests, He wants them to ask for forgiveness from Him so that he can have a relationship with them. *Ephesians 1:13 - in whom ye also trusted, after that ye heard the word of truth, the gospel of your salvation: in whom also after that ye believed, ye were sealed with that holy Spirit of promise.* Once they ask for forgiveness and "believe" in Him for salvation, then they will be "sealed" with the "holy Spirit of promise. The context of *Luke 11:13* speaks of answers to prayer requests. Jesus is telling us that if we as his children ask for the Holy Ghost, then we will receive Him. He will come "upon" us. We know that these people he's talking to are born again individuals because he says that God is their Father in a personal way.

Cate continues to write,

Therefore, when the Holy Spirit came on the day of Pentecost, we read these words "This same Jesus hath God raised up, whereof we all are witnesses. Therefore being at the right hand of God exalted, and HAVING RECEIVED of the FATHER the PROMISE OF THE HOLY GHOST, he hath shed forth this, which ye now see and hear" (Acts 2:32, 33) [51]

The truth is that Cate is right. They did receive the Spirit on the day of Pentecost. They received Him a second time as evidenced by the fact that they first received Him in *John 20:22 - And when he had said this, he breathed on them, and saith unto them, Receive ye the Holy Ghost:* So this passage contests the idea that we get all of the Holy Spirit that we are going to get when we get saved. Jesus is telling us to ask for more of Him! Where did we get that doctrine?

There are also many places in the book of *Acts* that the believers were baptized in the Spirit. I understand that *Acts* is not a doctrinal teaching book. However, we should be getting our doctrine from things that Jesus taught, that were continued through the book of *Acts*, and that were taught in the epistles. Let's look at a very familiar example of Philip in Samaria. *Acts 8:5-17 - Then Philip went down to the city of Samaria, and preached Christ unto them. 6 And the people with one accord gave heed unto those things which Philip spake, hearing and seeing the miracles which he did. 7 For unclean spirits, crying with loud voice, came out of many that were possessed with them: and many taken with palsies, and that were lame, were healed. 8 And there was great joy in that city. 9 But there was a certain man, called Simon, which beforetime in the same city used sorcery, and bewitched the people of Samaria, giving out that himself was some great one: 10 to whom they all gave heed, from the least to the greatest, saying, This man is the great power of God. 11 And to him they had regard, because that of long time he had bewitched them with sorceries. 12 But when they believed Philip preaching the things concerning the kingdom of God, and the name of Jesus Christ, they were baptized, both men and women. 13 Then Simon himself believed also: and when he was baptized, he continued with Philip, and wondered, beholding the miracles and signs which were done. 14 Now when the apostles which were at Jerusalem heard that Samaria had received the word of God, they sent unto them Peter and John: 15 who, when they were come down, prayed for them, that they might receive the Holy Ghost: 16 (for as yet he was fallen upon none of them: only they were baptized in the name of the Lord Jesus.) 17 Then laid they their hands on them, and they received the Holy Ghost.* Concerning this passage, Cate writes,

> The Samaritans believed and were baptized, as Peter instructed the JEWS to do on the day of Pentecost; yet they did not receive the Holy Spirit. They had the WAIT until Peter and John came down from Jerusalem to pray for them and lay hands on them before they received the Holy Spirit (Acts 8:12-17). No doubt the Lord worked in this way because of the division that had been between the JEWS and the SAMARITANS for so long (John 4:9). By giving the Holy Spirit to the Samaritans through two of the LEADING Jewish apostles, there was sure to be fellowship between the Jews and Samaritans that were Christians; otherwise this might not pray to receive the Holy Spirit. He was given to them through the apostles. So, there was nothing they did to receive the Spirit but WAIT for the apostles. It is obvious that this was an unusual occasion during the transition period, and is not an example for us to follow today.[52]

The Bible does not say that we have to "wait" to be sealed with the Holy Spirit. The Bible tells us that we are sealed with the Spirit after we believe. *Ephesians 1:13 - in whom ye also trusted, after that ye heard the word of truth, the gospel of your salvation: in whom also after that ye believed, ye were sealed with that holy Spirit of promise.* The Bible tells us that we are "sealed" with the holy Spirit of promise "after that ye believed". I understand that this was still after they believed, but if this refers to the sealing of the Spirit, and if Jesus Christ acts according to His Word "yesterday, to day, and for ever", then this should be the model for how we are sealed with the Spirit in our day. But, if this is an example of the baptism of the Spirit, and if Jesus Christ acts according to His Word "yesterday and to day and for ever", then we should receive the baptism of the Spirit today as these believers did in their day. Second, the Bible tells in *Acts 8:12 - But when they believed Philip preaching the things concerning the kingdom of God, and the name of Jesus Christ, they were baptized, both men and women.* We know that they "believed" what Philip preached to them concerning the "name of Jesus Christ". Peter told us in *Acts 4:12 - Neither is there salvation in any other: for there is none other name under heaven given among men, whereby we must be saved.* It is by His name that we are saved. It is interesting that the Samaritans "believed" what Philip preached to them concerning the "name of Jesus Christ". What was happening right now? The Bible tells us in *Acts 8:16 - (for as yet he was fallen upon none of them: only they were baptized in the name of the Lord Jesus.)* The Spirit was "fallen upon" none of the Samaritans yet. They had already believed in the Lord to be saved. They were "sealed" with that holy Spirit of promise, but Luke writes that they were only "baptized in the name of the Lord Jesus." They were only baptized with water baptism. They were not baptized in the Holy Spirit. Cate writes,

> No doubt the Lord worked in this way because of the division that had been between the JEWS and the SAMARITANS for so long (John 4:9). By giving the Holy Spirit to the Samaritans through two of the LEADING Jewish apostles, there was sure to be fellowship between the Jews and Samaritans that were Christians; otherwise this might not pray to receive the Holy Spirit. He was given to them through the apostles.[53]

That's right there had been division and hatred between the Jews and Samaritans for a long period of time. The Samaritans and the Jews hated each other. The Samaritans had Assyrian blood in them. When the Assyrian empire conquered Israel, they took the Jews captive. The Jews intermarried with the Assyrians, and settled in Samaria. Their descendants were known as Samaritans. The Jews were just flat out racist as they wouldn't have any dealings with the Samaritans. As a result the Samaritans did the same. They hated the Jews and didn't have any dealing with them either. There was definitely a great rift between the two groups. Cate is certainly right that this division needed to be given attention to bring unity. There are other explanations given by cessationists for why they only received the Spirit only after Peter and John laid hands on them and prayed for them. It is said that the apostles were the ones with authority so they ought to be the ones to witness it themselves. It is also said that the Samaritans also needed to see the authority of the apostles. They had their own temple and customs of worship for hundreds of years and if they were going to receive a new kind of worship, they needed to see the authority of the apostles. I would say to this that all three of these reasons are contrary to *Ephesians 1:13 - in whom ye also trusted, after that ye heard the word of truth, the gospel of your salvation: in whom also after that ye believed, ye were sealed with that holy Spirit of promise.* They received and were sealed with the Holy Spirit "after they had believed". If this passage pictures the sealing of the Spirit, and Jesus Christ acts according to his Word "yesterday, and to day, and for ever", then this passage should be an example of how we are to be sealed with the Spirit today. But, if Jesus Christ acts according to his Word "yesterday, and to day, and for ever", and if this passage pictures the baptism of the Spirit, then we should receive the baptism of the Spirit in like manner today.

All the reasons given by cessationists for why this passage pictures the sealing of the Spirit actually makes more sense being reasons for why it pictures the baptism of the Spirit, and could even explain a fourth reason. God could have been showing the apostles that the Samaritans could not only be saved, but also that they were fit for service. He didn't see them through men's eyes, but through the eyes of love, and He wanted to use them to spread His love throughout the world. The Bible says in *Acts 2:33 - Therefore being by the right hand of God exalted, and having received of the Father the promise of the Holy Ghost, he hath shed forth this, which ye now see and hear.* The baptism of the Spirit is "seen and heard". It was such a scene when the disciples were baptized in the Spirit, that those who were passing by thought they were filled with new wine. *Acts 2:13 - Others mocking said, These men are full of new wine.* They didn't know how right they were. They were filled with new wine, but not the way that they were thinking. If the Samaritans were baptised in the Spirit, then it would have been "seen and heard". If the Samaritans needed to know of the authority of the apostles, then they would've known it because what they were experiencing was "seen and heard". If the disciples who were the authorities in the church needed to know of the acceptance of God toward the Samaritans, then they would've known it because when the Samaritans were baptised in the Spirit, it was "seen and heard". If there needed to be unity among believers, then these Samaritans would've not only been unified by being part of the church, but they would've known that they had unity in purpose as well because the baptism of the Spirit was "seen and heard". Cate writes, "So, there was nothing they did to receive the Spirit" but WAIT for the apostles. It is obvious that this was an unusual occasion during the transition period, and is not an example for us to follow today."[54]

This passage in *Acts 8:15-17* does not contradict *Luke 11:13 - If ye then, being evil, know how to give good gifts unto your children: how much more shall your heavenly Father give the Holy Spirit to them that ask him?* Jesus simply tells us that we would receive the Holy Ghost "upon" us if we pray for Him. It does not mean that He couldn't be received from the prayer of someone else. It does not say that He couldn't be received by the laying on of hands. It just simply states that we will receive the Spirit if we ask for Him. As we have already seen that there was no "transition period". *Hebrews 13:8 - Jesus Christ the same yesterday, and to day, and for ever.* Jesus Christ is the same in character "yesterday, and to day, and for ever", which means that he is faithful yesterday, and to day, and for ever". This in turn means that He acts according to his Word yesterday, and to day, and for ever". He acts according to his Word concerning the baptism of the Spirit as well as the spiritual gifts, as He did in the early church. Cessationists are forced to believe that either he doesn't, or not his Word has changed, neither of which should be believed.

Then Peter opened his mouth, and said, Of a truth I perceive that God is no respecter of persons: 35 but in every nation he that feareth him, and worketh righteousness, is accepted with him. 36 The word which God sent unto the children of Israel, preaching peace by Jesus Christ: (he is Lord of all:) 37 that word, I say, ye know, which was published throughout all Judæa, and began from Galilee, after the baptism which John preached; 38 how God anointed Jesus of Nazareth with the Holy Ghost and with power: who went about doing good, and healing all that were oppressed of the devil; for God was with him. 39 And we are witnesses of all things which he did both in the land of the Jews, and in Jerusalem; whom they slew and hanged on a tree: 40 him God raised up the third day, and shewed him openly; 41 not to all the people, but unto witnesses chosen before of God, even to us, who did eat and drink with him after he rose from the dead. 42 And he commanded us to preach unto the people, and to testify that it is he which was ordained of God to be the Judge of quick and dead. 43 To him give all the prophets witness, that through his name whosoever believeth in him shall receive remission of sins. 44 While Peter yet spake these words, the Holy Ghost fell on all them which heard the word. 45 And they of the circumcision which believed were astonished, as many as came with Peter, because that on the Gentiles also was poured out the gift of the Holy Ghost. 46 For they heard them speak with tongues, and magnify God. Then answered Peter, 47 Can any man forbid water, that these should not be baptized, which have received the Holy Ghost as well as we? 48 And he commanded them to be baptized in the name of the Lord. Then prayed they him to tarry certain days. Cate writes concerning this passage,

> In Acts 10:1-11:18, we have the record of the gospel given to the GENTILES for the first time in this dispensation. See Acts 11:13, 14 for proof that they were not saved before that time. Peter climaxed his message to them by saying, "Whosoever BELIEVETH in [Christ] shall receive remission of sins" (Acts 10:43). "While Peter YET spake these words [concerning believing to receive the remission of sins], The Holy Ghost fell all them which heard the word" (Acts 10:44). They didn't have to WAIT for anything to receive the Holy Spirit. The very moment they were saved they received the Holy Spirit. "Then answered Peter, Can any man forbid water, that these should not be baptized, which HAVE received the Holy Ghost as well as we? Then he commanded them to be baptized in the name of the Lord" (Acts 10:47, 48). Thus it is clear that GENTILES were SAVED and (without WAITING) received the Holy Spirit BEFORE they were baptized.[55]

I'm going to sum up the context. Cornelius was a devout Roman centurion. He prayed and gave alms, but he wasn't saved so God sent an angel to him in a vision to tell him to send for Peter. He does as he is told. At the same time Peter is praying and becomes very hungry. But he falls into a trance and starts having a vision about unclean things. God told him in the vision three times to kill and eat. Peter said three times that he never ate anything common or unclean all the days of his life. God's response each time was that he should never call anything common that he has cleansed. While he is pondering on this vision, the men that Cornelius sent shows up at the house he was staying at. The men tell him the purpose for why they are there and he takes some believers from Joppa with him to Cornelius' house. When he arrives, Cornelius starts worshipping Peter. Peter abruptly stopped him and told them that he was a man as well. Peter then started telling him that God told him not to call any man common. He then asks Cornelius why he had called him. Cornelius reiterates what happened to him in his vision and that the angel that told him to send for Peter. Peter's eyes were opened to how God sees the Gentiles, and he preached to them about Jesus. As he was preaching, the Holy Ghost fell "on" them. This passage actually pictures the sealing of the Spirit, and the baptism of the Spirit at the same time. Cate writes,

> They didn't have to WAIT for anything to receive the Holy Spirit. The very moment they were saved they received the Holy Spirit. "Then answered Peter, Can any man forbid water, that these should not be baptized, which HAVE received the Holy Ghost as well as we? Then he commanded them to be baptized in the name of the Lord" (Acts 10:47, 48). Thus it is clear that GENTILES were SAVED and (without WAITING) received the Holy Spirit BEFORE they were baptized.[56]

The way that we know that this is a reference to the baptism of the Spirit is from the next chapter in *Acts 11:15-18 - And as I began to speak, the Holy Ghost fell on them, as on us at the beginning. 16 Then remembered I the word of the Lord, how that he said, John indeed baptized with water; but ye shall be baptized with the Holy Ghost. 17 Forasmuch then as God gave them the like gift as he did unto us, who believed on the Lord Jesus Christ; what was I, that I could withstand God? 18 When they heard these things, they held their peace, and glorified God, saying, Then hath God also to the Gentiles granted repentance unto life.* In context, Peter was reiterating what happened in the chapter before to his Jewish brothers. The Jews did not like the Gentiles. In fact, they hated them. This incident revealed to Peter the meaning of his vision. He said in *Acts 10:28 - And he said unto them, Ye know how that it is an unlawful thing for a man that is a Jew to keep company, or come unto one of another nation; but God hath shewed me that I should not call any man common or unclean.* Gentile salvation was a controversial topic in the early church. The Jerusalem council came together to determine the correct answer to the controversial matter. It is obvious from the words of the brethren which heard Peter speak that these Gentiles truly were saved. They said "Then hath God also to the Gentiles granted repentance unto life." But, by the words of Peter we know that these Gentile believers also experienced the baptism of the Spirit. He said the Holy Ghost "fell on them, as on us at the beginning." What beginning? Some have said that this refers to the beginning of the church. It does not, it refers to the beginning of the proclamation of the gospel. *Acts 1:8 - But ye shall receive power, after that the Holy Ghost is come upon you: and ye shall be witnesses unto me both in Jerusalem, and in all Judæa, and in Samaria, and unto the uttermost part of the earth.* After the Holy

Ghost came "upon" them, they would be his "witnesses". Right after they were baptized in the Spirit, Peter stands up and preaches to all that could hear him. The result was 3,000 people were saved! Praise God! In this passage, Peter refers to the baptism of the Spirit as an event when the Holy Ghost fell "on" them. Jesus refers to it as when the Holy Ghost came "upon" them. This means that when the Holy Ghost falls "on" a believer, and when he comes "upon" a believer, they both refer to the same experience which is the baptism of the Holy Ghost. It does in this passage, as it does in *Acts 8:16-17 - (for as yet he was fallen upon none of them: only they were baptized in the name of the Lord Jesus.) 17 Then laid they their hands on them, and they received the Holy Ghost.* These Gentile believers were baptized in the Spirit, just as the Samaritans had been baptized in the Spirit, just as the 120 disciples on the day of Pentecost had been. We know for a fact that these believers were baptised in the Spirit because of what the Bible says in *Acts 11:15-16 - And as I began to speak, the Holy Ghost fell on them, as on us at the beginning. 16 Then remembered I the word of the Lord, how that he said, John indeed baptized with water; but ye shall be baptized with the Holy Ghost.* As Peter was witnessing this event, the Holy Spirit brought to mind the words of the Lord like He said he would in *John 14:26 - But the Comforter, which is the Holy Ghost, whom the Father will send in my name, he shall teach you all things, and bring all things to your remembrance, whatsoever I have said unto you.* By the influence of the Holy Spirit, Peter remembered the word of the Lord when he said "ye shall be baptised with the Holy Ghost" applying it to the scene he was witnessing right before his eyes. This text proves to us that salvation and the baptism of the Spirit can happen at the same time. Why did they happen at the same time in this particular episode? I believe that these events happened at the same time in this case because God was trying to prove to Peter that not only did he accept penitent Gentiles who turn to Him for salvation, but he also wanted to prove that he wanted to use them as his vessels for his purposes as well.

There is another passage that speaks of the baptism of the Spirit in *Acts 19:1-7 - And it came to pass, that, while Apollos was at Corinth, Paul having passed through the upper coasts came to Ephesus: and finding certain disciples, 2 he said unto them, Have ye received the Holy Ghost since ye believed? And they said unto him, We have not so much as heard whether there be any Holy Ghost. 3 And he said unto them, Unto what then were ye baptized? And they said, Unto John's baptism. 4 Then said Paul,*

John verily baptized with the baptism of repentance, saying unto the people, that they should believe on him which should come after him, that is, on Christ Jesus. 5 When they heard this, they were baptized in the name of the Lord Jesus. 6 And when Paul had laid his hands upon them, the Holy Ghost came on them; and they spake with tongues, and prophesied. 7 And all the men were about twelve. Cate writes concerning this passage,

> The twelve disciples which Apollos had made at Ephesus (Acts 18:24-19:7), after being properly instructed by Paul, were baptized correctly. Yet they had to WAIT to receive Holy Spirit until Paul laid his hands on them. (See our comments on this passage under "Why Were Tongues Given?") This case is a little different than that of the Samaritans. Peter and John prayed and laid their hands on them. But here, neither Paul nor the recipients prayed. Paul simply laid his hands on them and they received the Holy Spirit. Here again is an occasion, which is obviously not an example for us to follow today.[57]

It is interesting in this passage that Paul asked the believers at Ephesus, "Have you received the Holy Ghost since ye believed?" The words "since ye believed" are all one Greek word. That Greek word is πιστεύσαντες. This word is a participle, particularly an antecedent temporal participle. This means that the action of believing came before receiving. It could be translated as, "Have you received the Holy Ghost after ye believed?" We know that it is not a contemporaneous temporal participle because it is in the wrong tense. It would be in the present tense indicating that receiving and believing would be happening at the same time, but it isn't. It is in the aorist tense indicating that it truly is an antecedent temporal participle which means that the action of receiving the Holy Spirit comes after the action of believing. Think about the implications of this. Paul is asking them if they received the Holy Spirit after they were saved. This is quite some time after they believed. We have no indication that these disciples weren't saved. Paul literally said that they had already "believed" in *Acts 19:2*. What did they believe? Well, Paul asks them what they were baptized unto. They responded by saying that they had been baptized unto John's baptism. The Bible then says in *Acts 19:4 - Then said Paul, John verily baptized with the baptism of repentance, saying unto the people, that they should believe on him which should come after him, that is, on Christ Jesus.* Paul flat out said that they believed. What did they believe? They "believed" "on him which should come after him". In other words, these people were saved, they believed in Christ, and these disciples were disciples of Christ. They were not the disciples of John the Baptist. In fact, the Greek word for "disciples" in this verse is μαθητής mathētés, math-ay-tes'; a learner, i.e. pupil:—disciple. This word was translated "disciples" in *Matthew 11:1 - And it came to pass, when Jesus had made an end of commanding his twelve disciples, he departed thence to teach and to preach in their cities.* I quoted this verse because in this verse, the Bible clearly refers to the twelve as "disciples". Though they weren't perfect, they had already made progress in their walk with God. This word is also frequently used in the book of *Acts* to refer to the disciples of Christ. *Acts 1:15 - And in those days Peter stood up in the midst of the disciples, and said, (the number of names together were about an hundred and twenty,).* This verse records that there were one-hundred and twenty disciples in the midst of them of whom Peter is the leader. Obviously this is referring to the disciples of Christ. *Acts 6:1-2 - And in those days, when the number of the disciples was multiplied, there arose a murmuring of the Grecians against the Hebrews, because their widows were neglected in the daily ministration. 2 Then the twelve called the multitude of the disciples unto them, and said, It is not reason that we should leave the word of God, and serve tables.* Though there was contention between the Grecians, and the Jews, they were all the disciples of Christ seeing that the "twelve" are the leaders of both of them. *Acts 6:11-12 - whom they set before the apostles: and when they had prayed, they laid their hands on them. And the word of God increased; and the number of the disciples multiplied in Jerusalem greatly; and a great company of the priests were obedient to the faith.* In context, it is the first deacons that were being set before the disciples. They were given their office so that the "twelve" wouldn't have to "leave the word of God, and serve tables". When these seven deacons were ordained, it gave the "apostles" the time to focus on the "word of God", and it increased. As a result the "disciples" were multiplied greatly. Obviously this is referring to the disciples of Christ seeing that it was the apostles that were preaching the Word of God. *Acts 9:1 - And Saul, yet breathing out threatenings and slaughter against the disciples of the Lord, went unto the high priest.* This verse specifically speaks of the disciples of the Lord meaning that they were disciples of Christ. *Acts 9:10 - And there was a certain disciple at Damascus, named Ananias; and to him said the Lord in a vision, Ananias. And he said, Behold, I am here, Lord.* Ananias was the man that God used to bring Paul into the faith. He specifically responds to the Lord. Obviously he was a disciple of Christ. *Acts 9:19-20 -And when he had received meat, he was strengthened. Then was Saul certain days with the disciples which were at Damascus. 20 And straightway he preached Christ in the synagogues, that he is the Son of God.* After spending time with these disciples, Paul immediately preached that Christ was the Son of God in the synagogues. Obviously these disciples were also disciples of Christ. *Acts 9:36-38 - Now there was at Joppa a certain disciple named Tabitha, which by interpretation is called Dorcas: this woman was full of good works and almsdeeds which she did. 37 And it came to pass in those days, that she was sick, and died: whom when they had washed, they laid her in an upper chamber. 38 And forasmuch as Lydda was nigh to Joppa, and the disciples had heard that Peter was there, they sent unto him two men, desiring him that he would not delay to come to them.* This passage specifically refers to a "disciple" named Tabitha. She had passed away, and the "disciples" that were in Joppa called for Peter. If they were calling for Peter, it should be clear that these people were also disciples of Christ. *Acts 11:26-29 - and when he had found him, he brought him unto Antioch. And it came to pass, that a whole year they assembled themselves with the church, and taught much people. And the disciples were called Christians first in Antioch. 27 And in these days came prophets from Jerusalem unto Antioch. 28 And there stood up one of them named Agabus, and signified by the Spirit that there should be great dearth throughout all the world: which came to pass in the days of Claudius Cæsar. 29 Then the disciples, every man according to his ability, determined to send relief unto the brethren which dwelt in Judæa:* These disciples were called Christians which literally means a follower of Christ. When Agabus prophesied, it was these same disciples that decided to send relief to the "brethren" in Christ. It is evident that they were disciples of Christ. *Acts 13:52 -And the disciples were filled with joy, and with the Holy Ghost.* These disciples were filled with the Holy Ghost proving that they were disciples of Christ. *Acts 14:19-20 - And there came thither certain Jews from Antioch and Iconium, who persuaded the people, and, having stoned Paul, drew him out of the city, supposing he had been dead. 20 Howbeit, as the disciples stood round about him, he rose up, and came into the city: and the next day he departed with Barnabas to Derbe. 22 And when they had preached the gospel to that city, and had taught many, they returned again to Lystra, and to Iconium, and Antioch, 22 confirming the souls of the disciples, and exhorting them to continue in the faith, and that we must through much tribulation enter into the kingdom of God.* These believers were standing around Paul after he had been stoned. They cared for him, and for his well-being proving that they must've been disciples of Christ. Paul got up and went to other cities "confirming the souls of the disciples and exhorting them to continue in the faith". Obviously these people were disciples of Christ. *Acts 14:28 - And there they abode long time with the disciples.* Paul is staying with these people which means that they must've been the disciples of Christ. *Acts 15:8-10 - And God, which knoweth the hearts, bare them witness, giving them the Holy Ghost, even as he did unto us; 9 and put no difference between us and them, purifying their hearts by faith. 10 Now therefore why tempt ye God, to put a yoke upon the neck of the disciples, which neither our fathers nor we were able to bear?* In this passage James stands up for the Gentiles saying that God had given them the Holy Ghost, and purified their hearts by faith. Because of this James refers to even the Gentiles as disciples, the disciples of Christ. *Acts 16:1 - Then came he to Derbe and Lystra: and, behold, a certain disciple was there, named Timotheus, the son of a certain woman, which was a Jewess, and believed; but his father was a Greek:* This verse tells us about Timothy. He has two whole books of the Bible that bear his name. He certainly was a disciple of Christ. *Acts 18:23 - And after he had spent some time there, he departed, and went over all the country of Galatia and Phrygia in order, strengthening all the disciples.* The "he" in this verse refers to Paul. He strengthened the disciples. If Paul is strengthening the disciples, then these disciples must be the disciples of Christ. *Acts 18:24-27 - And a certain Jew named Apollos, born at Alexandria, an eloquent man, and mighty in the scriptures, came to Ephesus. 25 This man was instructed in the way of the Lord; and being fervent in the spirit, he spake and taught diligently the things of the Lord, knowing only the baptism of John. 26 And he began to speak boldly in the synagogue: whom when Aquila and Priscilla had heard, they took him unto them, and expounded unto him the way of God more perfectly. 27 And when he was disposed to pass into Achaia, the brethren wrote, exhorting the disciples to receive him: who, when he was come, helped them much which had believed through grace:* This passage tells us of Apollos. It gives us a description of him. He was "an eloquent man", "mighty in the Scriptures", "was instructed in the way of the Lord", "being fervent in spirit", and "he began to speak boldly in the synagogue". These are very good descriptions of this man. It should be obvious that this man was a born again believer, and yet, he only knew of "the baptism of John." This means that a man that only knows of the baptism of John can still be saved. He wasn't only saved but he also was recommended to the "disciples" by the "brethren". If he was recommended to the "disciples" by the "brethren", then these "disciples" must be the disciples of Christ. I didn't quote every verse that mentions "disciples" in the book of *Acts*, I only quoted the verses up to the passage at hand. But if you continue to search through the book of *Acts*, you will find that every other time this Greek word is used, it refers to the disciples of Christ. *Acts 19:1 - And it came to pass, that, while Apollos was at Corinth, Paul having passed through the upper coasts came to Ephesus: and finding certain* disciples. Literally every other time that this word μαθητής is found in the book of Acts, it is translated as "disciple" referring to a disciple of Christ. Why would this verse be any different? Paul "laid his hands upon them, the Holy Ghost came on them". Cate writes, "But here, neither Paul nor the recipients prayed. Paul simply laid his hands on them and they received the Holy Spirit. Here again is an occasion, which is obviously not an example for us to follow today."[58] As we have already this does not violate *Luke 11:13 - If ye then, being evil, know how to give good gifts unto your children: how much more shall your heavenly Father give the Holy Spirit to them that ask him?* This passage tells us of one way to receive the baptism of the Spirit. This certainly is not the only way. As we have seen in the book of *Acts* that believers received the baptism of the Spirit at the moment of salvation. They received the baptism of Spirit by laying hands and prayer, and in this case they received the baptism of the Spirit simply by the laying on of hands. The Spirit is compared to wind in *John 3:8 - The wind bloweth where it listeth, and thou hearest the sound thereof, but canst not tell whence it cometh, and whither it goeth: so is every one that is born of the Spirit*. Jesus is not saying that the one who is born of the Spirit goes where he wants to, and you can't tell where he is coming, or where he is going. That sounds more like the world who walk after the imaginations of their heart. Anything that comes to their mind, they do. A born again child of God is much different. He is driven by the Spirit who is like the wind which blows where it wants to. You can't tell where it's coming or where it's going. If the Holy Spirit is like wind, you can't control Him, so stop trying. Just let Him be God, and let Him do according to His will.

    If this is not the baptism of the Spirit, then the only answer to explain what happened in this passage is to say that this occurred during the "transition period". In that case we are not to follow the example that the Bible gives because that was done during the "transition period". As we have already seen, there was no such thing as a "transition period". *Hebrews 13:8 - Jesus Christ the same yesterday, and to day, and for ever.* Jesus Christ is the same in character "yesterday, and to day, and for ever". This means that he is faithful "yesterday, and to day, and forever", and that he will act according to his Word "yesterday, and to day, and forever". To be a cessationist, one is forced to say that he doesn't, or that his Word has changed. The Bible says in *Ephesians 1:13 - in whom ye also trusted, after that ye heard the word of truth, the gospel of your salvation: in whom also after that ye believed, ye were sealed with that holy Spirit of promise.* I understand the the Greek word for "after that ye believed" is the same Greek word translated as "since ye believed" in *Acts 19:2.* But, if this passage is picturing the sealing of the Spirit which happens when we get saved, and Jesus Christ acts according to his Word "yesterday, and to day, and for ever", then this passage should be the model for how we are sealed with the Spirit today. On the other hand, if Jesus Christ acts according to his Word "yesterday, and to day, and for ever", and this passage pictures the baptism of the Spirit, then we should receive the baptism of the Spirit in like manner today as well. Both God and these believers were just operating in accordance to the Word of God which means that we actually are to follow the example of the exemplary believers that we read about in the book of *Acts*. Though this book is not a doctrinal teaching book, but it does record when doctrine is practically carried out such as the baptism of the Spirit, and communion, and the Spiritual gifts.

Our doctrine should be found in the gospels, is practically carried out in the book of *Acts*, and is also taught in the epistles. There isn't many places in the epistles that speak of the baptism of the Spirit. In fact, I only know of one clear direct reference of it, but once is good enough for me especially given the context. It is found in *Galatians 3:5 - He therefore that ministereth to you the Spirit, and worketh miracles among you, doeth he it by the works of the law, or by the hearing of faith?* Not much is written about the baptism of the Spirit in the epistles. I believe that it was so common that it didn't need to be written about very much. As we have seen, the baptism of the Spirit is pictured four times in the book of *Acts*. Once, at Pentecost, once with the Samaritan believers, once with Cornelius, and those that are with him, and once with the twelve believers in Ephesus. Not to mention it is simple enough that there doesn't need to be a whole lot of teaching on this. It is just an act of faith as it says in this verse. As we have seen it was just an answer to a prayer, or even simpler yet, the result of laying on of hands that facilitated the baptism of the Spirit. It simply requires faith, and God will respond. The Bible says in *Mark 16:15-20 - And he said unto them, Go ye into all the world, and preach the gospel to every creature. 16 He that believeth and is baptized shall be saved; but he that believeth not shall be damned. 17 And these signs shall follow them that believe; In my name shall they cast out devils; they shall speak with new tongues; 18 they shall take up serpents; and if they drink any deadly thing, it shall not hurt them; they shall lay hands on the sick, and they shall recover. 19 So then after the Lord had spoken unto them, he was received up into heaven, and sat on the right hand of God. 20 And they went forth, and preached every where, the Lord working with them, and confirming the word with signs following. Amen.* . Jesus said that these signs would follow those who stepped out to share the gospel, and those who had the faith to believe that God would confirm his Word with miracles. The disciples did just that. They believed, and the Lord l worked with them confirming his Word with signs following. Again, the disciples experienced miracles because they believed, not because they were apostles. But, notice where the Lord was. He was seated at the right hand of God. What's this mean? It means that when we believe, heaven responds. So it was, and still is with the baptism of the Spirit, it simply requires faith to facilitate it.

    The early church had much bigger problems to concern itself with than the lack of writing on the baptism of the Spirit. A much bigger problem was false teaching. There are entire epistles devoted to fighting false doctrine. Instead of spending so much writing about the baptism of the Spirit, the authors of Scripture wrote against one of the greatest threats to the church which was false doctrine. With that being said, Paul did leave us at least one verse concerning the baptism of the Spirit. One verse that mentions it, is enough to believe in it, and practically carry it out in our churches especially when we look at the context in which it was written. Paul in the book of Galatians is confronting the Judaizers that were teaching false doctrine to the Galatians. They were basically teaching that Christ was the way of salvation, but you must keep the law as well. Paul is confronting this thought, and reinforcing that salvation solely through Christ, and that we don't have to keep the law to be saved. In context, Paul writes this in *Galatians 3:1-4 - O foolish Galatians, who hath bewitched you, that ye should not obey the truth, before whose eyes Jesus Christ hath been evidently set forth, crucified among you? 2 This only would I learn of you, Received ye the Spirit by the works of the law, or by the hearing of faith? 3 Are ye so foolish? having begun in the Spirit, are ye now made perfect by the flesh? 4 Have ye suffered so many things in vain? if it be yet in vain.* This seems to be the way that the Christian life is supposed to be lived. He asks who taught them wrong doctrine, and tricked them into keeping the law and believing that they had to keep the works of the law to be saved. He asks whether they received the Spirit by the works of the law or by faith. Some people say that this is a reference to the baptism of the Spirit right here. Maybe it is, but I believe it is actually referring to the sealing of the Spirit. Why do I say that? Because the verse right before it, Paul writes that before their eyes "Jesus Christ hath been evidently set forth, crucified among you". It seems to me like Paul is saying that they heard the gospel, and then they received the Spirit, by believing the gospel. Then Paul asks if they begun in the Spirit, were they now made perfect by the flesh? When does flesh ever want to do the will of God? We are not able to keep the commandments of God in the flesh, we need the power of the Holy Spirit to live how we ought to live. It is not by the flesh that we can please God, it is by the Spirit. He then asks them if they suffered in vain. The sobering reality is that suffering is part of the Christian life. He has to prune out the branches in us that don't bear fruit. If you would like to refer it to pruning, testing, proving, or trying it is all the same process. God tests us to grow, and purify our faith. He is bringing out what is already inside of us. The Bible says in *Malachi 3:3 - and he shall sit as a refiner and purifier of silver: and he shall purify the sons of Levi, and purge them as gold and silver, that they may offer unto the Lord an offering in righteousness.* True holiness can only be found in a relationship with him, and through suffering. That is why following a set of rules in the flesh is vain. Then Paul writes in *Galatians 3:5 - He therefore that ministereth to you the Spirit, and worketh miracles among you, doeth he it by the works of the law, or by the hearing of faith?* I think this is undoubtedly a reference to the baptism of the Spirit. Paul writes that he that "ministereth to you the Spirit" does it by faith. If this is referring to salvation, then does that mean that the person ministering the Spirit to them would have the faith for them to be saved so that he could minister the Spirit to them? How could the person who is receiving the Spirit at the moment of salvation be saved by the faith of someone else? How could that person even minister Him anyway?

Ephesians 1:13 - in whom ye also trusted, after that ye heard the word of truth, the gospel of your salvation: in whom also after that ye believed, ye were sealed with that holy Spirit of promise. We receive the Spirit and are sealed with Him after we are saved. It doesn't make any sense that *Galatians 3:5* is speaking of salvation. Not to mention that this verse also speaks about the miracles, which goes right along with baptism of the Spirit. My biggest proof that this is speaking of the baptism of the Spirit is the Greek word for "ministereth". According to Strong's it is *ἐπιχορηγέω epichorēgéō, ep-ee-khor-ayg-eh'-o; to furnish besides, i.e. fully supply, (figuratively) aid or contribute:—add, minister (nourishment, unto).* So ministereth means to furnish besides, fully supply, aid, contribute, add, and minster (nourishment unto). This verse completely destroys the idea that we get all of the Holy Spirit that we'll ever get when we get saved. When you plug that meaning of the word into this verse, I really don't know how you can come up with any other conclusion than that Paul is speaking of the baptism of the Spirit. He therefore that furnishes besides to you the Spirit, he therefore that fully supplies to you the Spirit, he therefore that aids or contributes to you the Spirit, he therefore that adds to you the Spirit, he therefore that ministers (nourishment unto) to you the Spirit, doeth he by the works of the law, or by the hearing of faith? I really don't know how this verse can be taken any other way than the baptism of the Spirit. They had already received the Spirit when they were saved, and now someone is finishing besides to them the Spirit. Someone else is fully supplying to them the Spirit. Someone else is aiding or contributing to them the Spirit. Someone else is adding to them the Spirit. Let me reiterate this point, but they had already received the gospel in *Galatians 3:1*, and they had already received the sealing of the Spirit in *Galatians 3:2*. I actually tried to make this verse mean something else other than the baptism of the Spirit, but I couldn't do it. I remember sitting in a chapel service at college one day hearing a message on this passage, and the speaker completely ignored this verse by saying something like the greatest miracle that will ever happen is the salvation of someone's soul. No one is doubting that, but that's just not what this verse says. This verse says that someone can "minister" or fully supply, aid, contribute, and add the Spirit to someone else by faith. This is exactly what Peter and John did for the Samaritan believers. They prayed for them and laid their hands upon them, then the Spirit "was fallen upon" them. This is exactly what Paul did for the believers in Ephesus when he laid hands on them. To these same believers Paul asked them if they had received the Spirit since they believed, not when they believed. He says they do it by the hearing of faith. *Romans 10:17 - So then faith cometh by hearing, and hearing by the word of God.* The hearing of this verse refers to the Holy Spirit speaking to us. The Greek word for "word" here is *ῥῆμα rhēma, hray'-mah; an utterance (individually, collectively or specially),; by implication, a matter or topic (especially of narration, command or dispute); with a negative naught whatever:—+ evil, + nothing, saying, word.* All of these have to do with speaking. It's about the Holy Spirit speaking to us. It isn't the Word of God itself because if it was everyone walking about from a service listening to a message would increase in faith every time. Sometimes this is not the case. Sometimes people walk out from any given service very angry. This hearing comes from the Holy Spirit speaking to them through the Word of God. They would hear God speaking to them through the Word. Once they did so, then they would have the choice to act in faith on what they had heard. These believers would be able to do miracles and minister the Spirit because they exercised faith in what the Spirit spoke to them through the Word. The people in this verse had faith to pray for these believers because they had heard from the Holy Spirit confirming to them from the Word of God that this is real. Let me ask you, do you hear the Holy Spirit confirming this to you as well? Why don't you look over these Scriptures again, and ask the Holy Spirit for guidance? I encourage you to ask the Holy Spirit to guide you into truth concerning this subject.

Chapter 9

The Gift of Tongues

I saved this chapter for last because it deals with the one gift that causes many to shy away the spiritual gifts altogether. This has been a subject that has caused, and still does cause much division, strife, contention, and controversy. Let's endeavor to keep our opinions from creeping in instead of looking at the Scripture objectively. As I have already mentioned in chapter 3, there are many that misuse and abuse the gift of tongues. If that is the case, then what is the purpose of the gift of tongues? The Bible clearly tells a few things about it. First of all, the Bible tells us in *I Corinthians 14:2-4 - For he that speaketh in an unknown tongue speaketh not unto men, but unto God: for no man understandeth him; howbeit in the spirit he speaketh mysteries. 3 But he that prophesieth speaketh unto men to edification, and exhortation, and comfort. 4 He that speaketh in an unknown tongue edifieth himself; but he that prophesieth edifieth the church.* He that prophesies is edifying the church. Why is that? *I Corinthians 14:3 - But he that prophesieth speaketh unto men to edification, and exhortation, and comfort.* The person that is prophesying is speaking to men words of edification, exhortation, and comfort. This can be seen in the example of Timothy. *I Timothy 1:18 - This charge I commit unto thee, son Timothy, according to the prophecies which went before on thee, that thou by them mightest war a good warfare;* Paul charged Timothy that he would war a good warfare. This was done according to the prophecies that were specifically spoken to him. Most likely, they were words of edification, and exhortation encouraging him to do so. Again these words are not simply words of encouragement, but rather they are words that come directly from the heart of God to another individual concerning the secrets of their heart. The gift of prophecy was not used in the giving of Scripture, but it actually also was used to give other spiritual gifts. *I Timothy 4:14 - Neglect not the gift that is in thee, which was given thee by prophecy, with the laying on of the hands of the presbytery.* This makes sense seeing that the gift of prophecy speaks words of edification to individual men. I just wanted to show once again that the gift of prophecy was not used in the inspiration of Scripture, but for the purpose of speaking words of exhortation, edification, and comfort. This chapter is about the gift of tongues. Let's look at the gift of tongues in particular. The Greek word for "tongue" in this passage is γλῶσσα glōssa, gloce-sah'; of uncertain affinity; the tongue; by implication, a language (specially, one naturally unacquired):—tongue. It can imply a language. I believe that it does imply a language in this context. He that speaketh in an unknown language edifies himself. Why is that? The reason why he edifies himself is because he is speaking in tongues by faith, but he isn't going to edify anyone else by speaking in an unknown tongue because no one else can understand what he is saying unless there is an interpreter. That's why he is only edifying himself when he is speaking in this unknown language. As already stated earlier in this book, Paul gave specific guidelines for speaking in this unknown language. *I Corinthians 14:27-28 - If any man speak in an unknown tongue, let it be by two, or at the most by three, and that by course; and let one interpret. 28 But if there be no interpreter, let him keep silence in the church; and let him speak to himself, and to God.* If this unknown language were going to be spoken in a church service, it was only supposed to be spoken by two or at most three in any given service. They were to speak one at a time, and there must be an interpreter. Unfortunately, many times these guidelines are not followed. The fact that there must be an interpreter points to the fact that tongues is indeed an unknown language. I go back to the analogy in chapter 3. If I went into a Spanish speaking church, and the only language that was being spoken was Spanish, then I would be confused. If the people all started speaking Spanish to no one in particular, if they started off slow and worked themselves up to speaking really fast, loud, and out of control, then I would think that they are crazy. Too many times this is the way that tongues are used, but it ought not to be. Paul gives specific guidelines when it comes to speaking this unknown language that needs to be followed. Again, I am certainly not against Spanish speaking people. They are made in God's image, and are precious for it. It is simply an analogy. We should be able to be in a church service where someone is speaking in Spanish, and be edified through an interpreter. Speaking in this unknown language shouldn't be any different. In fact, someone that is speaking this unknown language through an interpreter should be very similar to the person speaking to the congregation in Spanish through the interpreter. They should be able to speak side by side through the interpreters without much noticeable difference. Paul flat out said that if there is no interpreter, then no one should be speaking this unknown language. These are the guidelines that he gives, and they need to be followed. As already stated, this is not the way that it is used many times in church services. But just because it is abused by some, does that mean it shouldn't be done at all? No, we are to speak this unknown language according to the guidance of Scripture. Some may object to all of this by saying that on the day of Pentecost, the people understood what the people were saying. I agree. Let's look at what the Scriptures says about it in *I Corinthians 12:10 - to another the working of miracles; to another prophecy; to another discerning of spirits; to another divers kinds of tongues; to another the interpretation of tongues:* Paul said that one person is given "divers kinds of tongues". The Greek word for tongues in this passage is the same Greek word used in *I Corinthians 14:2*. What's this mean? It means that this unknown language is one of these kinds of tongues or languages. This also means that there is more than one language that is given. On the day of Pentecost there were several people who heard those 120 disciples speak in their own language. Paul gives attention to the unknown language because guidelines must be laid down in order to speak it because no one could understand the language. If I was given the gift of tongues or languages, then it's not unlikely that I could go to that same Spanish speaking church and be able to speak and understand what they say. This means that the gift of tongues is not solely the ability to speak in this unknown language, but also the ability to speak other known human languages that are not native to the speaker. That would be really cool to be able to speak Spanish, German, or French without having to take classes! What is this unknown language then? *I Corinthians 13:1 - Though I speak with the tongues of men and of angels, and have not charity, I am become as sounding brass, or a tinkling cymbal.* Paul differentiates between speaking in the languages of men, and speaking in the languages of angels. Apparently it is possible to speak with the tongues of angels, as well as the tongues of men. The Greek word for "tongues" is the same Greek word that Paul has already been using when referring to the gift of tongues in *I Corinthians 12*, and will use *I Corinthians 14* when referring to the unknown language meaning that he is referring to the same language. Let me ask a question. Does anyone understand the language of angels? Most likely the answer is no. That is what is being spoken when someone is speaking in this unknown language. Again, we have seen that the problem with speaking in this unknown language is not the fact that it is done, but rather the problem is the manner in which it is done. When the guidelines that Paul gives are not used the result is confusion. That doesn't mean that the gift itself isn't of God because he is not the author of confusion because he is the one who gives the gift. The misuse of the gift which is the source of confusion is not of God because it contradicts the guidelines which Paul gives concerning the gift. With that being said, isn't it a privilege to be able to speak in the language of angels? That's amazing, and we should treat it as such! But, we should only speak it in accordance with the Scriptures guidelines. Some people might object to this concept of speaking in the language of angels by quoting the next couple verses. *I Corinthians 13:1-3 - Though I speak with the tongues of men and of angels, and have not charity, I am become as sounding brass, or a tinkling cymbal. 2 And though I have the gift of prophecy, and understand all mysteries, and all knowledge; and though I have all faith, so that I could remove mountains, and have not charity, I am nothing. 3 And though I bestow all my goods to feed the poor, and though I give my body to be burned, and have not charity, it profiteth me nothing.* I've heard people object to this concept of speaking in the language of angels by saying that Paul was speaking in hypothetical terms. They say that Paul never gave his body to be burned as a martyr. Therefore it is possible that he didn't really speak in the tongues of angels. I would respond by saying that though he didn't give his body to be burned as a martyr, it was still very possible that he could've. Nero persecuted Christians by lighting them on fire as torches in the city of Rome. It was very possible that he could've given his body to be burned as a martyr in this way. It was very possible that Paul gave all of his goods away to feed the poor seeing that he was a wealthy Pharisee before he was saved, not to mention the fact that many in the early church did so. He certainly did have faith to move mountains. Though he may not have known all mysteries, and all knowledge, he certainly did know a lot of them. It is likely that Paul had the gift of prophecy. So why wouldn't it be possible for him to speak in the tongues of angels? In fact, the Bible says in *I Corinthians 14:18 - I thank my God, I speak with tongues more than ye all:* Paul literally said that he spoke in tongues more than all the Corinthian believers who were zealous of the spiritual gifts. This Greek word for "tongues" is the same Greek word used in *I Corinthians 13:1*. If Paul wasn't talking about the unknown language of angels in *I Corinthians*

14, then what language was he talking about? Paul also specifically said no man understands someone speaking in this unknown language. If no man understands this unknown language, then this language must not be a human language which is evidenced by the fact that the interpretation of this language must be given by God. I do not write to condemn, but to ask thought provoking questions, that's all. I think it's safe to conclude that this unknown language was the language of angels. To say that Paul was speaking in hypothetical terms in these verses to prove that the unknown language does not refer to speaking in the tongues of angels is an invalid argument because Paul either very likely could've done most of everything else that he mentions, or he actually did do what he mentioned. What was being said when someone spoke in this language. *I Corinthians 14:14-17 - For if I pray in an unknown tongue, my spirit prayeth but my understanding is unfruitful. 15 What is it then? I will pray with the spirit, and I will pray with the understanding also: I will sing with the spirit, and I will sing with the understanding also. 16 Else when thou shalt bless with the spirit, how shall he that occupieth the room of the unlearned say Amen at thy giving of thanks, seeing he understandeth not what thou sayest? 17 For thou verily givest thanks well, but the other is not edified.* We do not need to dissect this passage, or look at it in depth since we already have in chapter 3. Paul is still talking about the unknown language, and is specifically talking about praying in the unknown language. He said that if he prayed in an unknown language, then his spirit was praying, and he didn't know what he was saying. Regardless, He still says that he would pray with his understanding, and he would pray with the spirit as well. Praying with his understanding referred to praying in a language that he personally knew, whereas praying with his spirit refers to praying in the unknown language that he did not understand. He said that when they are praying in the spirit, they are blessing with their spirit. They are praying, blessing, and giving thanks to God in this unknown language. But if there is no interpreter, how is someone going to receive that blessing seeing that they do not understand what they were saying? They would be giving thanks to God, but everyone around them wouldn't be edified. When someone speaks in this unknown language, they are speaking praise and thanks to God. They are not speaking anything against God as some claim. *I Corinthians 12:3 - Wherefore I give you to understand, that no man speaking by the Spirit of God calleth Jesus accursed: and that no man can say that Jesus is the Lord, but by the Holy Ghost.* If someone is truly speaking by the Spirit of God, he is not going to call Jesus accursed. He is going to call Him Lord. Anyone that does speak against God, or speaks curse words in a foreign language is simply not speaking by the Spirit of God. It is more likely that they are actually speaking by the flesh. We have already seen that speaking in tongues can mean speaking in an understood human language. *Acts 2:5-11 - And there were dwelling at Jerusalem Jews, devout men, out of every nation under heaven. 6 Now when this was noised abroad, the multitude came together, and were confounded, because that every man heard them speak in his own language. 7 And they were all amazed and marvelled, saying one to another, Behold, are not all these which speak Galilæans? 8 And how hear we every man in our own tongue, wherein we were born? 9 Parthians, and Medes, and Elamites, and the dwellers in Mesopotamia, and in Judæa, and Cappadocia, in Pontus, and Asia, 10 Phrygia, and Pamphylia, in Egypt, and in the parts of Libya about Cyrene, and strangers of Rome, Jews and proselytes, 11 Cretes and Arabians, we do hear them speak in our tongues the wonderful works of God.* There were many devout Jews at Jerusalem at this time. They were all amazed at these 120 disciples of the Lord. Why? Because they were supernaturally speaking in their own languages. The Bible literally says, "every man heard them speak in his own language." What did they hear them say? The wonderful works of God. Whether someone is speaking in the unknown language or in an understood human language, they can both speak praises to God. "Whether someone is speaking in the unknown language or in an understood human language, they can both speak praises to God. *I Corinthians 14:27-28 - If any man speak in an unknown tongue, let it be by two, or at the most by three, and that by course; and let one interpret. 28 But if there be no interpreter, let him keep silence in the church; and let him speak to himself, and to God.* If there is no unknown language of tongues, then why didn't any of these 120 exemplary disciples of the Lord follow these guidelines? The answer is simple, the people were speaking in known human languages, and these guidelines were given for the unknown language of tongues. This proves the unknown language of tongues does, in fact, exist. Cate writes concerning the gift of tounges,

> Paul tells us very clearly in I Corinthians 14:21, 22 why tongues were given. "In the law [Isaiah 28:11, 12] it is written, With men of other tongues and other lips will I speak to THIS people [Israel]; and yet for all that will THEY [Israel] not hear ME, saith the Lord. Wherefore

tongues are for a SIGN [to the Jews], but to them, not to them that BELIEVE [as the Modern Tongues preachers say], but to them that BELIEVE NOT." Here Paul applied the law of double reference. In Isaiah, the reference has to do with the Gentiles (men of other tongues) coming into the land of the Jews. But Paul applied it to the gift of tongues in the early church, showing that it also had a reference to the time when God would speak to the Jews by the gift of tongues which was a sign to them. If we use this KEY as given by Paul, it will unlock every problem concerning the tongues. [59]

Some people along with Cate have said that the gift of tongues was a sign to the unbelieving Jew as a witness to them of the gospel. Many times verses of the Scripture are quoted such as *I Corinthians 1:22 - For the Jews require a sign, and the Greeks seek after wisdom.* The Jews required a sign, therefore God used signs to confirm the Word to them. In fact, the Bible says in *Hebrews 2:3-4 - how shall we escape, if we neglect so great salvation; which at the first began to be spoken by the Lord, and was confirmed unto us by them that heard him; 4 God also bearing them witness, both with signs and wonders, and with divers miracles, and gifts of the Holy Ghost, according to his own will?* The Book of Hebrews was written to Jews, hence the name Hebrews. The "we" and "us" in this verse refer to Jews. The apostles gave witness of the salvation of the gospel to the Jews. When they did so, God confirmed the word and bore witness of it "with signs and wonders, and with divers miracles, and gifts of the Holy Ghost" to the Jews. The word "confirmed" is the same Greek word used for "confirming" in *Mark 16:20 - And they went forth, and preached every where, the Lord working with them, and confirming the word with signs following. Amen.* The Lord confirmed "the word with signs following." Which signs? *Mark 16:17-18 - And these signs shall follow them that believe; In my name shall they cast out devils; they shall speak with new tongues; 18 they shall take up serpents; and if they drink any deadly thing, it shall not hurt them; they shall lay hands on the sick, and they shall recover.* One of these signs was that "they shall speak with new tongues". Therefore the gift of tongues was used as a sign to confirm the word to the unbelieving Jews. Hold on a second. Paul wrote in *Romans 15:18-19 - For I will not dare to speak of any of those things which Christ hath not wrought by me, to make the Gentiles obedient, by word and deed, 19 through mighty signs and wonders, by the power of the Spirit of God; so that from Jerusalem, and round about unto Illyricum, I have fully preached the gospel of Christ.* The Greek word for "signs" is the same word used in *Hebrews 2:4, I Corinthians 1:22*, and *Mark 16:17, 20*. The Greek word for "wonders" is also the same Greek word used in *Hebrews 2:4*. In this passage, the Lord certainly is using Paul to work signs and wonders, but notice for whom they are being done. These signs and wonders are being done for the "Gentiles". What's this mean? The truth is that the gifts were a sign to the unbelieving Jews. But they were no more of a sign to the unbelieving Jews as they were to the unbelieving Gentiles. The sign of "speaking with new tongues" was no different. It was a sign to the Gentiles as much as it was a sign to the Jews. How could speaking in tongues be a sign to the Gentiles? If someone who was not native to a particular country without ever having been there came preaching the gospel in the native language, it probably would be a sign. If I was suddenly able to speak Spanish, then it would be a sign to those in Spanish speaking countries. Why? Because I'm a gringo! I don't understand the language, yet if I could speak it, then it would be a sign to the unbelieving Spanish-speaking people. It is true that throughout Israel's history, God used signs to speak to them. Moses was a great example, but even then the pagan magicians could recognize the finger of God. They said in *Exodus 8:19 - Then the magicians said unto Pharaoh, This is the finger of God: and Pharaoh's heart was hardened, and he hearkened not unto them; as the Lord had said.* Yes, signs and wonders, including the gift of tongues were a witness to the Jews, but they are also a witness to the Gentiles. Cate writes,

> Now in the light of the KEY given in I Corinthians 14:21-22, let us consider the four references given in the New Testament in which the people talked in tongues, and see how they apply to the JEWS that BELIEVED NOT. But remember that said, "tongues are for a sign to them who believe not," he did not necessarily mean an unsaved person. Thomas, the "doubter," was a saved person. But when he heard of the resurrection of Christ he said, "Except I shall see...I will not believe" (John 20:25). We will see that in some cases tongues were a sign to unsaved Jews. But in other cases they were a sign to saved Jews who were in "doubt" about certain things. Now let us consider four references. [60]

Though I do not agree that the gift of tongues was used as a sign to the Jews only, I do agree that it is a sign of unbelief in the Word of God, which as we have seen can be a sign to the Gentiles as well. Cate writes,

> 1) In the second chapter of Acts, the JEWS that were gathered at Jerusalem for the feast of Pentecost, heard the Lord speak unto them "WITH MEN OF OTHER TONGUES." That this demonstration on the day of Pentecost was for the Jews is seen in the fact that Peter's message was addressed to them. (See verses 14, 22, and 36.) In fact they "preached the Word to NONE but unto the JEWS ONLY" for some time AFTER Pentecost (Acts 11:19). In verses 32 to 36 of Acts 2, Peter makes it very clear why the sign of tongues were given to Israel. "This Jesus hath raised God up, whereof we are all witnesses. Therefore having received of the Father the promise of the Holy Ghost, HE HATH SHED FORTH THIS [SIGN] WHICH YE NOW SEE AND HEAR...Therefore let all the house of ISRAEL know assuredly, that God hath made this same Jesus, whom ye crucified, both Lord, and CHRIST [there Messianic King]." Thus we see that tongues were given to convince Israel that Jesus, the one they had rejected, was their Messiah. But as our KEY states, "yet for all that will they not hear ME, saith the Lord." And so the nation of Israel "BELIEVED NOT." The key works perfectly in this instance. [61]

The verse which Cate is quoting from to prove that the gift of tongues were strictly a sign to the unbelieving Jews in Jerusalem on the day of Pentecost is *Acts 2:33 - Therefore being by the right hand of God exalted, and having received of the Father the promise of the Holy Ghost, he hath shed forth this, which ye now see and hear.* Notice that Cate inserted a word in that verse. He inserted the word "sign" in this verse, yet it is not in the English or the Greek. Whether he purposely formatted this inserted word into the text to appear as though it is part of the English translation, or not, the fact stands that the way that it is written makes it appear as though it is. He is not talking about the gift of tongues. He is referring to the "promise of the Holy Ghost" which we have seen to be the baptism of the Holy Spirit. The Greek word for "promise" is ἐπαγγελίαν, while the Greek word for "this" is τοῦτο. They are both in the same Gender, Number, and Case in the Greek meaning that when Paul used the word "this" he was referencing the "promise" of the Holy Ghost.

> 2) In Acts 10:1 to 11:18, we find that Cornelius and his house (who were Gentiles) spake in tongues when they were saved. A careful study of this portion will show that this was a sign to the JEWS that the gospel was for the Gentiles. For until this time Peter (see Acts 10:28), his JEWISH co-workers (see Acts 10:45-36), and JEWS at Jerusalem (see Acts 11:1-18) did NOT BELIEVE that the gospel was for the Gentiles.[62]

As we have already seen, the gift of tongues truly was a sign to unbelieving Jews. *Mark 16:17 - And these signs shall follow them that believe; In my name shall they cast out devils; they shall speak with new tongues.* Speaking "with new tongues" was a sign to the Jews, but it was also a sign to the Gentiles. How do I know? The context indicates that these signs follow those who have the faith to share the gospel, and to believe in God that he will confirm his word with signs. The Greek word for "signs" in this verse is also the same Greek word for "signs" in *Romans 15:18-19 - For I will not dare to speak of any of those things which Christ hath not wrought by me, to make the Gentiles obedient, by word and deed, 19 through mighty signs and wonders, by the power of the Spirit of God; so that from Jerusalem, and round about unto Illyricum, I have fully preached the gospel of Christ.* Paul used these same "signs" to preach to the Gentiles meaning that these "signs" were just as much of a "sign" to the unbelieving Gentiles as they were to the unbelieving Jews. I am not trying to prove that the gift of tongues were not used to be a sign to the unbelieving Jews, I am however trying to prove that it was also a sign to the Gentiles. Cate writes,

> 3) In Acts 18:24 to 19:7, we find that Apollos had gone to Ephesus and preached in the "SYNAGOGUE" of the JEWS, "knowing ONLY the baptism of John." Then Paul to Ephesus and found certain disciples there. Of course, these were not disciples of Christ, having not believed on Him yet (Acts 19:4-5). For Apollos had preached unto them "knowing ONLY the baptism of John." So when Paul came, he had a different message. He preached unto them that they should "believe…on Christ Jesus." Inasmuch as Paul's ministry had been questioned by the Jews (Acts 15:1-2;

Galatians 1:6-9), whom were these disciples to believe, Paul or Apollos? It seems evident that Paul's message was right. The giving of the Holy Spirit and tongues through the laying on of Paul's hands were God's way of putting his approval upon Paul and his message.[63]

First of all, I will admit that I am not a specialist in Biblical Geography by any stretch of the imagination, but in every Biblical map that I looked at, Ephesus was not in Galatia, it was in Asia. Second, with no intention of condemnation toward Cate at all, I must say that he really twisted the Scripture to prove his point. The Scripture which Cate is quoting from in context is *Acts 19:1-7 - And it came to pass, that, while Apollos was at Corinth, Paul having passed through the upper coasts came to Ephesus: and finding certain disciples, 2 he said unto them, Have ye received the Holy Ghost since ye believed? And they said unto him, We have not so much as heard whether there be any Holy Ghost. 3 And he said unto them, Unto what then were ye baptized? And they said, Unto John's baptism. 4 Then said Paul, John verily baptized with the baptism of repentance, saying unto the people, that they should believe on him which should come after him, that is, on Christ Jesus. 5 When they heard this, they were baptized in the name of the Lord Jesus. 6 And when Paul had laid his hands upon them, the Holy Ghost came on them; and they spake with tongues, and prophesied. 7 And all the men were about twelve.* Paul found "certain disciples". Every other time that this word "disciple" is used in the book of *Acts*, it refers to disciples of Christ, why would it refer to the disciples of John the Baptist in this passage? Cate writes, "Of course, these were not the disciples of Christ, having not believed on Him yet (Acts 19:4-5). For Apollos had preached unto them "knowing ONLY the baptism of John." Therefore he knew nothing of the finished work of Christ on the cross. So when Paul came, he had a different message. He preached unto them that they should 'believe...on Christ Jesus.'"[64] First of all, notice that Paul flat out said that they had "believed". Second of all, Cate writes that Paul had a different message than Apollos because Apollos only knew of the baptism of John, yet it was John who said to the people "that they should believe on him which should come after him, that is on Christ Jesus." Paul flat out stated that they "believed". If these "disciples" already had "believed", what then did they believe? They believed "on him which should come after" John "that is, on Christ Jesus." In other words, this further proves that these "disciples" were saved, and truly did believe in Christ. Notice that Paul was simply quoting John. If Apollos preached to them "knowing only the baptism of John", and Paul was simply quoting John, then Paul and Apollos didn't have different messages. They were speaking the same message which originated with John. Cate tries to prove that these disciples were not saved, and that the gift of tongues was approval on Paul's message which was supposedly different from the message that Apollos preached for two reasons. One is that he is trying to prove that these "disciples" were not already saved when they received the Spirit so that he can discredit the baptism of the Spirit pictured in this passage. As we have already seen the Greek word "since ye believed" in this passage is πιστεύσαντες. It is an antecedent temporal participle meaning that Paul is asking if they received the Spirit after they believed. In fact, this same Greek word is found in *Ephesians 1:13 - in whom ye also trusted, after that ye heard the word of truth, the gospel of your salvation: in whom also after that ye believed, ye were sealed with that holy Spirit of promise*. This Greek word is translated as "after that ye believed". But, if this passage pictures the sealing of the Spirit, and if Jesus Christ acts according to his Word "yesterday, and to day, and for ever", then this passage should picture how we ought to receive the Spirit today, but if this passage pictures the baptism of the Spirit, and if Jesus Christ acts according to his Word "yesterday, and to day, and for ever", then we should receive the baptism of the Spirit in like-manner today as well. The second reason why Cate is trying to prove that these disciples were not yet saved until they met Paul, and that Paul preached a different message from the message of Apollos is because he is trying to prove that the gift of tongues was only used during the "transition period" strictly as a sign to the Jews who were in unbelief. By doing so, he is discrediting its valid use today for those who do so to edify themselves by speaking to God in faith. *I Corinthians 14:12 - For he that speaketh in an unknown tongue speaketh not unto men, but unto God: for no man understandeth him; howbeit in the spirit he speaketh mysteries. 3 But he that prophesieth speaketh unto men to edification, and exhortation, and comfort. 4 He that speaketh in an unknown tongue edifieth himself; but he that prophesieth edifieth the church*. The truth is that Cate has to twist the Scriptures to prove both of these things instead of believing the Scriptures for what they teach at face value. Cate writes.

4) Tongues were very prominent at Corinth. You will see the reason for this by reading the account in Acts 18:1-11 of the founding of the church there. Paul was preaching in the SYNAGOGUE and "testified to the JEWS that Jesus was CHRIST [their Messiah]. And when they opposed and blasphemed," it was a crisis for them. Paul said unto them, "from HENCEFORTH I sill go to the GENTILES." So he went NEXT DOOR to the SYNAGOGUE and established a church there. Therefore, the tongues at Corinth, NEXT DOOR to the SYNAGOGUE, were a SIGN to the JEWS that Paul's message concerning their Messiah was right. [65]

Tongues may very well have been a sign to the unbelieving Jews in Corinth, but as we have already seen that tongues were not just a sign to the Jews. For the sake of repetition, we will go through it again. The Bible says in *Mark 16:17 - And these signs shall follow them that believe; In my name shall they cast out devils; they shall speak with new tongues.* Speaking "with new tongues" truly was a sign to the unbelieving Jews. The context of this verse speaks of those who have the faith to share the gospel, and to believe that God will perform signs to confirm his Word. There were many unbelieving Jews in the days of the early church as there are today, but there were and still are many unbelieving Gentiles as well. Paul wrote in his epistle, which primarily deals with the doctrine of salvation, in *Romans 15:18-19 - For I will not dare to speak of any of those things which Christ hath not wrought by me, to make the Gentiles obedient, by word and deed, 19 through mighty signs and wonders, by the power of the Spirit of God; so that from Jerusalem, and round about unto Illyricum, I have fully preached the gospel of Christ.* The Greek word for "signs" in this verse is the same word for "signs" in *Mark 16:17*. Since Paul used these "signs" to preach the gospel to the Gentiles, the sign of "speaking with new tongues" was just as much of a sign to the Gentiles as it is to the Jews. Am I discrediting that tongues were a sign to the unbelieving Jews at the synagogue in Corinth? No, but I am pointing out that it was a sign to the Gentiles as well.

I Corinthians 14:20-25 - Brethren, be not children in understanding: howbeit in malice be ye children, but in understanding be men. 21 In the law it is written, With men of other tongues and other lips will I speak unto this people; and yet for all that will they not hear me, saith the Lord. 22

Wherefore tongues are for a sign, not to them that believe, but to them that believe not: but prophesying serveth not for them that believe not, but for them which believe. 23 If therefore the whole church be come together into one place, and all speak with tongues, and there come in those that are unlearned, or unbelievers, will they not say that ye are mad? 24 But if all prophesy, and there come in one that believeth not, or one unlearned, he is convinced of all, he is judged of all: 25 and thus are the secrets of his heart made manifest; and so falling down on his face he will worship God, and report that God is in you of a truth. Cate writes concerning the gift of tongues,

> Paul tells us very clearly in I Corinthians 14:21, 22 why tongues were given. "In the law [Isaiah 28:11, 12] it is written, With men of other tongues and other lips will I speak to THIS people [Israel]; and yet for all that will THEY [Israel] not hear ME, saith the Lord. Wherefore tongues are for a SIGN [to the Jews], but to them, not to them that BELIEVE [as the Modern Tongues preachers say], but to them that BELIEVE NOT." Here Paul applied the law of double reference. In Isaiah the reference has to do with the Gentiles (men of other tongues) coming into the land of the Jews. But Paul applied it to the gift of tongues in the early church, showing that it also had a reference to the time when God would speak to the Jews by the gift of tongues which was a sign to them. If we use this KEY as given by Paul, it will unlock every problem concerning the tongues.[66]

It should be evident by now that Cate believes that this passage teaches that the gift of tongues was given to be sign to Jews who were in unbelief. He mentions "the law of double reference" as the reason for why he believes that it was used for such a purpose. Before the law of double reference is applied, consider one very important fact. Just because Paul is quoting Isaiah, that doesn't mean that he is referring to the exact same circumstance as Isaiah. How do I know? Because if that was the case, then Isaiah would have been prophesying that God would use the gift of tongues to speak to his people, the people of Judah, in the Old Testament. As we will see, God was not saying that he would speak to his people, Judah, using the gift of tongues, he was going to use a people of another language to speak to them about their disobedience and unbelief. Paul is not trying to apply the same exact circumstance from Isaiah's prophecy to the Jews living in his day, he was simply making an analogy. Once we recognize that Paul was not referring to the exact same circumstance to which Isaiah wrote, we can see that Paul was referring to a different circumstance regarding the church, yet is similar in some ways to the circumstance which Isaiah wrote about. To understand what Paul is truly saying, we must put both passages in context, both the passage in Isaiah, and this passage which was penned by Paul. In context, Paul is writing to the church about speaking in the unknown tongue or language. He is saying that if anyone was going to be edified by what they were saying, then there must be an interpreter. If there's no interpreter, then there will be no understanding and therefore no edification (refer back to chapter 3). We have already seen that the context of these verses in *I Corinthians 14* speaks of being understood in the church setting. Paul makes this point over and over again in this passage. Being understood is necessary for the edification of the church. This can clearly be seen by looking at the verses right before it. *I Corinthians 14:18-20 - I thank my God, I speak with tongues more than ye all: 19 yet in the church I had rather speak five words with my understanding, that by my voice I might teach others also, than ten thousand words in an unknown tongue. 20 Brethren, be not children in understanding: howbeit in malice be ye children, but in understanding be men.* Paul spoke in tongues more than all of them, but in the church he would rather speak five words with his understanding than then thousand words in the unknown language so that he could be understood by the church, and edify the church. He was not referring to speaking in the "tongues of men". In context, he was referring to speaking in the tongues "of angels." Before we can even get to the "law of double reference", we better put the passage in context first. Let's look at the passage that Paul is referring to in *Isaiah 28:9-13 - Whom shall he teach knowledge? and whom shall he make to understand doctrine? them that are weaned from the milk, and drawn from the breasts. 10 For precept must be upon precept, precept upon precept; line upon line, line upon line; here a little, and there a little: 11 for with stammering lips and another tongue will he speak to this people. 12 To whom he said, This is the rest wherewith ye may cause the weary to rest; and this is the refreshing: yet they would not hear. 13 But the word of the Lord was unto them precept upon precept, precept upon precept; line upon line, line upon line; here a little, and there a little; that they might go, and fall backward, and be broken, and snared, and taken.* We must put passages in context if we are going to interpret them correctly. The teacher in this context is the Lord, we'll see this later on in this passage. Two questions are asked. Who will the Lord teach knowledge? Who will he make to understand doctrine? These questions are answered right after they are asked. He can teach doctrine and knowledge to those who are weaned from the milk. In other words, only to the ones who are mature. How does one grow in understanding? It can only happen step by step. Precept must be upon precept. In other words, the fundamental principles of the Scripture must be taught first before teaching any complex sections of Scripture. This makes sense to us. This is how learning is always accomplished. In mathematics, someone has to learn the principles of Algebra before they can get to Calculus. Precept must be upon precept. He said that he would speak to his people with "stammering lips and another tongue". This is the verse that Paul quotes in *I Corinthians 14:21*. What does Isaiah mean by this? *Isaiah 33:19 - Thou shalt not see a fierce people, a people of a deeper speech than thou canst perceive; of a stammering tongue, that thou canst not understand.* The word for "tongue" in this verse is the same word for "tongue" in *Isaiah 28:11*. Who is Isaiah writing to again? *Isaiah 1:1 - The vision of Isaiah the son of Amoz, which he saw concerning Judah and Jerusalem in the days of Uzziah, Jotham, Ahaz, and Hezekiah, kings of Judah.* He is writing to the people to the people of Judah. Isaiah was a great prophet of the Lord who prophesied, among other things, of the judgement which was to come upon them for their sins. He had already prophesied that God would raise up the Assyrian nation to be the instrument by which he judged them. The "fierce people" of which he spoke were the Assyrians. The Assyrians were known for their ferocity. We don't need to talk about the atrocities that they committed, for Paul writes that it is a shame to do so. Either way, they were the growing Empire at the time. They came down to Jerusalem and spoke to the people in the Assyrian language, a language which they could "not understand". But, God said that they would not see them. Why? Because Hezekiah was a very godly king who brought many reforms to Israel, and what some would call a national revival. He cried out to the Lord for help, and the Lord responded by sending his angel to destroy the Assyrian army, and as a result 185,000 Assyrian soldiers died. The Jews in Jerusalem truly didn't see the Assyrians soldiers because they didn't even have a chance to enter the city. Why was God using the Assyrian soldiers in this way? Let's look at the next two verses again. *Isaiah 28:12-13 - To whom he said, This is the rest wherewith ye may cause the weary to rest; and this is the refreshing: yet they would not hear. 13 But the word of the*

Lord was unto them precept upon precept, precept upon precept; line upon line, line upon line; here a little, and there a little; that they might go, and fall backward, and be broken, and snared, and taken. The Lord had a "rest" and a "refreshing" for his people Israel that was to be found in the "word of the Lord". The problem was that they didn't see it as rest. They didn't see it as refreshing. The "word of the Lord" was only principles and precepts. They continued on their own path until eventually they would "fall backward", "be broken, and snared and taken." The Lord saved them from the Assyrian army, but they continued to see the word of the Lord simply as the principles and precepts instead of the rest and refreshing that he wanted to give them. As a result they were taken away captive to Babylon by Nebuchadnezzar. How was God speaking to his people through the Assyrian soldiers anyway? He certainly wasn't speaking to them through the words that they spoke to the Jews. The Assyrians were an unregenerate pagan people that were speaking blasphemy. How was he speaking to his people? God was speaking to the Jews with their "stammering lips", with men that spoke a different language that they couldn't "understand". He was using them to speak to his own people, the same people that had made a covenant with Him. What was he saying? The Bible tells us in *Deuteronomy 28:49-50 - The Lord shall bring a nation against thee from far, from the end of the earth, as swift as the eagle flieth; a nation whose tongue thou shalt not understand; 50 a nation of fierce countenance, which shall not regard the person of the old, nor shew favour to the young:* He told his people in this passage that if they would not obey his law, and walk with Him, then He would send a nation to speak to them in a language that they did "not understand". This nation would be a "fierce" nation who wouldn't make any distinction between the old or the young, but would be fierce to all they encountered. This is exactly what happened. His people forsook Him, and started to worship false gods. As a response, God sent the Assyrians to them. God was telling his people that they had broken the covenant that they had made with Him. He was telling them that they were living in sin. He was telling them that they would not hear his voice, nor would they believe Him. He was telling them that His word of God was only principles and precepts to them, and not the rest which he had for them. He was telling them that did not know Him, nor did they have a relationship with Him. They didn't listen to Him, and as a result they were carried away as captives to Babylon.

What is the context of *I Corinthians 14:21*? The context spoke of understanding the words that are said in a church gathering. *I Corinthians 14:20 - I thank my God, I speak with tongues more than ye all: 19 yet in the church I had rather speak five words with my understanding, that by my voice I might teach others also, than ten thousand words in an unknown tongue. 20 Brethren, be not children in understanding: howbeit in malice be ye children, but in understanding be men.* Paul quotes the passage in *Isaiah 28* in this passage by likening how God spoke to Judah with the Assyrians about their unbelief with the gift of tongues in the church. It should be obvious that Paul was writing to the church. He is writing to the church about understanding the words spoken in a church gathering. In *Isaiah 28:9-13*, Isaiah is writing to the people of Judah who weren't obeying God. They had broken the covenant they made with God. As a result, God spoke to them with the Assyrians in a language that they didn't understand about their disobedience and unbelief in the Word of God. By comparing the language of the Assyrians which the Jews did not understand with the gift of tongues which cannot be understood, he is comparing the Jews who were disobedient, and who didn't believe in the Word of God, to those who have unbelief in what the Word of God teaches about the spiritual gifts. They were /are both living in unbelief. With that being said, when Paul makes his comparison to the church, he says in *I Corinthians 14:22 - Wherefore tongues are for a sign, not to them that believe, but to them that believe not: but prophesying serveth not for them that believe not, but for them which believe.* Tongues are for a sign to them "that believe not". What were they not believing? The Word of God. When people don't believe in the spiritual gifts, then the gift of tongues serves as a sign of their unbelief in what the Word teaches about them, any of the other gifts, and the baptism of the Spirit. It seems as though those that oppose the spiritual gifts have a major problem with the gift of tongues. Tongues seem to be the main issue that causes them to shy away from the gifts altogether. It is a sign to them of their unbelief in the Word of God that could bring rest and refreshing if they would just believe. How so? If they would believe in the Word of God, then they would make use of the gift of prophecy. The gift of prophecy serves those that believe in it because of what the Word of God teaches about it. The gift of prophecy serves them in such a way because the Bible says in *I Corinthians 14:3 - But he that prophesieth speaketh unto men to edification, and exhortation, and comfort.* Prophecy brings rest and refreshing to those that believe in it because those that do it are speaking words of exhortation, edification, and comfort to the secret of their hearts.

Boiling it down the gift of tongues is a sign of unbelief in those who do not believe in the spiritual gifts. I am not trying to be condemning towards Cate, but his unbelief is evident in his own words, He writes, "If we use this KEY as given by Paul, it will unlock every problem concerning the tongues."[67] He refers to problems concerning the gift of tongues. Though he does not specifically say that the gift of tongues is a problem in itself, it does seem that he believes that the gift of tongues is problematic which reveals his presupposition towards it. The gift of tongues is not a problem, and the only reason why it causes problems is because people do not follow the guidelines that Paul gives in *I Corinthians 14:27-28*. The problems arise from the misuse of the gift, not in the use of the gift. This misuse is not rooted in faith in the word of God, but neither is the cessationist argument. It is actually rooted in unbelief. They don't believe in what the Word of God tells us about the spiritual gifts. Proof of this unbelief can be found in *Matthew 10:5-8 - These twelve Jesus sent forth, and commanded them, saying, Go not into the way of the Gentiles, and into any city of the Samaritans enter ye not: 6 but go rather to the lost sheep of the house of Israel. 7 And as ye go, preach, saying, The kingdom of heaven is at hand. 8 Heal the sick, cleanse the lepers, raise the dead, cast out devils: freely ye have received, freely give.* Jesus sent forth his disciples to preach, and he commanded them to go to the lost sheep of the house of Israel, to preach that the kingdom of heaven is at hand, and to heal the sick, cleanse the lepers, raise the dead, and cast out devils. The words "heal", "cleanse", "raise", and "cast" are all in the imperative mood in the Greek, and are all imperatives of command meaning that all of these were commands given by Jesus to his disciples. This is corroborated in the context when Jesus sent his disciples forth, "and commanded them." It is very hard to say that all of these were not commands in the English, or the Greek. Jesus gave them another command in *Matthew 28:18-20 - And Jesus came and spake unto them, saying, All power is given unto me in heaven and in earth. 19 Go ye therefore, and teach all nations, baptizing them in the name of the Father, and of the Son, and of the Holy Ghost: 20 teaching them to observe all things whatsoever I have commanded you: and, lo, I am with you alway, even unto the end of the world. Amen.* Jesus came to his disciples and commanded them to teach all nations. The word "teach" is in the imperative in the Greek, and it is specifically an imperative of command meaning that teaching itself was a command. Jesus was commanding his twelve disciples to teach all nations. What were they supposed to teach them? They were to be "teaching them all things whatsoever I have commanded you". Remember the word "teach" in verse 19 was a command of Jesus. So they were to train the next generation to teach the generation after them to keep all the commands of Jesus. Since the teaching or discipling was a command itself, that same generation was to train the generation after them to keep all the commands of Jesus. And that generation was to train the next generation to keep all the commands of Jesus. The next generation was to teach the generation after them to keep all the commands of Jesus. How long was this to go on? It was to go on until the end of the world. Jesus was going to be with his disciples throughout the ages helping them to train the nations of the world until the end of the world. *Matthew 10:8 - Heal the sick, cleanse the lepers, raise the dead, cast out devils: freely ye have received, freely give.* It is hard to say that these are not the command of Jesus. That can be demonstrated both by the English translation, and the in the original Greek. Granted, they are not the only commands of Jesus, but they are just as valid as *Matthew 6:33 - But seek ye first the kingdom of God, and his righteousness; and all these things shall be added unto you.* To say that these four commands of Jesus were not given to his disciples is to deny the Scriptures. To say that these four statements were not really commands is to deny the Scriptures. To say that Jesus didn't really mean "all things whatsoever I have commanded you" when he said "all things whatsoever things I have commanded you" is to deny the Scriptures. The only way out of this is to deny that these four commands were not really commands. It can be said that it is not normative today, but that is also denying the Scriptures. If Jesus didn't mean "all things whatsoever I have commanded you" when he said "all things whatsoever I have commanded you", then what did he mean? If he didn't mean "all things whatsoever I have commanded you", then we had better find out what commands he was referring to. I am not ready to do that. If we wanted to we could attach a theological term to just about anything to prove what we want from Scripture. If I wanted to, I could say that we don't need missions today. I could say that teaching all nations was just a command to the early church before the Word of God was completed. They needed to spread out around the world. Now that the church is around the world, we don't need missions. I could come up with doctrines and ways to justify what I believe about missions. I could try to talk my way out of

Mark 16:15 - And he said unto them, Go ye into all the world, and preach the gospel to every creature. I could say that this command was only for the "transition period" of the church. Now that the Word of God is completed, people can read it for themselves. I could also question Jesus' command concerning the gospel. "Repent and believe the gospel"? That is not normative today. My truth is just as valid as your truth. That would be ridiculous. My point is if someone can do this with the passages that teach about the spiritual gifts, then what's to stopping them from doing it with anything else in the Word of God. I did not write this book because I'm zealous for the spiritual gifts. I wrote this book because I am zealous for the Word of God. I have given my life to study it, and I have a hard time seeing this attack on the Word of God, and doing nothing about it. By the way, the Greek word for "to observe is τηρέω tēréō, tay-reh'-o; from τερός terós (a watch); to guard (from loss or injury, properly, by keeping the eye upon, which is properly to prevent escaping, which implies a fortress or full military lines of apparatus), i.e. to note (a prophecy; figuratively, to fulfil a command); by implication, to detain (in custody; figuratively, to maintain); by extension, to withhold (for personal ends; figuratively, to keep unmarried); by extension, to withhold (for personal ends; figuratively, to keep unmarried):—hold fast, keep(- er), (pre-, re-)serve, watch. This Greek word is a military term. It means to hold on to, to guard, to not let go. It was the same word used in *Acts 12:5 - Peter therefore was kept in prison: but prayer was made without ceasing of the church unto God for him.* Peter was "kept" in prison. He was not to be let go. This word was also the same word used in *Acts 16:23 - And when they had laid many stripes upon them, they cast them into prison, charging the jailor to keep them safely:* This is when Paul and Silas were thrown in prison. The jailer was "to keep" them safely. This word is the word that was used both when Peter and Paul were thrown in prison. This means that the commands of God were to be kept that close. They were not to be let go. In other words, if these four commands were not kept throughout history, then it wasn't because they were supposed to. They were to be kept and taught to the next generation by every generation throughout the history of the church. Someone might object by saying that we don't have the ability to do these things. Remember what Nicodemus said? *John 3:1-2 - There was a man of the Pharisees, named Nicodemus, a ruler of the Jews: 2 the same came to Jesus by night, and said unto him, Rabbi, we know that thou art a teacher come from God: for no man can do these miracles that thou doest, except God be with him.* Nicodemus said that no one can do the miracles of Jesus unless God is with him. But if God is with him, then he is able to do the same miracles that Jesus did. Isn't it interesting that the one that has been given all authority in heaven and earth is with us always, even to the end of the world? The church has always had the ability to do the miracles of Jesus, and always will have that ability even unto the end of the world. What disease can stand in the way of Jesus? The Bible records in *Matthew 9:35 - And Jesus went about all the cities and villages, teaching in their synagogues, and preaching the gospel of the kingdom, and healing every sickness and every disease among the people.* Jesus healed every disease and every sickness. What disease or sickness can stop him? What disease or sickness is too hard for him to heal? There isn't a single one. What is death to Jesus? The Bible tells us that he has been the keys to it. *Revelation 1:18 - I am he that liveth, and was dead; and, behold, I am alive for evermore, Amen; and have the keys of hell and of death.* He rose from the dead himself, and now he holds the keys of hell and of death. What is death to him? He already conquered it. What are devils to him? The Bible tells us in *I Timothy 6:13-15 - I give thee charge in the sight of God, who quickeneth all things, and before Christ Jesus, who before Pontius Pilate witnessed a good confession; 14 that thou keep this commandment without spot, unrebukeable, until the appearing of our Lord Jesus Christ: 15 which in his times he shall shew, who is the blessed and only Potentate, the King of kings, and Lord of lords;* Jesus Christ is that blessed and only Potentate. He is the King of kings. He is the Lord of lords. What devil can stand before him? If that is not enough, the Bible also tells us in *Revelation 19:15-16 - And out of his mouth goeth a sharp sword, that with it he should smite the nations: and he shall rule them with a rod of iron: and he treadeth the winepress of the fierceness and wrath of Almighty God. 16 And he hath on his vesture and on his thigh a name written, KING OF KINGS, AND LORD OF LORDS.* When he comes back he will have a name written on his clothes in all capital letters signifying that He, and He alone truly is the KING OF KINGS AND LORD OF LORDS. What devil can stand before Him? This is the one that is with us always even unto the end of the world. The one that has been given all authority in heaven and earth. The one that is the KING OF KINGS AND LORD OF LORDS. The one that has the keys of death and hell. The one that healed every disease, and every sickness among the people. He is with us to help us do the same things. What excuse do we have? The Greek word τηρέω is found in another place in Scripture. *John 14:15 - If ye love me, keep my commandments.* This same Jesus told us that if we love him, we are to "keep" his commandments. The way that we show that we love Him is by "keeping" his commandments, by keeping all of them. How much do you love Jesus? This is not written to condemn anyone, but to encourage you to seek the Lord for yourself, and ask Him what He says. If you truly love Him, isn't it worth spending time in prayer asking him about all these things? He truly does love you, and He won't lead you astray. Why not spend time with the Lord, who laid down his life for you in love, to ask him about these things. Jesus himself told us the two greatest commandments in *Matthew 22:37-40 - Jesus said unto him, Thou shalt love the Lord thy God with all thy heart, and with all thy soul, and with all thy mind. 38 This is the first and great commandment. 39 And the second is like unto it, Thou shalt love thy neighbour as thyself. 40 On these two commandments hang all the law and the prophets.* I encourage you to do just that. I encourage you to love the Lord with all your heart, with all your soul, and with all your mind, and then to love your neighbor as yourself. Amen!

Notes

1. Reinhard Bonnke, *Taking Action* (Lake Mary, FL: Charisma House, 2012), 262
2. Bonnke, *Taking Action*, 88
3. Jon Courson, *Jon Courson's Application Commentary: New Testament* (Thomas Nelson, 2013), 1070
4. Courson, *Jon Courson's Application Commentary*, 1070
5. Courson, *Jon Courson's Application Commentary,* 1070
6. Courson, *Jon Courson's Application Commentary*, 1070-1071
7. Courson, *Jon Courson's Application Commentary*, 1071
8. Courson, *Jon Courson's Application Commentary*, 1071
9. Courson, *Jon Courson's Application Commentary*, 1071
10. B.F. Cate, *The Nine Gifts of the Spirit are not in the Church Today* (Lorain, Oh: Lorain Book and Bible House, 1956), 15-17
11. Cate, *The Nine Gifts of the Spirit*, 18
12. Cate, *The Nine Gifts of the Spirit*, 15
13. Cate, *The Nine Gifts of the Spirit*, 15-16
14. Cate, *The Nine Gifts of the Spirit*, 16
15. Cate, *The Nine Gifts of the Spirit*, 16
16. Cate, *The Nine Gifts of the Spirit*, 34.
17. Cate, *The Nine Gifts of the Spirit*, 21-22.
18. Cate, *The Nine Gifts of the Spirit*, 22.
19. Cate, *The Nine Gifts of the Spirit*, 22
20. Cate, *The Nine Gifts of the Spirit*, 22
21. Cate, *The Nine Gifts of the Spirit*, 22
22. Cate, *The Nine Gifts of the Spirit*, 23-24
23. Cate, *The Nine Gifts of the Spirit*, 24
24. Cate, *The Nine Gifts of the Spirit*, 39
25. Cate, *The Nine Gifts of the Spirit*, 39-40
26. Cate, *The Nine Gifts of the Spirit*, 41-42
27. Cate, *The Nine Gifts of the Spirit*, 61-62

28. Cate, *The Nine Gifts of the Spirit*, 61
29. Cate, *The Nine Gifts of the Spirit*, 61
30. Cate, *The Nine Gifts of the Spirit*, 61-62
31. Cate, *The Nine Gifts of the Spirit*, 42-43
32. Cate, *The Nine Gifts of the Spirit*, 43
33. Cate, *The Nine Gifts of the Spirit*, 43
34. Cate, *The Nine Gifts of the Spirit*, 58
35. Cate, *The Nine Gifts of the Spirit*, 64-67
36. Cate, *The Nine Gifts of the Spirit*, 64-65
37. Cate, *The Nine Gifts of the Spirit*, 65
38. Cate, *The Nine Gifts of the Spirit*, 66
39. Cate, *The Nine Gifts of the Spirit*, 66-67
40. Cate, *The Nine Gifts of the Spirit*, 54-56
41. Cate, *The Nine Gifts of the Spirit*, 55
42. Cate, *The Nine Gifts of the Spirit*, 56
43. James Orr, *Progress of Dogma* (New York, NY: A.C. Armstrong, Hodder and Stoughton, 1901), 21-31 by J. Dwight Pentecost, *Things to Come: a Study in Biblical Eschatology* (Grand Rapids, MI: Zondervan, 1964), 166-168.
44. Cate, *The Nine Gifts of the Spirit*, 69-70
45. Cate, *The Nine Gifts of the Spirit*, 69
46. Cate, *The Nine Gifts of the Spirit*, 69
47. Cate, *The Nine Gifts of the Spirit*, 69-70
48. Cate, *The Nine Gifts of the Spirit*, 68
49. Cate, *The Nine Gifts of the Spirit*, 68
50. Cate, *The Nine Gifts of the Spirit*, 68
51. Cate, *The Nine Gifts of the Spirit*, 68
52. Cate, *The Nine Gifts of the Spirit*, 70-71
53. Cate, *The Nine Gifts of the Spirit*, 70-71
54. Cate, *The Nine Gifts of the Spirit*, 71
55. Cate, *The Nine Gifts of the Spirit*, 71-72
56. Cate, *The Nine Gifts of the Spirit*, 71-72
57. Cate, *The Nine Gifts of the Spirit*, 71
58. Cate, *The Nine Gifts of the Spirit*, 71

59. Cate, *The Nine Gifts of the Spirit,* 27-28
60. Cate, *The Nine Gifts of the Spirit,* 30
61. Cate, *The Nine Gifts of the Spirit,* 30-31
62. Cate, *The Nine Gifts of the Spirit,* 31
63. Cate, *The Nine Gifts of the Spirit,* 31-32
64. Cate, *The Nine Gifts of the Spirit,* 31-32
65. Cate, *The Nine Gifts of the Spirit,* 32
66. Cate, *The Nine Gifts of the Spirit,* 27-28
67. Cate, *The Nine Gifts of the Spirit,* 27-28

Caleb Stahl

Bibliography

Bonnke, Reinhard. *Taking Action*. Lake Mary, FL: Charisma House, 2012.

Cate, B. F. *The Nine Gifts of the Spirit Are Not in the Church Today = or, The Answer to the Modern Tongues and Healing Movements*. Lorain, Oh.: Lorain Book and Bible House, 1956.

Courson, Jon. *Jon Courson's Application Commentary: New Testament*. Thomas Nelson, 2013.

Orr, James. *Progress of Dogma*. New York, NY: A.C. Armstrong, Hodder and Stoughton, 1901, p. 21-31 quoted by Pentecost, J. Dwight. *Things to Come: a Study in Biblical Eschatology*. Grand Rapids, MI: Zondervan, 1964.

Caleb Stahl

Caleb Stahl is available for interviews and personal appearances. For more information or requests email the publisher at: info@advbooks.com

To purchase additional copies of this book, visit our bookstore website at: www.advbookstore.com

"we bring dreams to life"™
www.advbookstore.com

www.ingramcontent.com/pod-product-compliance
Lightning Source LLC
Chambersburg PA
CBHW050857160426
43194CB00011B/2195